SAILING TO FREEDOM

Fight in the Delaware Bay; Crossing the Bay in a Batteau. In June 1860, a party of six fugitives (four men and two women) fled from Worcester County, Maryland, to a point near Cape May lighthouse in New Jersey. En route near the Delaware shore, they drove off five white men in a boat who tried to apprehend them. Illustration in William Still, *The Underground Rail Road: A Record of Facts, Authentic Letters, Narratives, &c.* (Philadelphia: Porter & Coates, 1872); image from Digital Collections, General Research Division, The New York Public Library, https://digitalcollections.nypl.org/items/510d47df-79d2-a3d9-e040-e00a18064a99.

SAILING TO FREEDOM

MARITIME DIMENSIONS OF THE UNDERGROUND RAILROAD

EDITED BY
TIMOTHY D. WALKER

University of Massachusetts Press
AMHERST AND BOSTON

Printed in the United States of America

ISBN 978-1-62534-592-9 (paper); 593-6 (hardcover)

Designed by Jen Jackowitz
Set in Minion Pro and Understock
Printed and bound by Maple Press, Inc.

Cover illustration by C. H. Reed, *Escaping from Portsmouth, Virginia; Escaping from Norfolk in Captain Lee's Skiff*, ca. 1872. From The New York Public Library, https://digitalcollections.nypl.org/items/510d47e0-fc1a-a3d9-e040-e00a18064a99.

Library of Congress Cataloging-in-Publication Data
Names: Walker, Timothy Dale, 1963– editor.
Title: Sailing to freedom : maritime dimensions of the Underground Railroad / edited by Timothy D. Walker.
Other titles: Maritime dimensions of the Underground Railroad
Description: Amherst : University of Massachusetts Press, 2021. | Includes bibliographical references and index.
Identifiers: LCCN 2020053343 (print) | LCCN 2020053344 (ebook) | ISBN 9781625345929 (paperback) | ISBN 9781625345936 (hardcover) | ISBN 9781613768488 (ebook) | ISBN 9781613768495 (ebook)
Subjects: LCSH: Underground railroad. | Fugitive slaves—Atlantic Coast (U.S.)—History—19th century. | African Americans—History—19th century. | Antislavery movements—United States—History. | Waterways—Atlantic Coast (U.S.)—History—19th century.
Classification: LCC E450 .S25 2021 (print) | LCC E450 (ebook) | DDC 973.7/115—dc23
LC record available at https://lccn.loc.gov/2020053343
LC ebook record available at https://lccn.loc.gov/2020053344

British Library Cataloguing-in-Publication Data
A catalog record for this book is available from the British Library.

A portion of chapter 2 was previously published in *Working on the Dock of the Bay: Labor and Enterprise in an Antebellum Southern Port* (Columbia: University of South Carolina Press, 2015). Published by permission. All rights reserved. Chapter 3 abridges and revises material from *The Waterman's Song: Slavery and Freedom in Maritime North Carolina*, by David S. Cecelski. Copyright © 2001 by the University of North Carolina Press. Used by permission of the publisher. All rights reserved. www.uncpress.org.

Sailing to Freedom has been supported by a UMass Dartmouth Subvention Grant awarded by the Office of the Dean of the College of Arts & Sciences.

To my son, Sebastian Dale de Melo e Walker, in the hope that he will grow to be fortified with a clear understanding of the profound human capacity for malevolence and benevolence.

CONTENTS

ACKNOWLEDGMENTS xi

INTRODUCTION 1

TIMOTHY D. WALKER

CHAPTER 1

Sailing to Freedom 14

Maritime Dimensions of the Underground Railroad

TIMOTHY D. WALKER

CHAPTER 2

Working on the Docks 36

Waterfront Labor, Coastal Commerce, and Escaping Enslavement from Charleston, South Carolina

MICHAEL D. THOMPSON

CHAPTER 3

Black Watermen, Fugitives from Slavery, and an Old Woman on the Edge of a Swamp 54

Maritime Passages to Freedom from Coastal North Carolina

DAVID S. CECELSKI

CHAPTER 4

Hampton Roads and Norfolk, Virginia, as a Waypoint and Gateway for Enslaved Persons Seeking Freedom 80

CASSANDRA NEWBY-ALEXANDER

CHAPTER 5

The Underground Railroad in Maryland's Ports, Bays, and Harbors 99

Maritime Strategies for Freedom

CHERYL JANIFER LAROCHE

CHAPTER 6

Claiming Liberty by Sea 123

The Port of New York as a Fugitive's Gateway from Enslavement

MIRELLE LUECKE

CHAPTER 7

Abolitionists and Seaborne Fugitives in Coastal Eastern Connecticut 140

Escaping Slavery in New London, Mystic, and Stonington

ELYSA ENGELMAN

CHAPTER 8

Seaborne Fugitives from Slavery and the Ports of Eastern Massachusetts 160

KATHRYN GROVER

CHAPTER 9

Making a Living in the "Fugitive's Gibraltar" 179

People of Color in New Bedford, 1838–1845

LEN TRAVERS

CHAPTER 10

Freedom on the Move by Sea 198

Evidence of Maritime Escape Strategies in American Runaway Slave Advertisements

MEGAN JEFFREYS

CONTRIBUTORS 219

INDEX 221

ACKNOWLEDGMENTS

Not only does this book have many mothers and fathers, but it has taken a village—combined synergies of effort from a community of dedicated scholars and public history professionals—to produce. First among them is Lee Blake, president of the New Bedford Historical Society, who approached me in 2009 with the idea for organizing a series of teacher training workshops, supported by the National Endowment for the Humanities Landmarks in American History and Culture grant program, focused on the extraordinary role that New Bedford, Massachusetts, played as an Underground Railroad waypoint and terminus. Lee and I successfully presented this program, titled "Sailing to Freedom: New Bedford and the Underground Railroad," three times over five years (2011, 2013, 2015). We are deeply grateful to the NEH, and the NEH program officers—Deborah Hurtt foremost among them—who worked with us, providing the guidance and funding that made these summer workshops possible. Profound thanks are due, too, to the dedicated workshop presenters and teacher participants, who came from all over the United States, for their inspiration and ideas that, in time, became the genesis of this book project. "Sailing to Freedom" workshop presenters include Jeffrey Bolster, Kathryn Grover, David Cecelski, Kate Clifford Larson, Len Travers, Elysa Engleman, Laurie Robertson-Lorant, John Stauffer, Kit Dunlap, Mary Malloy, Delores Walters, Michael Dyer, Polly Zajac, Jessica Ross, Richard Legault, and Kim and Reggie Harris. Additionally, for their scholarly guidance and inspiration, I wish to thank David Blight and Michelle Zacks of the Gilder Lehrman Center for the Study of Slavery, Resistance, and Abolition at Yale University, and Marcus Rediker of the University of Pittsburgh.

A number of institutions and their resourceful staff members assisted by providing source documentation, illustration materials, or other aid for this volume. These include New Bedford Whaling Museum staff members Michael Dyer, Mark Procknick, Robert Rocha, Christina Connett Brophy, and Judy Lund; Superintendent Jennifer White Smith and the rangers of the New Bedford Whaling National Historical Park; Jodi Goodman and Alexandra Copeland of the New Bedford Free Public Library; the staff of the Boston African American National Historic Site; Amelia Holmes and James Russell of the Nantucket Historical Association; Paul J. O'Pecko and Carol Mowrey of the G. W. Blunt White Library at the Mystic Seaport Museum; and Glenn Gordinier and Eric Roorda of the Frank C. Munson Institute of American Maritime Studies at the Mystic Seaport Museum. In addition, I am indebted to Lynda Ames of the Wareham Public Library and Jonathan Schroeder of the University of Warwick for key information referenced in these pages.

At the University of Massachusetts Dartmouth, I have many colleagues and friends to thank for their direct or indirect support of this book. Mary Hensel and Deborah Dolan (UMass Dartmouth Sponsored Research Administration) did outstanding work coordinating and advising on the NEH application process. It has been a pleasure to collaborate with Anthony Arrigo of the UMass Dartmouth English Department on the 2021 iteration of the NEH "Sailing to Freedom" summer workshops for teachers. UMass Dartmouth graduate Dan Everton provided indispensable help with computer-generated graphics included in the volume.

My sincere thanks go to Amy Shapiro and the UMass Dartmouth College of Arts & Sciences Dean's Office, and Lee Blake of the New Bedford Historical Society, for providing financial assistance for tasks necessary to the production of this volume. This work was supported by a publication subvention grant from the UMass Dartmouth College of Arts & Sciences, and with funds from the New Bedford Historical Society.

To my colleagues of the University of Massachusetts Press, whose enthusiasm for this project was a spur to my labors right from the start, I offer many thanks: Matthew Becker (editor in chief); Mary Dougherty (director); Brian Halley (senior editor); Courtney Andree (marketing); and Rachael DeShano and Sally Nichols (editing and production). Their editorial guidance and support has been indispensable in bringing this work to fruition.

Finally, I wish to express my deep gratitude to my partner, Daniela Flôr Coelho Melo, whose critical reading of portions of the text, to say nothing of her constant support and encouragement, was invaluable throughout the entire process, from inception to completion.

New Bedford, Massachusetts
21 September 2020

SAILING TO FREEDOM

INTRODUCTION

TIMOTHY D. WALKER

This volume of curated essays focuses exclusively on the maritime dimension of the Underground Railroad, as antebellum pathways to freedom for enslaved African Americans have collectively become known.[1] The contributors examine and contextualize the experiences of many enslaved persons in the United States who, prior to the Civil War, fled to freedom by sea and of the people who facilitated those escapes. Maritime escape episodes figure prominently in the majority of published North American fugitive slave accounts written before 1865: of 103 extant pre-Emancipation slave narratives, more than 70 percent recount the use of oceangoing vessels as a means of fleeing slavery.[2] Similarly, in William Still's classic, widely read account of his activities as an Underground Railroad "Station Master" in Philadelphia during the mid-nineteenth century, many of the most striking engravings that accompany the text illustrate dramatic descriptions of waterborne, maritime escapes.[3] Clearly, the sea should rightly constitute a central component of the full Underground Railroad story. But the topic remains surprisingly understudied. Maritime fugitives have drawn minimal attention in the historiography of the field, and the specific nautical circumstances of their flight garner little discussion in classrooms when the Underground Railroad is taught.[4]

To date, public scholarship, academic research, and pedagogical materials examining the Underground Railroad have focused almost exclusively on inland, landlocked regions of the United States. Such publications highlight and prioritize persons who used overland routes and interior river crossings, often

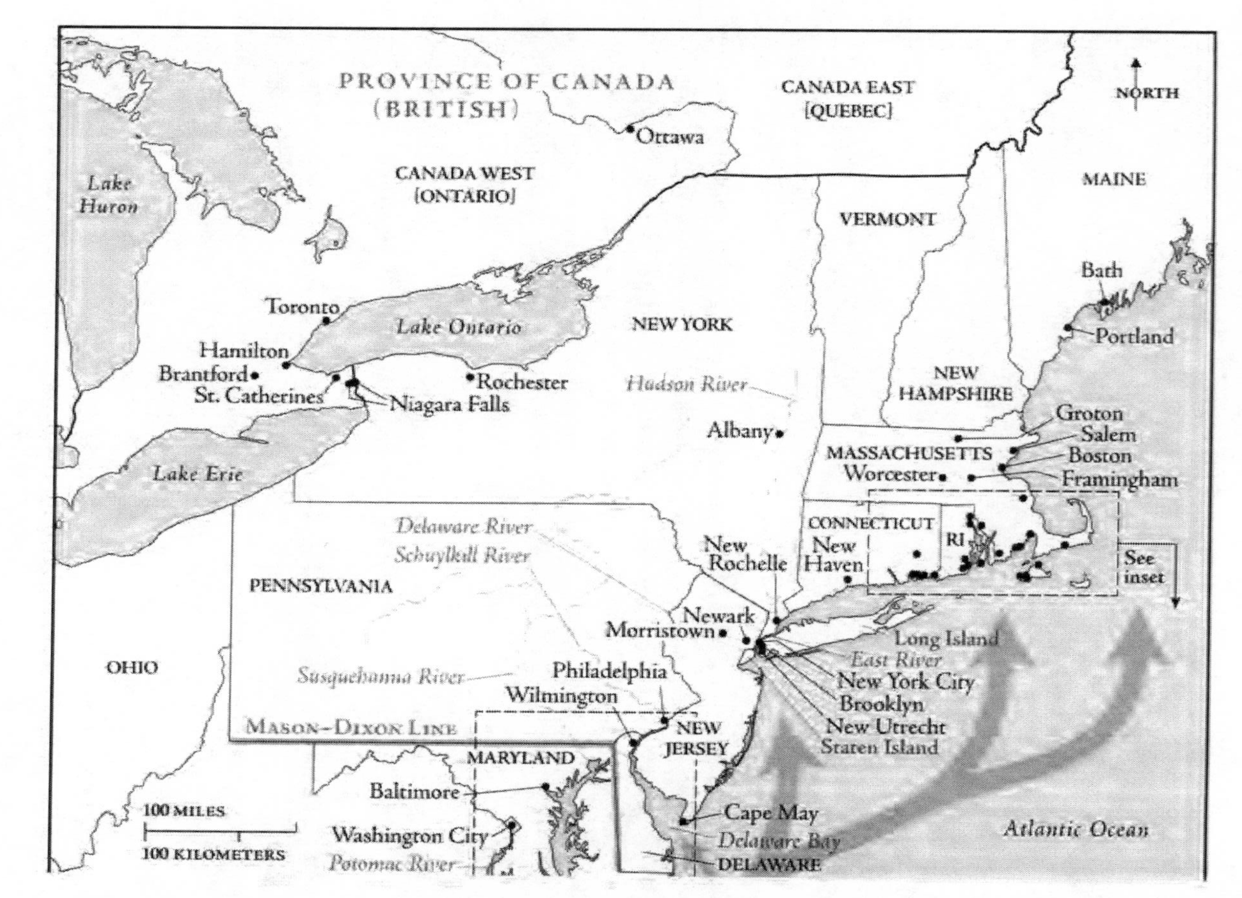
PROVINCE OF CANADA
(BRITISH)
CANADA EAST
[QUEBEC]
NORTH
Ottawa
CANADA WEST
[ONTARIO]
MAINE
Lake Huron
VERMONT
Bath
Portland
Toronto
Lake Ontario
NEW YORK
Hamilton
Brantford
St. Catherines
Niagara Falls
Rochester
Hudson River
NEW HAMPSHIRE
Groton
Salem
Boston
Framingham
Albany
MASSACHUSETTS
Worcester
Lake Erie
Delaware River
Schuylkill River
CONNECTICUT
RI
New Haven
New Rochelle
See inset
PENNSYLVANIA
Newark
Morristown
Long Island
East River
New York City
Brooklyn
New Utrecht
Staten Island
OHIO
Susquehanna River
Philadelphia
Wilmington
MASON–DIXON LINE
NEW JERSEY
MARYLAND
Baltimore
100 MILES
100 KILOMETERS
Washington City
Potomac River
Cape May
Delaware Bay
DELAWARE
Atlantic Ocean

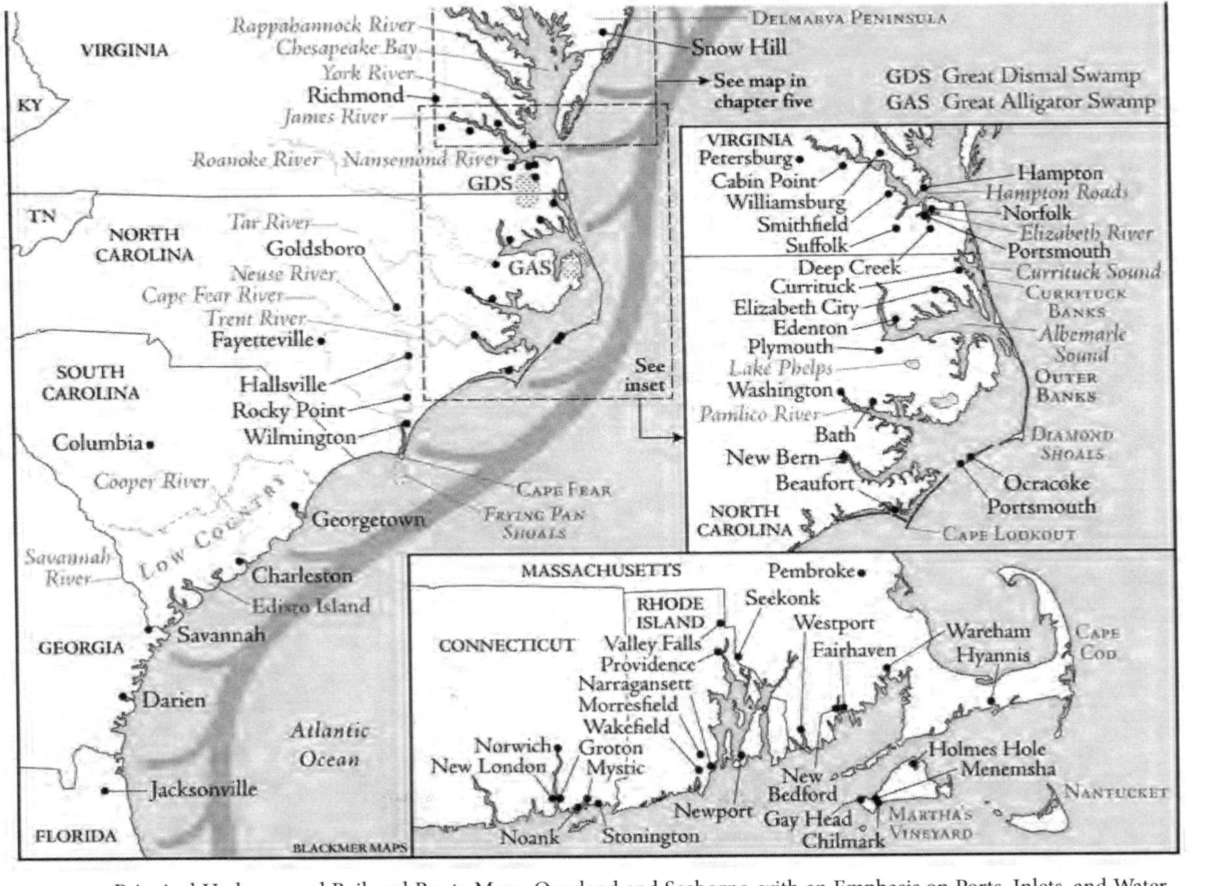

FIGURE 1. Principal Underground Railroad Route Maps, Overland and Seaborne, with an Emphasis on Ports, Inlets, and Waterways of the Maritime Underground Railroad. Maps by Kate Blackmer.

traveling clandestinely by night, as they sought to escape enslavement in the Antebellum South. However, recent academic historiography and public history research for museum exhibitions amply demonstrate that, because of the myriad practical difficulties consequent to being a northbound African American fugitive fleeing through hostile slaveholding territory, where vigilante patrols for escapees were an ever-present danger, successful escapes overland almost never originated in the Deep South.[5] In fact, prominent Underground Railroad historian Fergus M. Bordewich states flatly, "Escape by land from the Deep South was close to impossible."[6] Instead, the extant scholarship shows that the overwhelming majority of successful overland escapes were relatively short journeys that began in slave states (Virginia, Maryland, Kentucky, Missouri) sharing a border with a free state (Pennsylvania, Ohio, Indiana, Illinois, Iowa).[7]

What has been largely overlooked, however, is the great number of enslaved persons who made their way to freedom by using coastal water routes (and sometimes inland waterways), mainly along the Atlantic seaboard but also by fleeing southward from regions adjacent to the Gulf of Mexico. Because most historians of the Underground Railroad typically have not cultivated a maritime dimension to their research, they have generally neglected this essential component of the Underground Railroad, leaving the sea out of the various means employed to convey enslaved persons to the northern free states and Canada. Such neglect is deeply unfortunate; the absence of a detailed assessment and understanding of the maritime dimension of the Underground Railroad distorts the broader historical picture and hinders the formation of a more-accurate and -comprehensive knowledge of how this secretive, decentralized "system" operated. A revision of the traditional land-bound view of the Underground Railroad is therefore long overdue. This volume is intended to address this lacuna.

Research undertaken and presented for a series of "Landmarks in American History" workshops was sponsored by the National Endowment for the Humanities and realized through the University of Massachusetts, Dartmouth. The series, titled "Sailing to Freedom: New Bedford and the Underground Railroad" and running from 2011–2015, demonstrated that a far larger number of fugitives than previously supposed actually escaped bondage by sea—especially those fleeing from coastal areas in the far South, where the employment of slaves in diverse maritime industries was ubiquitous. (The far South was any slave region that lay beyond a relatively close journey by foot to the permeable border zones where slave states lay adjacent to free states.) Enslaved laborers worked as shipyard artisans, quayside stevedores and longshoremen, river boatmen and ferrymen, coastwise cargo-vessel crewmen, and estuary or near-coastal fishermen, among many other occupations connected to the water. Such work allowed enslaved persons to develop expert seafaring skills and knowledge in myriad areas: handling watercraft; gaining a detailed knowledge of coastal geography and hydrography (currents, tides, channels, navigation hazards); and establishing direct or indirect contacts with ocean-going ships' crews from northern free states. Equally valuable was their ready access to vessels heading out to sea. For enslaved persons in the southern Virginia and Maryland tidewater areas, the Carolina Low Country, and the Georgia and Florida seaboard, or along the coast of the Gulf of Mexico, escape by water was the logical option and, in reality, the only viable way to achieve an exit from their enslaved circumstances.

The new scholarship presented in this volume convincingly establishes that a markedly high proportion of successful escapes from the slaveholding South to sanctuary in the North were achieved using coastal seaways rather than overland routes. It is tempting to argue deductively that, given the circumstantial evidence, potentially even the majority of North American escapes from enslavement may have been accomplished by sea, but absent a definitive body of statistical data that would allow for a comparison between overland and waterborne escapes, this point is nearly impossible to prove. Still, of the known and documented fugitives who made successful escapes from the far South, almost all their escapes were achieved by sea.

Unfortunately, there is no way to conclusively quantify clandestine, illegal Underground Railroad activity or to reliably count the precise numbers of fugitive escapees by land or by sea.[8] Even so, the research contained in this book establishes definitively that escape by sea must be seen as a significant, indispensable component of the Underground Railroad story. Moreover, this analysis demonstrates that waterborne travel provided the only practical method of escape to a free territory from the coastal far South, because escape by long-distance overland routes would have been in most cases impractical: too slow, too dangerous, too logistically complicated, and therefore unsustainable.[9] By contrast, sailing to freedom was relatively simple and less hazardous. Once the fugitive was aboard a northbound vessel, escape by sea was direct; traveling by ship, whether powered by wind or steam, proceeded far more quickly and with much less effort than undertaking any terrestrial journey of comparable distance.[10]

This maritime fugitive dynamic was not only present but prominent in all slaveholding regions along the U.S. Eastern Seaboard. Consider, for example,

the perspective of historian Kate Clifford Larson, a specialist on Harriet Tubman and a contributing scholar of the "Sailing to Freedom" NEH workshops in 2015. Regarding her examination of Underground Railroad activity in and unassisted escapes from one distinct coastal district of antebellum Maryland along the Eastern Shore of Chesapeake Bay, Larson writes:

> It is very clear that escapes from anywhere along a water route—not just ports themselves, but rivers, streams, marshes—vastly outnumbered escapes from as little as ten miles away from any shoreline. This doesn't mean that people were grabbing canoes and small sailboats and sailing away, but rather, they were clearly getting information and making connections that would be valuable for escape. The plantations, homes, small farms, and businesses along the roads that linked villages and towns that hugged the Choptank River (which empties into the Chesapeake), for instance, witnessed hundreds of escapes over the 30-year period before the Civil War. Further inland—10 to 20 miles inland—you see just a few dozen escapes over that period.[11]

Although not all those hundreds of escaped slaves from along the Choptank River absconded by water—some few fled overland northward to freedom in adjacent Pennsylvania—most did. That being the case, Larson then wondered why historians have not seen "similar [elevated] escape rates from interior [slaveholding] communities?" Scholars of the Underground Railroad, she says, can provide a more nuanced understanding by "exposing the broader and more inclusive resources that maritime communities and workers could offer an escapee—those resources included more than just a vessel, but vital information and connections."[12]

Providing a more nuanced understanding is precisely what this volume aims to do. By highlighting the people involved in waterborne escapes, telling their little-known stories, and describing the less understood means by which the nautical side of the Underground Railroad functioned, this work hopes to reshape the overall scholarly view of it, to assemble a more accurate, more comprehensive, and better informed perspective. Taken together, these essays will address an important gap in the scholarly literature of the Underground Railroad and serve to reorient the traditional interpretive framework of scholarship on the topic, broadening it to include little-considered seaborne routes used by fugitives from enslavement in the South prior to the American Civil War.

The primary goal of this book, then, is to build a more authentic and precise description of how two distinct historical spheres—American slavery and maritime experience—intersected, while establishing conclusively through

FIGURE 2. A Sperm Whale Crushing a Whaleboat during a Hunt and Tossing the Boat's Multiracial Crew into the Pacific Ocean. Fugitives from slavery often served on long whaling voyages to evade capture and re-enslavement. (Detail from illustration by anonymous whaleman, ca. 1830s, courtesy, New Bedford Whaling Museum, Massachusetts.)

documented cases that enslaved people frequently used waterborne means to escape to freedom. A parallel aim, however, is to reinforce the idea that maritime escapes could be and often were effected without any assistance from individuals who saw themselves as deliberate Underground Railroad operatives. In the nineteenth century, after all, there was little in the way of an organized network to assist would-be freedom seekers in the far South of the United States. The Underground Railroad, according to the prevailing scholarly conception based on available evidence, seems to have functioned as an organized, albeit a loose, network mainly in free northern states.[13] Though assisted seaborne escapes from the southern states certainly happened, as indicated in several of the incidents described in the following pages, far more frequently such acts of escape were impulsive and unplanned. Any assistance provided to fugitives was the result of chance meetings, often with persons who were in no way connected to any organized resistance to slavery.

An important question that this volume asks, therefore, is to what extent are maritime escapes rightfully referred to as part of the Underground Railroad, as the term is commonly understood and used by historians? According to the evidence collected in this collection, many maritime escapes were achieved without organized, premeditated outside help of the kind typically provided by Underground Railroad operatives. To be sure, some of the escapes by sea recounted here did require extensive planning, with multiple persons involved; a handful of these episodes are well known to historians.[14] But many other escapes were spontaneous, opportunistic, and entirely self-directed by enslaved persons using only their own maritime knowledge, skills, and resources. Such incidents happened quietly, surreptitiously, with the ingenuity and personal agency of the successful fugitive remaining largely unknown, except for tantalizing hints available in runaway slave advertisements in newspapers or until the freedom seekers themselves told their stories publicly once they were long out of danger of recapture.

Consequently, one of the contentions of this book is that, by taking ship from coastal regions far south of the Mason-Dixon line and following the Gulf Stream offshore to northern free ports, enslaved individuals in the eighteenth and nineteenth centuries usually bypassed entirely much of the terrestrial infrastructure of the Underground Railroad. Their experiences rightly comprise part of the Underground Railroad story but typically entailed sailing directly to a free territory and engaging with its personnel, resources, and strategies only once safely arrived in a northern port of refuge. These fugitives escaped slave states by sea, without confronting most of the impediments and potential dangers consequent to a protracted journey along an overland escape route. Thus, seaborne escapes were potentially faster, safer, and more efficient than attempting to run away from enslavement overland. This dimension of Underground Railroad operations would have been readily apparent to anyone living near the Atlantic or Gulf coast of the southern United States during the antebellum period—but to modern readers in the twenty-first century, this dimension isn't at all obvious, in part because we have largely forgotten the centrality of the sea to early American economic and social life. The following essays reframe the Underground Railroad story, placing the sea back in its proper place as an essential stage and backdrop for this history.

The team of scholars who contributed to this publishing project—an interdisciplinary mix of experts at varying stages of their careers—was assembled deliberately to cover key geographic regions along the Eastern Seaboard. These authors have researched and written extensively about slavery and abolitionism, the Underground Railroad, port communities, and coastal areas such as New York, New Bedford, the Chesapeake Bay, and the Carolina Low Country, and the intersection of maritime industries with the African American experience during the late eighteenth and nineteenth centuries. In their chapters, they have asked penetrating questions to create an interpretive framework that will allow casual readers and Underground Railroad scholars alike to draw distinctions between the typical characteristics of fugitives who escaped from slavery by land and those who fled by sea, and to compare their experiences. Such questions include, for example: What is the profile of a typical seaborne fugitive in terms of gender, age, occupation, skills, and marriage status? What strategies and methods did freedom seekers use to acquire a boat or to get aboard a northbound ship? What personal skills did the they carry with them—particularly maritime-related skills that may have helped in making good their escape or that helped the fugitive to find work and survive after reaching a wage-based economy in a free state? How did maritime communities in the South react to, respond to, accommodate, or try to thwart escapes via water? Insofar as available data and evidence have allowed, the featured authors have tried to answer these and other related questions.

Together, the ten essays that make up this volume create a mosaic describing the nautical routes and waterborne methods that allowed so many freedom seekers to accomplish their liberation from enslavement. The text is primarily aimed at scholars and teachers of the Underground Railroad or the experience of slavery in the United States, including museum and public history professionals. However, the structure and focus of the text makes it suitable for classroom use by undergraduate and graduate students as well as by advanced secondary school students and interested general readers.

The volume is organized geographically, with the focus of each succeeding chapter proceeding from south to north along the Atlantic Seaboard from the Carolinas to New England. The analysis thus follows the coastwise route of untold numbers of enslaved persons who sought freedom aboard northbound vessels following the Gulf Stream toward sanctuary in states and territories where human bondage was illegal. Each chapter covers a different coastal location or region wherein extensive waterborne Underground Railroad activity took place. The exceptions are the general conceptual opening chapter and the closing tenth chapter, which describes emerging digital tools that will open new pathways of research on this subject.

Because this project was first conceived as an examination of coastal waterborne escape routes northward toward the ports and abolitionist communities of northern free states, it focuses principally on the U.S. Atlantic Seaboard, thereby leaving out southern Florida, the Gulf of Mexico coast, and New

Orleans, all important slaveholding regions with strong and varied connections to the sea. Clearly, enslaved persons in these areas sought and achieved freedom through seaborne means as well, fleeing by boat or ship. Our hope is that the present volume will stimulate new scholarship to explore these southward seaborne conduits of escape from the United States, and so further expand our understanding of the operation and geographic dimensions of the saltwater Underground Railroad.

Timothy D. Walker's essay opens the volume with a consideration of some practical and methodological issues surrounding the maritime Underground Railroad—issues that motivated him to undertake a study of this critical central theme. Walker offers a brief review of the scant historiography on the subject, then sketches a number of maritime Underground Railroad episodes as examples to contextualize the rest of the book, laying the groundwork to introduce and set up the essays that follow.

In chapter two, Michael D. Thompson provides an incisive examination of waterfront labor, coastal commerce, and the varied means of escaping enslavement by sea from Charleston, South Carolina. Thompson, a historian at the University of Tennessee, Chattanooga, shows how many runaway slaves had deliberately sought waterfront work in the Charleston seaport, which presented them with opportunities for embarking on northbound vessels. The port provided an ideal bridge on the road to freedom.

Next, David S. Cecelski's chapter focuses on the Carolina Low Country, where local African American watermen, sometimes free but usually held in bondage, provided the labor that merchants and planters depended on to guide their vessels and land valuable cargo. Cecelski shows that enslaved dock workers, fishermen, and transport boatmen were ubiquitous in the coastal areas of the Carolinas, but they also steered fugitives toward freedom along furtive maritime routes that endured throughout the slavery era. His meticulous research provides valuable insights about practical means frequently used to escape enslavement by sea through the Carolina coasts and wetlands.

In chapter four, Cassandra Newby-Alexander, director of the Joseph Jenkins Roberts Center for the Study of the African Diaspora at Norfolk State University in Virginia, describes the maritime Underground Railroad as it functioned in the neighboring ports of Hampton Roads and Norfolk, Virginia, and the surrounding hinterland. The entire region of Hampton Roads served as the gateway and starting point for incalculable numbers of enslaved Blacks who made their way by sea to freedom in the North.

Chapter five by Cheryl Janifer LaRoche of the University of Maryland, discusses the strategies that enslaved persons employed to escape bondage through Baltimore Harbor, the Chesapeake Bay, and other key maritime locales in Maryland. Significant as a border area just across the Mason-Dixon line from free territory, Maryland nevertheless saw exceptional numbers of fugitives use waterborne means to flee their intolerable circumstances.

Mirelle Luecke, whose recent doctorate in Atlantic history from the University of Pittsburgh focuses on maritime labor in New York City, provides in the sixth chapter a detailed consideration of the metropolitan harbor and waterfront, which served as a transitional port for fugitive Blacks. For many freedom seekers recently departed from lives of bondage in the southern states, New York represented a "gateway to freedom," a waypoint *en route* to other more secure destinations farther north. Maritime networks that assisted and protected such fugitives are the subject of her contribution to this volume.

Chapter seven is authored by Elysa Engelman, the director of exhibits for the Mystic Seaport Museum. She uses her experience as a public historian and museum professional in an innovative approach to analyzing research material for our volume. In her contribution, she sets about explaining how smaller shipbuilding towns such as Mystic, Connecticut, and whaling ports such as nearby Stonington and New London also proved to be destinations for fugitives escaping to the northern free states. Engelman's analysis focuses particular attention on the case of one local abolitionist shipbuilding family, the Greenmans of Mystic, and considers their complicated role in a community where abolition was not a cause favored by a majority of elites.

Independent scholar Kathryn Grover has worked on fugitive slave documentation in Massachusetts for over two decades. Her chapter eight synthesizes and expands the corpus of her research to examine the formal and informal ties between abolitionists who assisted fugitives in Boston and New Bedford and on Cape Cod and the islands of Martha's Vineyard and Nantucket. In so doing, her contribution explores the critical role that free African American communities in these places played in sheltering, supporting, and otherwise aiding fugitives from slavery.

In chapter nine, Len Travers of the University of Massachusetts, Dartmouth, asks to what extent did New Bedford actually encourage and develop Black participation in maritime work. His incisive analysis of the New Bedford city directory for 1838 (the year of Frederick Douglass's escape and arrival) provides readers with detailed, nuanced data, and fresh insights concerning the size of this port town's community of color, where they lived, and how they supported themselves mainly in waterfront trades or services in support of the whaling industry.

The tenth and final chapter describes opportunities for new research using digitized primary-source documentation collected in a cutting-edge online resource: the *Freedom on the Move* (FOTM) project database being compiled at Cornell University. Cornell doctoral candidate Megan Jeffreys introduces the database and guides the reader through it, demonstrating its utility for scholarly Underground Railroad investigation and providing some preliminary observations about how this tool can help historians understand the seaborne escape methods that enslaved peoples used to seek freedom.

This innovative book addresses an important gap in the scholarly literature and understanding of the Underground Railroad. Collectively, these *Sailing to Freedom* essays provide a fresh approach that will reframe the salient interpretive model of Underground Railroad scholarship, recasting it to be more inclusive and incorporating the historically indispensable seaborne routes and strategies that fugitives from enslavement employed during the antebellum era.

NOTES

1. *Underground Railroad* is a term of contested meaning and some imprecision. In this volume, it is meant broadly and collectively to include all the formal and informal means, methods, strategies, and tactics by which enslaved African Americans escaped their circumstances and achieved freedom prior to 1865. Its first appearance in common usage dates to the period 1839–1842. See Eric Foner, *Gateway to Freedom: The Hidden History of the Underground Railroad* (New York: W. W. Norton, 2015), 6.
2. Survey of authors represented in the University of North Carolina's "North American Slave Narratives," Documenting the American South, https://docsouth.unc.edu/neh/. I am grateful to Professor Jonathan Schroeder of the University of Warwick for this reference.
3. William Still, *The Underground Rail Road: A Record of Facts, Authentic Letters, Narratives, etc.* (Philadelphia: Porter & Coates, 1872).
4. This despite the fact that the earliest systematic and widely known learned work on the Underground Railroad acknowledged manifold instances of escape by sea and plotted coastal maritime routes on an iconic, often-reproduced map of Underground Railroad networks that accompanied the volume. See William H. Siebert, *The Underground Railroad from Slavery to Freedom* (New York: MacMillan, 1898), 81–82, 144–45.

5. Foner, *Gateway to Freedom*, 5; Fergus Bordewich, *Bound for Canaan: The Underground Railroad and the War for the Soul of America* (New York: Amistad, 2005), 109–10; 271–72.
6. Bordewich, *Bound for Canaan*, 271.
7. Ibid., 115.
8. The ongoing scholarly discussion on the difficulty of obtaining quantitative Underground Railroad data and the ultimate unknowability of escape numbers is alluded to by Spencer Crew in his foreword to *Passages to Freedom: The Underground Railroad in History and Memory*, ed. David W. Blight (New York: Harper Collins/Smithsonian Books, 2004), *x*.
9. Though, to be sure, this dynamic leaves aside the estimated fifty thousand annual runaways who fled their enslaved circumstances *within* the South during the late antebellum period. These fugitives were usually recaptured and rarely achieved freedom. See John Hope Franklin and Loren Schweninger, *Runaway Slaves: Rebels on the Plantation* (New York: Oxford University Press, 1999), 282.
10. Bordewich, *Bound for Canaan*, 272.
11. Kate Clifford Larson, email to the author, 18 August 2015. See her *Bound for the Promised Land: Harriet Tubman, Portrait of an American Hero* (New York: Random House, 2004).
12. Larson, 18 August 2015.
13. Bordewich, *Bound for Canaan*, 197, 307–9.
14. The protracted seven-year escape effort of Harriet Ann Jacobs provides a good example. See Jean Fagan Yellin, ed., et al., "September 1810—November 1843: Slavery and Resistance," pt. 1 of *Harriet Jacobs Family Papers,* (Chapel Hill: University of North Carolina Press, 2008), 1:1–51.

1

SAILING TO FREEDOM

Maritime Dimensions of the Underground Railroad

TIMOTHY D. WALKER

> No sooner, indeed, does a vessel, known to be from the North, anchor in any of these waters [in the Chesapeake Bay]—and the slaves are pretty adroit at ascertaining from what state a vessel comes—than she is boarded, if she remains any length of time, and especially overnight, by more or less of them, in hopes of obtaining a passage in her to a land of freedom.
>
> —Captain Daniel Drayton, *Personal Memoir of Daniel Drayton*

ISSUES AND CONCEPTS

Given the strong popular interest in and scholarly activity focused on the history of slavery in the United States, including the means by which desperate enslaved individuals escaped bondage, what explains the surprising dearth of historiographical material written on the maritime dimensions of the Underground Railroad? A brief review of the available scholarly literature focused on this volume's research theme will provide some context for our project and its intended goal: to challenge and reshape the salient perception that the Underground Railroad was primarily a terrestrial undertaking. This view dominates the extant Underground Railroad historiography. Only a handful of academic works stand out for their treatment of the nautical means freedom seekers used. Not surprisingly, several of the authors noted below are contributors, either directly or indirectly, to the research presented in this volume.

Jeffrey Bolster's award-winning study, *Black Jacks: African American Seamen in the Age of Sail* published in 1997, is an early example of this line of inquiry. His book raises incisive questions and provides useful insights about how escaped slaves and free Black mariners came to serve in large numbers aboard U.S. merchant and naval vessels, especially those sailing from northern states prior to the Civil War. Chapter five in particular, titled "Possibilities for Freedom," discusses how coastal maritime activities provided a portal for escape to enslaved African Americans.[1] The present inquiry into the maritime dimensions of the Underground Railroad proceeds directly from Bolster's groundbreaking scholarship.

In 2001, Kathryn Grover's assiduous, comprehensive research resulted in *The Fugitive's Gibraltar: Escaping Slaves and Abolitionism in New Bedford, Massachusetts*. Her fine-grained work demonstrates clearly that, in America's principal whaling port, the large Black community was replete with people who had likely been born into slavery, had escaped the South by sea, and who had ample reason to sign on to whaling voyages that would keep them away from slave-catching bounty hunters for years at a time. Also appearing in 2001 was David Cecelski's *The Waterman's Song: Slavery and Freedom in Maritime North Carolina*. Beautifully written, this book highlights the ubiquity of maritime coastal slave labor in the antebellum South, which in turn afforded slaves with necessary training and opportunities to facilitate waterborne flight.[2]

Historian Jane Landers touches on the theme of maritime escape in passing in her chapter titled "Southern Passage: The Forgotten Route to Freedom in Florida," published in 2004 as part of the collected volume, *Passages to Freedom*, edited by David Blight. In 2005, Harvey Amani Whitfield published *From American Slaves to Nova Scotian Subjects: The Case of the Black Refugees, 1813–1840* (Pearson/Prentice Hall), an adroit study of those who had fled slavery in the United States to the protection offered by British forces during the War of 1812 and were subsequently transported by the Royal Navy as freed people to maritime Canada.[3]

Fergus Bordewich's excellent comprehensive volume, *Bound for Canaan: The Underground Railroad and the War for the Soul of America*, also came out in 2005. Bordewich repeatedly mentions fugitive slaves' frequent recourse to coastal shipping as a means to reach the North, describing seaborne escape episodes throughout his text. He even devotes a brief chapter, "The Saltwater Underground," to maritime dimensions of the Underground Railroad, but his work does not recognize the overall magnitude or relative historic importance of such waterborne fugitive activity; his focus remains squarely on the conventional narrative of terrestrial Underground Railroad routes. The following year, Cassandra Pybus published her fine volume, *Epic Journeys of Freedom: Runaway Slaves of the American Revolution and Their Global Quest for Liberty*, which chronicles enslaved peoples who fled from their American owners to seek freedom with the British and describes the challenges they faced as they subsequently dispersed throughout the British maritime empire, pursuing lives as free women and men of color in social contexts where legal slavery continued to be the norm.[4]

Though historical attention to waterborne flight southward toward the Caribbean Sea has been especially scant, the theme was picked up in one groundbreaking study from 2013. Echoing Bordewich, historians Irvin D. S. Winsboro and Joe Knetsch employ in their article published in *The Journal of Southern History* the term "southern Saltwater Railroad" to refer to fugitive routes from the United States into the Bahamas—but it could also accurately describe nautical pathways to jurisdictions in Mexico, Haiti, and other Caribbean islands where laborers held in bondage could find sanctuary during the nineteenth century. Winsboro and Knetsch point out that, in 1825, when the British Colonial Office declared that any U.S. slave "who reaches British ground" would be declared "free," the ruling immediately liberated approximately three hundred runaway bondspeople who had fled to the Bahamas.[5]

This policy caused great diplomatic tension between the United States and Britain, never more so than when, in 1841, just two years after the well-known uprising on the schooner *Amistad*, another shipboard rebellion on the American brig *Creole* led to 128 enslaved people gaining their freedom in the Bahamas. Although this incident—the most successful revolt and liberation of enslaved people in U.S. history—made headlines at the time, the *Creole* slave mutiny at sea is barely known today. The *Creole* was transporting 135 enslaved people from Richmond and Hampton Roads, Virginia, to be sold in the slave markets of New Orleans, Louisiana. On 7 November 1841, as the *Creole* approached the Bahamas, 19 enslaved persons, reportedly led by a man named Madison Washington, who had been re-enslaved after living in freedom in Canada, rose up against the crew and successfully took control of the vessel. Two days later, the mutineers brought the *Creole* into Nassau Harbor. Because slavery had been outlawed in all British colonies in 1833, the Bahamian colonial authorities considered the majority of the enslaved people on the ship to be free. The outraged U.S. consul, however, demanded that those involved in overtaking the ship be arrested and charged with mutiny. Despite the U.S. government's remonstrances, the British Admiralty Court in Nassau ordered on 16 April 1842 that the surviving 17 mutineers be released and declared free men.[6]

In 2015, Eric Foner published *Gateway to Freedom: The Hidden History of the Underground Railroad*, which describes the central role that New York City played as an Underground Railroad waypoint. While not the book's primary focus, much of Foner's narrative revolves around clandestine maritime activity in the port and along the city's waterfront; his index lists dozens of instances of seaborn escape from enslavement. Finally, the most recent work in this vein, Cassandra Newby-Alexander's *Virginia Waterways and the Underground Railroad* appearing in 2017, narrates and documents the multiple ways that resourceful enslaved people used their access to Virginia's waterways to escape bondage and achieve freedom. Here at last is a work of scholarship wholly and explicitly focused on the central nautical aspect that characterized so much Underground Railroad activity along the eastern seaboard.[7]

In addition, an ambitious online research project currently underway promises to shed new light on seaborne escapes from enslavement. Historian and researcher Edward Baptist of Cornell University heads the "Freedom on the Move" project (FOTM), which aims to compile all North American runaway slave advertisements from regional newspapers of the eighteenth and nineteenth centuries into one master digital research tool. Such notices—classified advertisements placed by owners seeking to recover escaped slaves—have never before been systematically and comprehensively collected. Project researchers are compiling the advertisements collaboratively and entering them into a searchable online database. The project will integrate existing runaway-slave advertisement projects and allow archivists and researchers nationwide to add advertisements and search terms.[8] According to the Library of Congress, between 1730 and 1865, an estimated two hundred thousand fugitive slave notices appeared in U.S. newspapers; as of January 2020, just over 10 percent of these are available via the FOTM website.[9] Because such advertisements often provide details from owners about the means slaves used to escape, the project will provide significant new data regarding maritime strategies used to seek liberation. Moreover, initial analysis of the FOTM database undertaken for this volume indicates that, once a full reckoning of these newspaper notices is possible, cases of waterborne escape may figure as prominently in the historic record as overland escapes.[10]

Why has the historiography of the Underground Railroad, so rich in studies of overland escape routes, overlooked the broad maritime dimension of strategies employed by freedom seekers to escape bondage? One explanation is that, in recent decades, few scholars who investigate fugitives from slavery in North

America are trained in the perspectives, methodologies, and skills of maritime history.[11] The influence of the sea on historical events on land has become neglected as a field of scholarly inquiry, rarely figuring in terrestrial historical causality.[12] But this neglect is in turn part of a larger contemporary misconception about the past: most people alive today, particularly those who live inland and experience no direct contact with seaborne trades, have no real concept of how important water transport was to daily life in the United States of the eighteenth and nineteenth centuries. Once railroads and motor vehicle traffic reshaped settlement and transportation patterns, people forgot how vital the sea and waterborne commerce were to the fabric of everyday life in the United States prior to the early decades of the twentieth century.

Quite simply, coastwise shipping along the Eastern Seaboard dominated the American economy until the late 1800s. Almost all personal and business travel of more than a relatively few miles and virtually all shipping of heavy goods were conducted predominantly by water, because watercraft offered by far the fastest, cheapest, and most efficient means of transport. Coastal schooners, sloops, and brigs were the workhorses of this internal trade, in which slave-produced raw materials such as cotton and molasses were shipped northward to New England and New York factories, and northern industrial manufactured goods were shipped south. These items included finished cotton cloth, iron and steel tools, agricultural machinery, as well as third-rate salted fish used as a cheap food for enslaved populations.

For much of the pre–Civil War era, travel along the North American Atlantic Coast, where the great majority of the U.S. population resided, was made particularly difficult by the numerous unbridged rivers that cut the coastline.[13] As a telling example, Frederick Douglass's escape from Baltimore, Maryland, to New York City in 1838, though conducted along an "overland" route of less than two hundred miles, nevertheless entailed three river or estuary crossings by ferry and a steamboat passage between Wilmington, Delaware, and Philadelphia.[14]

The few American roads at the time—mostly rudimentary and vulnerable to seasonal rains—linked coastal ports to regional hinterland communities and industries but did not tie together distant and disparate regions north and south. So coastwise navigation on innumerable small merchant vessels

> provided a service that was at once more comfortable, safer, and cheaper than travel by land. Moreover, these vessels brought publications from other colonies and distributed European news from whichever American port had received it first from overseas. In the end, one cannot measure the importance to ordinary seaboard inhabitants of this connection to American coastal communities beyond their immediate neighbors. . . .[15]

The ubiquity of the maritime industry and therefore of maritime work, performed universally in the southern states by chattel laborers, whether as on-board seagoing crew, ferrymen and pilots, coastal and river watermen, or on the working waterfronts of port towns, provided many enslaved people with abundant opportunities for escape—opportunities that persons held in bondage in the hinterland and interior simply did not have. For example, William Grimes, "self-emancipated" in 1814, stowed away aboard the Boston sloop *Casket*, bound from Savannah, Georgia, to New York, with the assistance of the vessel's sympathetic crew of New Englanders, one of whom even helped him to buy provisions for the trip in town before departure. He revealed details about seizing this fortunate opportunity in an account of his seaborne escape published in 1855:

> I went . . . to assist in loading her. I soon got acquainted with some of these Yankee sailors, and they appeared to be quite pleased with me. Her cargo chiefly consisted of cotton in bales. After filling her hold, they were obliged to lash a great number of bales on deck. The sailors, growing more and more attached to me, they proposed to me to leave, in the centre of the cotton bales on deck, a hole or place sufficiently large for me to stow away in, with my necessary provisions. Whether they then had any idea of my coming away with them or not, I cannot say; but this I can say safely, a place was left, and I occupied it during the passage, and by that means made my escape.[16]

By the mid-nineteenth century, fleeing enslavement in the South by being secreted on a northbound ship had been commonplace for decades. For their part, southern slaveholders and civil authorities were well aware of the danger that seaports and commercial shipping represented to their property, as a means by which fugitive slaves often slipped away to freedom. So great was their concern that, beginning in the early 1800s, municipal and state lawmakers in the South enacted a series of regulations to limit interaction between northern free Black mariners and enslaved waterfront workers. Southern authorities in Virginia, the Carolinas, and Georgia passed statutes requiring northern sailors of color to either remain aboard ship or be confined on land while their vessels were in port.[17] Further, to staunch this inexorable flow of absconding human property, by the 1850s lawmakers in several southern states passed statutes requiring a systematic search for stowaway slaves before any northbound vessel could clear harbor. Southern port officers regularly contracted agents to fumigate ships as they prepared to get underway, using a noxious mixture of pitch, tar, vinegar, and brimstone (sulfur) to drive any would-be fugitives from their hiding places below decks. For example, in late 1854, the Florida legislature passed An Act to Prevent the Abduction and Escape of Slaves from this State, which created an officer of inspection and fumigation charged with locating slaves attempting to escape aboard northbound vessels.[18]

Such measures were only partially effective. Ingenuity and determination overcame adversity, and seaborne escapes to destinations in northern port towns continued unabated. In the earliest systematic scholarly work on the Underground Railroad, published at the end of the nineteenth century, author William H. Siebert compiled hundreds of firsthand accounts through correspondence with witnesses and operators who had engaged in clandestine assistance of fugitives. Siebert wrote: "The advantages of escape by boat were early discerned by slaves living near the coast or along inland rivers. Vessels engaged in our coastwise trade became more or less involved in transporting fugitives from Southern ports to Northern soil."[19] He went on to describe, with documented examples, how small trading vessels, returning from their voyages to Virginia, landed slaves on the New England coast. An Underground Railroad station keeper of Valley Falls, Rhode Island, reported to Siebert: "'Slaves in Virginia would secure passage either secretly or with the consent of the captains, in small trading vessels, at Norfolk or Portsmouth, and thus be brought into some port in New England.' . . . The reporter gives several instances coming with her knowledge of fugitives that escaped from Virginia to Massachusetts as stowaways on vessels."[20]

Clearly, such seaborne escapes were neither isolated incidents nor in any way considered unusual. In another telling instance, Thomas H. Jones, born a slave in North Carolina in 1806, described in his published narrative how he worked for years as a stevedore or longshoreman, loading and unloading vessels in Wilmington harbor. In 1849, he bribed a steward on the cargo brig *Bell*, bound for New York, paying $8.00 (well over a week's wages for a laborer at the time) to be hidden in the vessel's hold. Discovered by the captain while underway and fearing re-enslavement, Jones made a dramatic escape when the *Bell* arrived in New York Harbor; using a hastily assembled raft of boards for flotation, he attempted to swim a mile to shore. Pursued by the *Bell's* chief mate, who noticed his absence, Jones was providentially rescued by some boatmen with abolitionist sentiments who happened to be passing by.[21] In yet another remarkable case early in the Civil War, a seasoned waterman, Dempsey Hill, about thirty years old and a slave since birth, took advantage of the turmoil in Beaufort, North Carolina, caused by the Union blockade and advancing northern forces. One night in autumn 1861, Hill deliberately broke into the Beaufort Customs House to steal nautical charts detailing the complex and hazardous coastal waterways of the region, hiding them in the city cemetery. A few nights later, he and four enslaved companions, all experienced boatmen, stole a pilot vessel and escaped, delivering the valuable charts to the blockading Union naval squadron anchored "down the bay" near a passage through the Outer Banks. When Hill and his friends told the officers aboard the Union warships that they "wanted to become sailors and freemen," they were immediately mustered in as able seamen.[22] Hill served throughout the war, after which he worked as a crewman aboard coastal trading vessels before settling in Wareham, Massachusetts, where he became well known and highly regarded as the captain of a Buzzards Bay fishing and pleasure craft.[23]

Northern naval blockading operations during the Civil War occasioned many such waterborne escapes, yet they are rarely discussed as part of the broader Underground Railroad story. For example, in a well-known photograph of the crew of the USS *Monitor*, the Union's first ironclad naval vessel, the African American crewman sitting in the foreground is Josiah "Siah" Hulett Carter, a former slave who had escaped directly to that warship in a stolen boat. On the night of 16 May 1862, the USS *Monitor* rode at anchor in the James River off City Point, Virginia. Around midnight, twenty-two-year-old Siah, having just escaped from the Shirley Plantation of Charles City County, approached the

FIGURE 3. Josiah "Siah" Hulett Carter, *front right*, with the USS *Monitor* crew. Carter joined the ship on 19 May 1862. He had escaped enslavement in Virginia days before and fled down the James River in a stolen boat, sailing directly to the famed Union ironclad warship. Photograph, "James River, Va. Sailors on Deck of U.S.S. Monitor; Cookstove at Left" by James F. Gibson, Civil War Photographs, Prints and Photographs Division, Library of Congress, Washington, D.C., LC-DIG-cwpb-00306.

ship in his purloined skiff. The startled crewmen on watch first challenged, then shot at him before realizing he was "contraband"—a runaway slave. Siah's owner, Colonel Hill Carter, had tried to frighten his slaves so they would not attempt to flee to blockading Union vessels; the Yankees, he said, would carry them out to sea and throw them overboard to drown. Though terrified, Siah rowed alongside the *Monitor*, seeking sanctuary, work, and a passage to freedom. By 19 May 1862, Siah Hulett Carter had officially signed on for a three-year enlistment as a member of the warship's crew. Carter survived the *Monitor*'s sinking off Cape Hatteras on 31 December 1862 and afterward served in the Union Navy for the duration of the war; he was honorably discharged on 19 May 1865.[24]

Even as early as the final quarter of the eighteenth century, escape by sea was a common strategy for enslaved persons in the southern coastal United States—so common, in fact, that in northern ports such as New Bedford, Massachusetts, local newspapers developed a standardized text that ship captains published as a legal notice whenever such an event occurred. Consider, for example, the following classified advertisement that appeared as a boxed text published in the *Medley or New Bedford Marine Journal* on 20 April 1797:

> Public Notice! To all whom it may concern, Know Ye, THAT I William Taber, commander of the sloop *Union*, sailed from *York River*, in *Virginia*, on or about the 28th of March last, bound to this Port [New Bedford]—That on the day after sailing, I discovered a NEGRO on board said sloop, who had concealed himself unbeknown to me.—It appearing inconsistent for me to return, the wind being ahead, I proceeded on my voyage, and landed him in this Port.—He calls himself JAMES, is about 27 years old, and says he belongs to Mr. Shacleford, a Planter, in *Kings* [*sic*] and *Queen's County, Virginia*. Any person claiming him, will know by this information where he is—For which purpose it is made public in this manner, and every legal method has been taken to prevent the Owner losing the property, in my power.—WILLIAM TABER. New Bedford[25]

Such notices appeared regularly in newspapers published in seaports along the New England coast and maintained precise language that varied little from one region to the next. The principal variation was in the details reported: name of the captain; name and type of vessel; point of departure; date; and so on. Printers even used a purpose-made illustration that appeared alongside these texts. It was a small stylized image of a running African male figure dressed in stereotyped "native" clothing (a kind of loose skirt) and carrying a spear or staff, with a capital "R" signifying "runaway" emblazoned on his chest.

By federal law—the Fugitive Slave Act of 1793—knowingly aiding or harboring someone fleeing legal bondage was a crime punishable by an exceptionally large fine of up to five hundred dollars and a prison term of not more than a year.[26] So, following the passage of the act of 1793, masters of vessels who arrived in northern ports with fugitive slaves on board found it legally prudent to post public notices in newspapers stating the circumstances by which an escaped slave had come to be discovered aboard their vessel, that they had done everything in their power not to aid and abet the runaway, and to publicly report the fugitive's last known location. Captains typically took out these advertisements over three successive weeks in a weekly publication.

These advertisements served several purposes. Taken at face value, such legal notices were meant simply to alert a slave's owner regarding the last known whereabouts of valuable human property. However, reading between the lines, a knowing reader may understand that this type of public notice was printed to provide legal cover to the captain and crew of any vessel that had, knowingly or unknowingly, transported a fugitive from his or her place of enslavement. One may even suspect that the practical circumstances of the publication and dissemination of such notices—many newspapers came out only weekly—actually provided an advantage to fugitive slaves: it gave them valuable time for onward travel to get beyond the reach of masters bent on recovering their "self-emancipated" property and of the federal law that supported them.

It is striking that the text of this advertisement provided no concrete information about the identity, legal status, or whereabouts of the person in question. The fugitive was described in neutral terms—a "negro" only, neither slave nor free—implicitly suspected but not confirmed to be a fugitive from enslavement. The ad's primary purpose, from the perspective of the sloop *Union*'s owners and commander, was to absolve the captain and crew of the vessel of any criminal liability for having transported a likely fugitive slave—to establish and circulate a narrative that created a kind of plausible deniability that would protect the captain and his vessel from legal repercussions. The reader must take the captain at his word that this lone man, "James," had stowed away aboard his vessel without his knowledge and that sailing conditions did not allow the vessel to return to port in Virginia and deliver a possible freedom seeker to his owner.

Regional newspapers circulated with merchant vessels up and down the Atlantic Seaboard, and southern slave-owners read them avidly to seek news of their missing property.[27] The stated goal of such advertisements was to inform owners of the location of their human chattels, but by the time news reached the owners in the South, the fugitives could have been anywhere. According to the Fugitive Slave Act of 1793, it became the responsibility of the state or territory where escaped slaves were discovered to arrest and secure known fugitives. However, owing to the vague language of the law, the fugitive effectively

—*Public Notice !*—

TO all whom it may concern, KNOW YE, THAT I WILLIAM TABER, commander of the ſloop Union, ſailed from *York River*, in *Virginia*, on or about the 28th of *March* laſt, bound to this Port—That on the day after ſailing, I diſcovered a NEGRO on board ſaid ſloop, who had concealed himſelf unbeknown to me.—It appearing inconſiſtent for me to return, the wind being ahead, I proceeded on my voyage, and landed him in this Port—He calls his name JAMES, is about 27 years old, and ſays he belongs to Mr. SHACLEFORD, a Planter, in *Kings* and *Queen's County*, *Virginia*. Any perſon claiming him, will know by this information where he is—For which purpoſe it is made public in this manner, and every legal method has been taken to prevent the Owner loſing the property, in my power.—

WILLIAM TABER.

Newbedford, April 20th, 1797.

FIGURE 4. Classified Advertisement Placed by Captain William Taber in the *Medley or New Bedford Marine Journal*, 20 April 1797. The item gives legal notice of the whereabouts of a suspected fugitive slave who had arrived in New Bedford, Massachusetts, aboard the sloop *Union* in the previous month. Ad, courtesy, New Bedford Whaling Museum, Massachusetts.

became a free person if, after six months following arrest, he or she remained unclaimed by the legal owner or the owner's agent.[28]

Left unstated was that, once the fugitive came into port, his or her movements were not controlled or impeded in any way. As interpreted in Massachusetts after 1783, even before the passage of explicit federal runaway slave legislation, the state's law did not compel authorities to arrest and detain suspected fugitives.[29] Instead, Massachusetts jurisprudence, which at the time also covered all the ports down east along the Maine coast, held that a ship's principal officer had fulfilled his duty under the law once he had served public notice of what had transpired aboard his vessel without his consent. The larger lesson here is that events like these happened with such frequency in the late eighteenth century (not just in Massachusetts but in other northern free states, as well) that standard legal language and iconography evolved in the public press to report the circumstances in a way calculated to benefit all parties involved or implicated in a seaborne escape from enslavement.

NEW BEDFORD: A PORT TOWN WINDOW ON THE MARITIME UNDERGROUND RAILROAD

No northern maritime community exemplifies the multiple themes embodied in this volume better than does the whaling port of New Bedford, Massachusetts. The story of the Underground Railroad comprises a series of epic narratives detailing individual sacrifices and acts of heroism by many people of diverse ethnic backgrounds who attempted to escape enslavement or who sought to help enslaved people gain their freedom. Because whaling was typically an industry dominated by antislavery-minded Quakers, New Bedford became a hotbed for abolitionism in the antebellum North. For runaway slaves from south of the Mason-Dixon line, New Bedford was known as a safe haven. The port town was a beacon of hope at the end of the Underground Railroad, where southern slave catchers in pursuit of fugitives and the sizeable bounties on their heads received a distinctly hostile reception. As a northern port city closely linked by commercial water routes to the Deep South, New Bedford provides the historian a prime microcosm in which to explore and understand the maritime dimension of the Underground Railroad.

New Bedford became a vitally important station in this clandestine network for a number of reasons. Foremost among them were its population of dedicated Quakers and free African Americans for whom slavery was a moral outrage and the vitality, heterogeneity, and resourcefulness of its maritime community. Although seafaring was considered a "contemptible occupation" for white men, it was "an occupation of opportunity for slaves and recent freedmen," as Jeffrey Bolster writes in *Black Jacks*.[30] New Bedford was one hub in an extensive coastal seaborne trading system that exchanged goods in southern ports and the West Indies. Sympathetic New England ship captains and crewmen assisted fugitives by stowing them away amid bales of trade goods and other cargo until they reached a northern port and eventual sanctuary in places such as New Bedford, Boston, or Canada. Indeed, escaping slaves termed New Bedford "the Fugitive's Gibraltar" in admiration of the lengths to which its residents would go to safeguard them.[31] Thus, the town became not so much a stop *along* the Underground Railroad; rather, it was a *terminus*—a community where ex-slaves knew they could settle and prosper. By 1853, nearly 9 percent of New Bedford's residents were African American, the highest percentage of any city in the antebellum northern United States. Moreover, in 1855, according to the Massachusetts state census taken that year, nearly 43 percent of New Bedford's African American population admitted to having been born in the southern United States. That statistic indicated an extraordinary migration pattern for Blacks from a region of the country where slavery was legal (and the overwhelming majority of Black people were enslaved) to a specific northern city where slavery was emphatically held to be intolerable.[32] Such statistics strongly support the view, as historian Kathryn Grover notes, "that a considerable number of fugitives lived in New Bedford, before and especially after the Fugitive Slave Act" of 1850.[33]

Even in the 1830s and 1840s, New Bedford was a primary hub of abolitionist activity; sympathetic residents founded the New Bedford Anti-Slavery Society in the fall of 1833. "The town was antislavery from the start, being full of Quakers . . . and the people were all Abolitionists before William Lloyd Garrison began his wonderful work," wrote journalist Charles T. Congdon.[34] In *The Underground Railroad in Massachusetts* published in 1936, author Wilbur Siebert credits residents of New Bedford early on with "befriending the runaway . . . in a manner often employed later by Underground operators."[35]

Quaker owners of whale-ships usually welcomed runaways as much for practical as moral reasons. Freedmen often made good sailors, and "self-emancipated" men might seek convenient employment on a whaling voyage, knowing that their multiyear absences at sea would confound bounty hunters sent to haul them back into involuntary servitude. After the passage of the Fugitive Slave Act in 1850, New Bedford's citizens, such as prominent shipowners Rodney French, William C. Taber, and the Rotch and Rodman families, protected runaway slaves even though aiding and abetting fugitives was an illegal activity that placed all the involved participants in danger of punishment by fine, imprisonment, or re-enslavement.

In September 1838, with the help of Underground Railroad agents, Frederick Augustus Washington Bailey, who had been born into slavery in Maryland, escaped to New York and then to New Bedford with his wife, Anna, who was a free woman. Dressed as a mariner to allay suspicions, he traveled overland and by sea and carried an official seaman's protection certificate borrowed from a free Black sailor.[36] Taking the last name Douglass to escape detection, Frederick found work as a day laborer on the New Bedford docks. The town's people of color, he recalled, were "much more spirited than I had supposed they would be," with a "determination to protect each other from the blood-thirsty kidnapper [bounty hunters who sought fugitive slaves], at all hazards."[37] Douglass and his family made New Bedford their home for seven years.

In addition to the employment opportunities in the whaling, fishing, and maritime-support trades that drew fugitive African Americans to New Bedford, booming textile mills later brought untold numbers of immigrants from Ireland, French-speaking Canada, Portugal and even the South Pacific, transforming the town into one of the most cosmopolitan places in the United States. Contemporaries saw this community as a wonder, a model of social diversity and racial harmony in an America North and South generally hostile to foreign immigrants of any race or ethnicity. In 1858, local scion Daniel Ricketson, a friend of Henry David Thoreau, observed in his *History of New Bedford* that "owing to the influence of the anti-slavery principles of the Society of Friends, there is but little prejudice against color, and a general willingness and desire that the colored population may enjoy equal rights and privileges with themselves."[38] During the Civil War, New Bedford was a recruiting site for the celebrated African American Fifty-Fourth Massachusetts Infantry Regiment. Many local residents—often fugitive ex-slaves, including some with seagoing experience—joined the ranks to fight for slave emancipation. One volunteer, Sgt. William H. Carney, who had been born a slave in 1840 in the port of Norfolk, Virginia, and had escaped to New Bedford most likely by ship, became the nation's first Black soldier to earn the Congressional Medal of Honor.[39] Two of Frederick Douglass's sons, Charles and Lewis, served in the Fifty-Fourth Massachusetts as well, while a third son, Frederick Jr., worked as a regimental recruiter alongside the Union Army campaigning in Mississippi.[40]

EVADING THE BOUNTY HUNTER: FUGITIVES AT SEA ON WHALING VOYAGES

Once arrived in New Bedford or a nearby whaling port, one expedient option for work open to an escaped male slave was to go to sea as a foremast jack on whaling voyages to avoid re-enslavement. While one might expect that many instances of such artifice would be well known, in fact there is only a small selection of concretely documented cases of fugitive slaves who signed aboard a whaling vessel as novice "green hands" for a protracted voyage specifically to avoid detection after fleeing slavery. Upon consideration, the reasons for this lack of abundant documentation are clear enough: the practice was illegal; and the men in question were fugitives, technically stolen legal property. Maintaining anonymity and a low profile were in the best interests of everyone involved, whether freedom seeker, ship's master, or shipowners. The use of aliases complicates attempts by modern researchers to compile data on this matter.

Still, oblique and direct references to runaway slaves serving as crew aboard Yankee whaling vessels are not difficult to find. In 1834, a knowledgeable observer gave an insider's account of the disparate origins of the men who made up a typical Massachusetts whaling crew:

> There are often found on the same deck the lingering remnants of the aborigines of this State, in specimens of Gayhead and Mashpee tribes,—the runaway slave,—a renegade tar from the British navy,—the Irish, the Dutch,—the mongrel Portuguese from the Azores, and the natives of the Sandwich Islands, from which the captains make up the complements of crews diminished by accident or disease, or scanty by design.[41]

John Thompson, who was born into slavery in 1812 but who escaped from Maryland by traveling overland to Pennsylvania, provided one of the most detailed accounts of a fugitive who went to sea to avoid arrest by bounty-hunting slave catchers. In his self-published narrative of these events, Thompson recounted how he determined to go to sea after seeing freedom seekers in Philadelphia recaptured and sent back to enslavement in the South. On arriving in New Bedford, he deliberately joined the crew of a whaling vessel, which he identified as the bark *Milwood*, and served as the ship's steward during a lengthy voyage to the Indian Ocean.[42] The *Milwood*'s logbook and crew list show that Thompson shipped under his own name; the voyage lasted two full years, from June 1842 to June 1844.[43]

Other examples of fugitive slaves who are known to have signed as crew aboard New Bedford whaling ships include John S. Jacobs, the brother of Harriet Ann Jacobs. He sailed as a green hand on the whaleship *Frances Henrietta*, beginning a four-year voyage to the Pacific in August 1839[44] and later going aboard the *Draper* on a three-year voyage from 1844–1847.[45] Also George Weston, at age twenty-two, sailed aboard the whaling bark *Ocean* in May 1854, giving peninsular Northampton County, Virginia, as his birthplace, and later worked as cook on the whaling bark *Edward* (1856–1860), this time claiming falsely to be from Philadelphia when he signed on.[46] Philip Piper was another case. Although he had escaped from Alexandria, Virginia, his shipping papers listed New York City as his home. Piper completed multiple voyages on whalers out of New Bedford, including the ships *Frances Henrietta,* most likely from April 1837–April 1839, and *America* from July 1840–May1842. He gave his age as twenty-one when he signed on with the *America.*[47]

At least two members of the crew of the whaling brig *Rising States,* which sailed from New Bedford in 1837 under the command of African American captain William Cuffe, were likely to have been fugitives trying to evade re-enslavement by going to sea on a long voyage. Green hand "Lisbon" Johnson is described on the vessel's muster roll in terms that identify him as a man of African descent; he gave his age as forty and his place of birth as Bladensborough, Virginia. His thirty-five-year-old shipmate James Roselle, also an African American, stated that his place of birth was Washington, North Carolina, a port on the Pamlico River.[48] While it is possible that each was a free man of color seeking maritime employment for the first time, the circumstances suggest that they had ulterior motives for going aboard a whaler. The wealthy Cuffe family, based a few miles from New Bedford in Westport, Massachusetts, were outspoken abolitionists, and as shipowners during the first half of the nineteenth century, they were notable for shipping whaling and merchant crews composed entirely of men of color.[49] In any event, the *Rising States* left U.S. waters in July 1837; seamen Johnson and Roselle were paid off and discharged that December when the vessel was condemned in the Cape Verde Islands off the northwest coast of continental Africa.[50]

Determining precisely who were in fact fugitive slaves among the many known African American whaling ship crewmen is a task fraught with potential pitfalls for the investigator. Regarding primary-source documentation held by the New Bedford Whaling Museum, Mark Procknik, that institution's head librarian, comments:

> The crew lists that we have in our collections are full with whalers who may have been freed slaves, but . . . locating concrete documentation brings its own set of challenges. For example, the crew list for the maiden whaling voyage of the *Lagoda* included a man named Joseph Wilson, who is listed as having a black complexion and "wooly hair" and hailing from Baltimore. The ship *Martha* of Fairhaven shipped another seaman with "wooly hair" and a black complexion named Charles Flowers [who claimed to be] from Pennsylvania. The ship *Condor* of New Bedford shipped a black-skinned "wooly-haired" seaman named Felix Hutchinson who came from New Orleans. The trick, however, is determining which of these

> African-American whalers, as per the available documentation, were actually [self-emancipated] slaves. It gets even trickier when you factor in the fact that the names provided in the crew lists may not even be their real names. In my opinion, our crew lists are full of freed slaves who shipped onboard whaling voyages.[51]

Corroborating evidence from other contemporary sources indicates that fugitives from slavery frequently set their course toward New Bedford. One of those sources is the work of a well-known African American abolitionist, William Still, who was chairman of the Vigilance Committee of the Pennsylvania Anti-Slavery Society prior to the Civil War. Still operated an exceptionally active Underground Railroad safe house near the waterfront in Philadelphia during the mid-1850s. As many as eight hundred fugitive slaves passed through his care; many had arrived in the free state of Pennsylvania by ship via the Philadelphia seaport. Still kept a detailed record of his work, which he published in 1872. Among the many examples of maritime escape that he documented is a report of five men brought to Philadelphia by an anonymous schooner captain from Wilmington, North Carolina, in November 1856. At least one man was bound for New Bedford, where he believed his brother and cousin were then living.[52]

On the topic of gender, recorded incidents of successful maritime escape demonstrate a strong predominance of male fugitives. What explains this gender discrepancy? The practical circumstances of male-dominated waterfront and shipboard labor practices favored escape attempts made by male slaves. In commercial ports, there simply were not many women employed on the docks or in shipyards and virtually none on board vessels. Most women who frequented the waterfront worked in conspicuous service industries as street vendors, tavern workers, and other occupations. Consequently, they were usually well known by local authorities and laborers. The presence of unfamiliar Black women in any of these areas would have been noticeable and suspect, marking them as potential fugitives. Even so, it was not unknown for women and girls to escape enslavement by sea.

For example, another case that William Still documented is that of Mary Millburn, using the alias Louisa F. Jones, who escaped to Philadelphia from Norfolk, Virginia, in May 1858 aboard an express steamship carrying U.S. mail. With the assistance of agents arranged by Still, she boarded the vessel in disguise, wearing "male attire," and avoided detection when state authorities searched the ship before departure.[53] In another instance, Still recounted how a large group of fifteen enslaved men, women, and children were landed at the foot of Philadelphia's Broad Street in the dead of night from an unnamed schooner on the Schuylkill River. They had been spirited away from Norfolk, Virginia, in July

1854 with the full knowledge and cooperation of the vessel's captain, who later assisted with getting the fugitives ashore on League Island in Philadelphia, after a coastal voyage fraught with danger of discovery for the contraband cargo. The schooner successfully endured two separate searches by government officials while *en route*, with terrifying potential consequences—arrest and imprisonment for the crew and re-enslavement for the African Americans.[54]

Subsequent research has identified this vessel as the passenger schooner *City of Richmond*, commanded by a Virginia-based captain named Albert Fountain. He conducted a regular packet service between New York, Norfolk, and Richmond, with occasional stops in Philadelphia and Wilmington, Delaware. Fugitive slaves, male and female, often traveled aboard as clandestine cargo.[55] Perhaps the most-active documented maritime operator involved in conducting fugitives along the saltwater Underground Railroad, however, was a mysterious schooner owner whom William Still refers to in his records only as "a law-breaking captain by the name of B." This sea-going abolitionist sympathizer was responsible for numerous voyages in the 1850s, ferrying dozens of fugitive slaves (and sometimes entire family groups) to sanctuary in Philadelphia in exchange for a hefty fee per illicit passenger.[56]

Only two escaped slaves were ever arrested in Boston and returned to slavery by federal marshals under the Fugitive Slave Act of 1850. Both had arrived in that city by sea as fugitives from the South. Seventeen-year-old Thomas Sims had escaped from Georgia as a stowaway aboard a coastal trading vessel; authorities arrested him in Boston and returned him to his owner in April 1851. Three years later in 1854, twenty-one-year-old Anthony Burns escaped from Richmond, Virginia, and traveled to Boston by boat with the assistance of an empathetic African American mariner. Burns was also captured and returned, despite the efforts of a crowd of abolitionists in Boston, who tried to rescue him from federal custody and spirit him to safety.[57]

Shifting the long-established, terrestrial-dominated historical narrative about the Underground Railroad to include its counterpart maritime dimension is a matter of raising awareness and improving scholarly accuracy. However, the reorientation is also an exercise in doing justice to the memory of Underground Railroad operatives, known and unknown, free and unfree, who risked imprisonment, brutal corporeal punishment, or death in North America's ports and coastal waterways to provide untold numbers of enslaved persons a chance to live in freedom. Their experiences have always been available to researchers, with archival evidence in abundance, yet their agency has been chronically obscured in the salient narrative by a century or more of historiographic predisposition to privilege the stories of fugitives who traveled by land over those who went by sea. Perhaps the emphasis on overland sojourners resulted from their usually requiring more time and more assistance to flee; they thus had greater contact with formal networks of Underground Railroad operatives, and so left more written and material vestiges of their ordeal. By contrast, those slaves who sailed far offshore, expeditiously over the pathless sea, necessarily left fewer traces of their passing. Their tales, though no less significant, have therefore taken longer to come to the attention of contemporary land-bound scholars.

NOTES

1. Jeffrey Bolster, *Black Jacks: African American Seamen in the Age of Sail* (Cambridge, Mass.: Harvard University Press, 1997).
2. Kathryn Grover, *The Fugitive's Gibraltar: Escaping Slaves and Abolitionism in New Bedford, Massachusetts* (Amherst: University of Massachusetts Press, 2001); David S. Cecelski, *The Waterman's Song: Slavery and Freedom in Maritime North Carolina* (Chapel Hill: University of North Carolina Press, 2001).
3. Jane Landers, "Southern Passage: The Forgotten Route to Freedom in Florida," in *Passages to Freedom: The Underground Railroad in History and Memory*, ed. David W. Blight (New York: Harper Collins/Smithsonian Books, 2004), 117–31; Harvey Amani Whitfield published *From American Slaves to Nova Scotian Subjects: The Case of the Black Refugees, 1813–1840* (Toronto: Pearson/Prentice Hall, 2005).
4. Fergus Bordewich, *Bound for Canaan: The Underground Railroad and the War for the Soul of America* (New York: Amistad/HarperCollins, 2005), 268–92; Cassandra Pybus, *Epic Journeys of Freedom: Runaway Slaves of the American Revolution and Their Global Quest for Liberty* (Boston: Beacon Press, 2006).
5. Irvin D. S. Winsboro and Joe Knetsch, "Florida Slaves, the 'Saltwater Railroad' to the Bahamas, and Anglo-American Diplomacy," in *Journal of Southern History* 79, no. 1 (February 2013): 51–78. They discuss the British Colonial Office's declaration of freedom on p. 56.
6. Walter Johnson, "White Lies: Human Property and Domestic Slavery Aboard the Slave Ship *Creole*," *Atlantic Studies* 5, no. 2 (2008): 237–63; Anita Rupprecht, "'All We Have Done, We Have Done for Freedom': The Creole Slave-Ship Revolt (1841) and the Revolutionary Atlantic," *Internationaal Instituut voor Sociale Geschiedenis* 58 (2013): 253–77; Jeffrey R. Kerr-Ritchie, *Rebellious Passage: The Creole Revolt and America's Coastal Slave Trade* (Cambridge, U.K.: Cambridge University Press, 2019), 10–11, 96–98, 103–30, 159–61.
7. Eric Foner, *Gateway to Freedom: The Hidden History of the Underground Railroad* (New York: W. W. Norton, 2015); Cassandra Newby-Alexander, *Virginia Waterways and the Underground Railroad* (Charleston, S.C.: The History Press, 2017).

8. "About the Project," Freedom on the Move, CISER Institute, Cornell University, accessed 27 September 2019, https://freedomonthemove.org/#about.
9. Library of Congress, Research Guides, Topics in Chronicling America, "Fugitive Slave Ads," accessed 15 September 2019, https://guides.loc.gov/chronicling-america-fugitive-slave-ads.
10. Correspondence with Megan Jeffreys, 11–12 October 2019. Jeffreys is a doctoral candidate at Cornell University and a researcher with the FOTM project.
11. The recent publications of historian Marcus Rediker, Sowande M. Mustakeem, and Jeffrey R. Kerr-Ritchie are notable exceptions. See Rediker, *The Slave Ship: A Human History* (New York: Viking-Penguin, 2007) and *The Amistad Rebellion: An Atlantic Odyssey of Slavery and Freedom* (New York: Viking-Penguin, 2012); Muskateem, *Slavery at Sea: Terror, Sex, and Sickness in the Middle Passage* (Urbana: Unniversity of Illinois Press, 2016); and Kerr-Ritchie, *Rebellious Passage.*
12. A recent shining exception is Nathaniel Philbrick, *In the Hurricane's Eye: The Genius of George Washington and the Victory at Yorktown* (New York: Viking Press, 2018). Philbrick, a competitive sailor, masterfully demonstrates the centrality of nautical concerns—weather, tides, sea power, fleet movements—to General George Washington's strategy in the Yorktown campaign of 1781, his climactic operation during the American Revolutionary War.
13. Benjamin Woods Labaree, William M. Fowler Jr., John B. Hattendorf, Jeffrey J. Safford, Edward W. Sloan, and Andrew W. German, *America and the Sea: A Maritime History* (Mystic, Conn.: Mystic Seaport, 1998), 94–95.
14. Foner, *Gateway to Freedom: The Hidden History of the Underground Railroad* (New York: W. W. Norton, 2015), 2.
15. Labaree et al., *America and the Sea*, 94–95.
16. William Grimes, *Life of William Grimes, the Runaway Slave, Brought Down to the Present Time. Written by Himself* (New Haven, Conn: published by the author, 1855), cited in Kathryn Grover, "Fugitive Slave Traffic and the Maritime World of New Bedford" (research paper prepared for New Bedford Whaling National Historical Park, Massachusetts, and the Boston Support Office of the National Park Service, Massachusetts, September 1998), 8.
17. Cecelski, *The Waterman's Song*, 143–48.
18. Florida, *An Act to Prevent the Abduction and Escape of Slaves from this State, Acts and Resolutions of the General Assembly of the State of Florida* (1855), chap. 635, 52–53.
19. William H. Siebert, *The Underground Railroad from Slavery to Freedom* (New York: MacMillan, 1898), 81.
20. Ibid., 144–45.
21. Thomas H. Jones, *The Experience of Thomas H. Jones, Who Was a Slave for Forty-three years* (New Bedford, Mass.: A. Anthony & Sons, 1871), 32, 43–44; U.S. Bureau of Labor Statistics, *History of Wages in the United States from Colonial Times to 1928*, rev. of Bulletin No. 499 with suppl., 1929–1933 (Washington, D.C.: GPO, 1934), 253.

22. Obituary of Captain Dempsey Hill, *New Bedford (Mass.) Evening Standard*, 14 May 1894; and "Many Have Sailed with Him. The Late Capt. Dempsey Hill Was Well Known," *Boston Herald*, 16 May 1894.
23. "Dempsey Hill Has Passed Away," *Boston Herald*, 16 May 1894. I am grateful to Lynda Ames of the Wareham Public Library for this and the above references regarding Dempsey Hill.
24. Keeler to his wife, 19 May 1862, in *Aboard the USS Monitor: 1862; The Letters of Acting Paymaster William Frederick Keeler, U.S. Navy, to His Wife, Anna*, ed. Robert W. Daly (Annapolis, Md.: United States Naval Institute Press, 1964); and John V. Quarstein, Cindy L. Lester, and Diana Martin, *The Monitor Boys: The Crew of the Union's First Ironclad* (Charleston, S.C.: The History Press, 2015), 15, 31, 123, 126–29, 137, 170–71, 200, 252, 270.
25. "Public Notice," *Medley or New Bedford (Mass.) Marine Journal*, 20 April 1797. The notice appeared in two successive editions.
26. *Fugitive Slave Act of 1793*, U.S. Statutes at Large 1 (1793): 302.
27. Labaree et al., *America and the Sea*, 94.
28. The Library of Congress, *A Century of Lawmaking*, 1414.
29. Emily Blanck, "Seventeen Eighty-Three: The Turning Point in the Law of Slavery and Freedom in Massachusetts," in *The New England Quarterly* 75, no. 1 (2002): 24–51; Margot Minardi, *Making Slavery History: Abolitionism and the Politics of Memory in Massachusetts* (New York: Oxford University Press, 2012), 15–19.
30. Bolster, *Black Jacks*, 4.
31. F. N. Boney, Richard L. Hume, and Rafia Zafar, eds., *God Made Man, Man Made the Slave: The Autobiography of George Teamoh* (Macon, Ga.: Mercer University Press, 1990), 106, cited in Grover, "Fugitive Slave Traffic," 11.
32. Grover, *The Fugitive's Gibraltar*, 54–60.
33. Grover, *The Fugitive's Gibraltar*, 60; and Grover, "Fugitive Slave Traffic," 5–7.
34. Congdon cited in Grover, *The Fugitive's Gibraltar*, 17.
35. Wilbur H. Siebert, *The Underground Railroad in Massachusetts* (Worcester, Mass.: The American Antiquarian Society, 1936), 5.
36. Frederick Douglass, *Life and Times of Frederick Douglass, Written by Himself, new. rev. ed., intro. George L. Ruffin* (Boston: De Wolfe & Fiske, 1892), 242–56; and David W. Blight, *Frederick Douglass: Prophet of Freedom* (New York: Simon & Schuster, 2018), 80–86.
37. Frederick Douglass, *Narrative of the life of Frederick Douglass, an American Slave* (Boston: Anti-Slavery Office, 1845), 115.
38. Daniel Ricketson, *The History of New Bedford, Bristol County, Massachusetts* (New Bedford, Mass.: published by the author, 1858), 253.
39. Massachusetts, Adjutant General's Office, *Massachusetts Soldiers, Sailors, and Marines in the Civil War, vol. 4* (Norwood, Mass.: printed at the Norwood Press, 1932), 670.
40. William S. McFeely, *Frederick Douglass* (New York: W. W. Norton, 1991), 226; Blight, *Frederick Douglass*, 385–86, 392, 396.

41. "The Whale Fishery," *North American Review*, January 1834, 108. I am indebted to Michael Dyer of the New Bedford Whaling Museum for this reference.
42. John Thompson, *The Life of John Thompson, a Fugitive Slave: Containing His History of 25 Years in Bondage, and His Providential Escape* (Worcester, Mass.: published by the author, 1856), 103, 107–32.
43. Logbook of the whaling bark *Milwood*, 1842–1844, no. 0996, Kendall Collection, Research Library, New Bedford Whaling Museum, Massachusetts; and Crew list of the bark *Milwood*, folio 44, in "Register for seaman's names, their descriptions, and remarks pertaining to their vessel, its destination, and further remarks regarding next of kin," 1842, manuscript, New Bedford Port Society, Research Library, New Bedford Whaling Museum (hereafter NBPS "Seaman's Register").
44. Alexander Starbuck, *History of the American Whale Fishery from Its Earliest Inception to the Year 1876* (Washington, D.C.: GPO, 1878), 1: 354–55. I am grateful to Lee Blake, president of the New Bedford Historical Society, for references in this paragraph.
45. "A True Tale of Slavery," an anonymous slave narrative serialized in *The Leisure Hour: A Family Journal of Instruction and Recreation*, February 1861, 125–27. This anonymous, serialized article is attributed to John S. Jacobs. See crew list of the ship *Draper*, folio 44, in NBPS "Seaman's Register," 1844.
46. George Weston's seamen's protection paper, 29 April 1854, Manuscripts, Special Collections, New Bedford Free Public Library, Massachusetts, cited in Grover, *The Fugitive's Gibraltar*, 245.
47. Crew list of the ship *America*, folio 224, in NBPS "Seaman's Register," 1832–1843.
48. Crew list of the brig *Rising States*, folio 102, in NBPS "Seaman's Register," 1832–1843.
49. *Times* (London), 2 August 1811, 3. See also Rosalind Cobb Wiggins, ed., *Captain Paul Cuffe's Logs and Letters* (Washington, D.C.: Howard University Press, 1996), 97–130, 157–94, 221–48.
50. Dennis Wood, "Abstracts of Whaling Voyages, 1831–1873," n.p., manuscript, 1981, New Bedford Free Public Library, Massachusetts; Charles F. Batchelder, "Whaleship Index," 1960, card file, Research Library, New Bedford Whaling Museum, Massachusetts.
51. Mark Procknik (Librarian, New Bedford Whaling Museum); correspondence with author, 24 May 2018.
52. William Still, *The Underground Rail Road: A Record of Facts, Authentic Letters, Narratives, &c.* (Philadelphia: Porter & Coates, 1872), 379–81.
53. Ibid., 558–59.
54. Ibid., 559–65.
55. Foner, *Gateway to Freedom*, 153–54, 209.
56. Still, *The Underground Rail Road*, 74–79, 177–89, 200–201, 250–54, 262–63, 293, 307–9.
57. Foner, *Gateway to Freedom*, 148–49.

2

WORKING ON THE DOCKS

Waterfront Labor, Coastal Commerce, and Escaping Enslavement from Charleston, South Carolina

MICHAEL D. THOMPSON

> The captain . . . asked me how I came there? I said, 'I got stowed away.' He asked me if some white man did not stow [me] away to get him in trouble? I assured him he was mistaken, as I stowed myself away.
>
> —John Andrew Jackson, *The Experience of a Slave in South Carolina*

In 1862 a former South Carolina slave named John Andrew Jackson published an account of his enslavement and escape from bondage during the winter of 1846–1847.[1] In this narrative Jackson claimed to have become aware of the geographical limits of slavery from northern travelers passing through rural South Carolina. "The 'Yankees,' or Northerners, when they visited our plantations," the former slave explained, "used to tell the negroes that there was a country called England, where there were no slaves, and that the city of Boston was free; and we used to wish we knew which way to travel to find those places." Jackson often had been tasked with driving his master's cattle to market in Charleston, located approximately 150 miles away, and it occurred to Jackson that "if I could hide in one of the vessels I saw lading at the wharfs, I should be able to get to the 'Free country,' wherever that was." During a three-day Christmas holiday in 1846, Jackson slipped away from the festivities of the slave quarters and made his way to Charleston on a pony. Recalling that it was the custom in the city for masters to hire out their bondsmen, he joined a gang of slave wharf-hands on the docks and—despite lacking the mandatory badge used to visibly identify and regulate the city's enslaved workers—earned wages "without arousing any suspicion."[2]

After laboring on the docks for several weeks, Jackson boarded a ship and inquired of the free Black cook whether the vessel was bound for Boston. After the cook affirmed that it was, the runaway asked, "Can't you stow me away?" The free Black seaman immediately said that he could, but having second thoughts, he asked Jackson, "Did not some white man send you here to ask me this?" The cook elucidated that under the provisions of South Carolina's controversial Negro Seamen Acts—passed between 1822 and 1856 and designed to prevent seditious communications between southern slaves and northern or foreign free Blacks—the Black members of the crew had been in jail since the vessel's arrival but that in preparation for departure the captain had paid to release them from confinement the day before. Despite his misgivings, the free Black cook agreed to look for a place to hide Jackson but beseeched the fugitive not to betray him.[3]

When Jackson returned to the vessel the next morning, the cook again expressed apprehension and told the slave to go ashore and that he wanted nothing to do with him. Jackson obeyed him but snuck on board after the cook entered the ship's galley. Tiptoeing to the cargo hatch, the runaway waited there for the captain or mate to emerge from the cabin. When the mate appeared, Jackson asked permission to remove the hatch, and "he thinking that I was one of the gang coming to work there, told me I might." Jackson descended and soon was joined in the hold by a gang of slave laborers, who began questioning him about his occupation and owner. "Just then they were all ordered on deck, and as soon as I was left," he recalled, "I slipped myself between two bales of cotton, with the deck above me, in a space not large enough for a bale of cotton to go; and just then a bale was placed at the mouth of my crevice, and shut me in a space about 4-ft. by 3-ft., or thereabouts. I then heard them gradually filling up the hold; and at last the hatch was placed on, and I was left in total darkness." Cramped, dehydrated, and nearly asphyxiated—conditions not unlike those experienced by millions of enslaved Africans during the Atlantic crossing—John Andrew Jackson was forced to reveal himself *en route* to Boston. The captain, like the free Black cook, was convinced that he was being entrapped and that a white Charlestonian had ordered Jackson to stow away in the vessel. The captain therefore resolved to return the runaway aboard the first southward ship encountered, but "he met no vessel." On the evening of 10 February 1847, the ship, with the stowaway, docked in Boston, and Jackson obtained his freedom.[4]

As evidenced by Jackson's account, laboring on an urban waterfront had its advantages, even for the enslaved. The antebellum South's bustling wharves and levees offered slaves more than the capacity to hire out one's own time, earn wages, and claim a measure of autonomy. Situated on the western rim of the Atlantic World in what might be characterized as an amphibious or littoral borderland, slaves toiling along Charleston's seaboard also were afforded ample occasion to interact with northern and foreign mariners, receive abolitionist literature, stow away in dockside vessels, and abscond to northern ports via the Underground Railroad. These labor and life experiences were in many ways unique. Due to the nature of their indispensable work, enslaved dock laborers in this coastal port were daily subject to outside influences and presented with remarkable opportunities and enticements not accessible to most plantation slaves or even other urban bondsmen not employed along the water's edge. Not even the slaves of New Orleans' crowded levees or those manning the hundreds of steamboats plying the Mississippi quite enjoyed all the potential and inherent benefits of perpetual exposure and access to ocean-going vessels of the nearby Atlantic and their Black and white crews. Consequent legislation, such as South Carolina's Negro Seamen Acts and the little-studied New York Ship Inspection Law of 1841, aimed to further control the communications and movements of the city's bondsmen. But as with measures censuring work songs and prescribing slave badges, hiring locations, and fixed wages, enslaved dock workers were not so easily dominated by authorities and masters and found ways to resist and circumvent such restrictions. Long before enslaved waterman Robert Smalls famously drew on his experience, knowledge, and skills as a stevedore, rigger, and pilot to boldly guide the Confederate steam-powered gunboat *Planter* out of Charleston Harbor and into Civil War immortality, scores of unheralded slaves employed waterfront labor to embark on maritime conveyances of the Underground Railroad and so find their way to freedom.[5]

With hundreds, then thousands of vessels annually entering and exiting Charleston Harbor, runaway slaves were drawn to the city's waterfront. In fact, countless bondsmen had escaped enslavement by stowing away in northbound vessels during the colonial period, and maritime runaways continued their flight during and after the American Revolution. In a runaway advertisement published in August 1781, William Sams announced that his slave Will "has been seen about the wharfs in town."[6] James Lynah similarly informed readers in May 1784 that his man Guy "has been frequently seen about Rose's wharf."[7] Some slave-owners plainly stated their fears. Among them was William McWhann, whose "stout made negro lad named SAM" was supposed to be "lurking about

FIGURE 5. The Confederate Gunboat *Planter*, a Converted Cotton Transport Steamer, and Twenty-two-year-old Enslaved Waterman Robert Smalls (*inset*). Smalls commandeered the vessel on 13 May 1862, along with eight Black crewmen and their relatives (five women and three children). He navigated the ship safely out of Charleston Harbor and delivered it to blockading Union warships, winning freedom for all on board. Engraving of *Planter*, *Harper's Weekly*, 14 June 1862, 372; portrait of Robert Smalls courtesy of Hagley Museum and Library, Wilmington, Delaware.

till he gets an opportunity of going on board some vessel."[8] A master named G. Hooper likewise assumed that his slave Jupiter would "endeavour to get away by sea."[9] Slave masters were so concerned that their absconded slaves would stow away and sail to freedom, hundreds of runaway advertisements issued warnings to ship captains who frequented South Carolina ports. A typical notice read, "Masters of vessels are hereby cautioned against suffering such a slave to be harboured by their crews, concealed on ship board [*sic*] or carried off."[10]

Though "inveigling, stealing and carrying away" slaves became a capital offense in South Carolina in 1754, the problem remained so acute that Charleston's grand jury complained in September 1797 that "great numbers of Negroes and other Slaves, are carried off the State to the great injury of the Citizens thereof."[11] Taking notice, Governor Charles Pinckney called on the General Assembly to pass legislation requiring all departing vessels to stop at Fort Johnson, located on James Island near the mouth of Charleston Harbor, where they would be searched for runaway slaves. A legislative committee subsequently reported that laws formerly designed to thwart such "mischief" had fallen into disuse after the Revolution. The committee therefore recommended the passage of a new act "to prevent the Evil complained of."[12]

Lawmakers failed to enact such legislation, and hundreds of slaves continued to run away, using maritime strategies that constituted an important but little understood dimension of the Underground Railroad. Leaders of the South Carolina Association, a group of prominent white Charlestonians formed after the Denmark Vesey conspiracy to maintain order and implement stricter controls over the city's Black population, again warned the state legislature in the early 1820s that there were increasing attempts to "inveigle away our slaves." So many packet-ship lines now existed between Charleston and New York, not to mention other northern ports, that "the opportunities for embarking are occurring almost every day in the year," and consequently there was "no security, that our slaves, will not be seduced from the service of their masters, in greater numbers than heretofore."[13] When in 1821 three enslaved sailors fled their vessel anchored in the Cooper River, the ship's captain surmised that the runaways would attempt "to get on board some vessel bound to the northward."[14] A free Black New Yorker named Joseph Lawrence, meanwhile, had arrived in the low country aboard the schooner *Fair Play* in June 1822, and was convicted and imprisoned for "endeavoring to inveigle" a slave named Macklin. This incident was reprinted in the *Charleston Courier* explicitly as "a warning to others, who are in the habit of being employed on board our packets, in the Southern States" and who similarly might consider secreting slaves in the holds of coastal trading vessels.[15] And Augusta slave-owner Jonathan Hand was convinced in July 1828 that his slave Harry, an absconded drayman, would "probably endeavor to escape out of the country, either by the way of Charleston or Savannah."[16] The historical record therefore demonstrates that most runaway slaves were not, in fact, unwillingly "inveigled" or "seduced, swerved from their allegiance to their masters." That slaves were no more passively acted on than they were contented and docile, slave-owners privately knew well. "Slaves are . . . capable of evil purposes as well as good," admitted a Charleston judge in January 1860. "They are, to a certain extent, free agents. They have brains, nerves, hands, and thereby can conceive and execute a malignant purpose," including freeing themselves from bondage.[17]

But rather than merely loitering about the wharves and awaiting a chance occasion to slip into a ship's hold, many runaway slaves actively sought waterfront work that presented these "opportunities for embarking," especially when loading cotton or rice below decks. Waterfront employment, in other words, was an ideal halfway house on a runaway's road to freedom. In an account similar to that of John Andrew Jackson's escape from bondage, *The Emancipator* chronicled the firsthand narrative of another slave's flight from Charleston's waterfront during the winter of 1837. This unnamed bondsman detailed the beatings and abuse he had received while working for a railroad company in rural South Carolina. The day after a particularly severe whipping, he slipped away into some nearby woods. That night, under the cover of darkness, the slave returned to the railroad, boarded a car, and hid among cotton bales bound for Charleston. After arriving in the city, the runaway made his way to the waterfront and, though lacking the requisite slave badge, "waited there with the rest of the hands to get work." Before long, a white stevedore approached and offered the fugitive a job, and he followed the employer to a wharf where he worked alongside other slaves "stowing away cotton in a vessel" from Boston.

Each day the enslaved wharf-hands went to a cook-shop for meals. But lacking money, the runaway returned to the vessel, where he became acquainted with the white steward, who gave the slave something to eat. When asked one day, "how much of your wages do you have to give your master," the slave answered all, to which the steward responded that "it was not so where he came from" and that "there the people are all free." Apparently having never heard of Black freedom, the former slave recalled, "When he told me this I began to think that there was a free country, and to wish that I could get there." During subsequent conversations, the steward proposed assisting the slave to run away to the North: "He said the vessel was all loaded and would sail next morning. That day was Saturday, and he told me that after I knocked off work and had got my pay, I must stay about there till it was dark and all the people in the ship were asleep and that he would wait for me. He said he had got a place made to hide me in, and that if I was sure not to cough, or make any noise, he thought he could get me away safe." After dark, the fugitive crept along the wharf to the vessel where he was greeted by the white steward, who hastily opened the scuttle and instructed the slave to quietly jump in. Once the hatchway was closed, the stowaway "crowded in between the bales." After a harrowing four-week voyage to Boston, the steward assisted the runaway out of his hiding place and directed him to walk up the street and inquire for a colored boarding house. The newly freed slave soon encountered a Black man who quickly perceived "from my dress and the cotton on my head and clothes" that he was a runaway and saw to it that he was cared for.[18]

Another episode of waterfront labor facilitating escape from bondage comes from the Works Progress Administration (WPA) interview of former slave Susan Hamlin, recorded in dialect amid the Great Depression and Jim Crow South. Hamlin's father, Adam Collins, was a slave coachman on Edisto Island, located about twenty miles south of Charleston. The day after Collins received a whipping, the slave drove his master four miles into the woods, tied him to a tree, "an' give him de same 'mount of lickin' he wus given on Sunday." Collins frequently had been permitted to go to Charleston on errands, so he made his way to a landing and boarded a boat taking agricultural products to the city. Once in Charleston, "he gone on de water-front an' ax for a job on a ship so he could git to de North." Evidently not required to present a slave badge or provide proof of free status, Collins was hired and eventually sailed to New York where he worked as a store clerk.[19]

Meanwhile, slave-owner A. J. Huntington of Augusta offered an eye-catching thirty dollars for the arrest of his mulatto slave Ben Elliott, who had absconded in October 1834. In advertisements continuously appearing in the *Charleston Courier* between 4 February and 9 April 1835, the master expressed concern that Ben had returned to Charleston, the city in which the slave was raised and his mother still "sells fruit in the market." Prior to being sold to Huntington eighteen months before—and despite being "rather dandyish"—Ben was "in the habit of working about the wharves and on board vessels as a Stevedore or an Assistant." Although Huntington's slave disappeared into the relative anonymity and liminality of Charleston's waterfront and the master advertised for capture and return in a Charleston newspaper, his runaway ad, paradoxically, reemerged in the New York abolitionist newspaper, *The Emancipator,* in May 1836. After nineteen months of searching for his valuable bondsman, A. J. Huntington reasonably concluded that Ben was no longer in South Carolina and likely had exploited his employment and familiarity on Charleston's docks to stow away to freedom in New York City.[20]

Of course, many slaves were not successful in their attempts to run away via Charleston's waterfront. From September 1838 to August 1839, for instance, city authorities apprehended 115 runaway slaves, many of whom undoubtedly had planned to stow away.[21] Wharfinger Thomas Marshall, in fact, reported that one of his slaves—who "writes well enough & has the capacity to write his free papers, passes &c."—was confined in the Work House after attempting "to take his departure for the north" by engaging with "the Yankey [*sic*] Capt. of a fishing smack."[22] In June 1837 two slaves owned by lawyer and legislator Langdon Cheves were discovered at sea aboard the brig *New York* and transported back to Charleston on a pilot boat.[23] Under the title, "Another Attempt at Escape," the *Savannah Georgian* reported in May 1845 that a slave named James, the property of Charleston's mercantile firm Williams and McBarney, was "fortunately discovered" hiding between a water cask and a cotton bale aboard a British bark anchored off Long Island, New York, and bound for Liverpool, England.[24] This English seaport also was the intended destination for a fugitive named Billy, whom Charleston City Guard officer Moses Levy found "concealed in the long boat of the British ship *Coronet* . . . prepared to make his escape." A year earlier, the same slave had nearly stolen out of Charleston Harbor before he was discovered and returned to town. Conceding that "the city of Charleston render[ed] it comparatively easy for the said slave to accomplish his purpose to abscond in some future attempt," Billy's master resolved to sell the "unruly" but valuable bondsman.[25] In another instance, waterfront master cooper Jacob Schirmer recorded in his diary the daring but failed attempt of a slave who stowed away on the steamer *S. R. Spaulding*, which was bound for Boston and carried delegates from the Democratic National Convention held in Charleston in late April and early May 1860. This fugitive was discovered at sea, transferred to a vessel that took him to Baltimore, and returned from there to Charleston by rail.[26] And former slave Amie Lumpkin recalled the episode of "one big Black man, who tried to steal a boat ride from Charleston" in or around 1856. This slave absconded from his master's plantation in Fairfield and made it to the city before being apprehended. According to Lumpkin, the returned runaway admitted to the overseer: "Sho', I try to git away from this sort of thing. I was goin' to Massachusetts, and hire out 'til I git 'nough to carry me to my home in Africa."[27]

Evidence suggests that New York and Boston—the latter being the cradle of the American antislavery movement and home to prominent abolitionists such as David Walker and William Lloyd Garrison—were the preferred destinations of Charleston's maritime runaways. Though many seafaring New Yorkers and Bostonians, white and Black, offered stowaways aid ranging from benign neglect to active assistance, not all people in these northern ports were abolitionists. In April 1852, less than one month after the publication of Harriet

Beecher Stowe's *Uncle Tom's Cabin* unleashed a firestorm of sectional enmity and contentious debate over the federal Fugitive Slave Act of 1850, the *Charleston Courier* printed with "considerable gratification" a letter sent from a Boston merchant house to one of the firm's ship captains in Charleston: "See that you do not bring any negroes—slaves—away. If you find any secreted after you get to sea, no matter if in Boston Bay, we wish you to return to [Charleston] and deliver any such slaves to their owners, or the proper authorities. We would spare neither expense [n]or trouble in restoring to our Southern friends their slaves." These Bostonians, it seems, if we accept their letter as sincere, valued commercial trade relations and prosperity more than freedom for Black southerners. The newspaper commended these "Northern brethren" for their "praiseworthy conduct" and for exercising the "right spirit."[28] When a Charleston slave was discovered hiding aboard a New York–bound steam packet in October 1836, the *Courier* similarly announced, "The Commanders and Managers of these boats have in every such instance, taken effectual means to restore such property—no matter at what risk or inconvenience."[29] Such sectional harmony, however, was the exception rather than the rule, a fact that was no more evident than during the aftermath of the "Virginia Controversy."

In the summer of 1839 the schooner *Robert Center* sailed into Norfolk, Virginia, for repairs with three free Black seamen aboard.[30] As an enslaved ship carpenter named Isaac worked on the schooner, these three Black sailors advised the slave that he was "'foolish to remain in Virginia as he could get good wages in the north.'"[31] After the *Robert Center* was repaired and departed Norfolk, the slave carpenter could not be found, the disappearance prompting his owner, John G. Colley, to suspect that the skilled, valuable bondsman had escaped on the New York–bound vessel. Colley immediately dispatched a party to New York City with the object of recovering the absconded slave, who indeed was found hiding in the ship's hold. The runaway was returned to Virginia, but New York governor William Henry Seward, an antislavery Whig, refused to arrest and extradite the three Black mariners for prosecution in the Old Dominion.[32]

Then in May 1840, the New York State Legislature passed a fugitive slave act that was viewed by some south of the Mason-Dixon Line as "manifestly designed . . . to throw obstacles in the way of the recovery by Citizens of the Southern states of their fugitive slaves." This New York law granted runaways the right to jury trials and provided them with legal counsel and representation. The legislation furthermore required payment of a one-thousand-dollar "penal sum" from those suing for recovery of supposed fugitive slaves to cover legal fees in unsuccessful cases.[33] Outraged authorities in Virginia responded with an appeal to fellow slaveholding states for support and collaboration.[34] Legislators in South Carolina answered this call and, on 17 December 1841, passed An Act to Prevent the Citizens of New York from Carrying Slaves or Persons Held to Service out of this State and to Prevent the Escape of Persons Charged with the Commission of Any Crime, which was more commonly known as the New York Ship Inspection Law. This law, which was similar to one enacted in Virginia, was said to be a "retaliatory measure" against New York and "was passed in testimony of the high confidence which South Carolina reposed in the Counsels of Virginia and as a manifestation of her determination to cooperate with the Commonwealth and other States in maintaining by all proper methods an institution in which she has a common interest."[35]

South Carolina's New York Ship Inspection Law stipulated that vessels owned in any proportion whatsoever by a citizen of New York could not depart Charleston before undergoing an inspection or search for runaway slaves or fleeing criminals. Given that valuable slaves had long used northbound vessels to escape bondage, this legislation struck many slave-owning South Carolinians as an imperative and a commonsensical policy. The law seemingly would have been more practical and effective, however, had it also obliged the examination of vessels owned by Bostonians and northerners besides those from New York. But as a reactive rather than proactive measure, southern legislators targeted New Yorkers for reasons other than the Virginia Controversy. It was the New York–based American Anti-Slavery Society that had mailed thousands of abolitionist tracts to slaveholding Charlestonians in July 1835, prompting a mob to seize the offending pamphlets and publicly burn them along with effigies of Arthur and Lewis Tappan. Other New York abolitionists and moral reformers in 1839 established the Colored Sailors' Home, where hundreds of fugitive slaves were secreted and free Black mariners, such as those who assisted slave stowaways and disseminated seditious literature to bondsmen in southern ports such as Charleston, were encouraged to join the struggle against the institution of slavery. Abolitionists also founded the nation's first antislavery political party, the Liberty Party, in New York City in 1840. And in 1841, New York lawmakers reversed a long-standing law permitting southern slaveholders to bring their bondsmen into the Empire State for up to nine months without surrendering their human property.[36] As abolitionist attacks on the southern institution intensified, slavery's defenders responded with vigorous and pointed salvos aimed directly at their harshest northern critics—New Yorkers in this case.

Like the vexed Negro Seamen Acts, meanwhile, the sectionally divisive New York Ship Inspection Law had local detractors and unintended consequences for Charleston's commercial waterfront and its workers. And arguments similar to those both for and against the Black sailor laws were often applied to this 1841 legislation. Opponents insisted that the New York Ship Inspection Law was unconstitutional, inefficient, and ineffective, inhibited free trade, and drove much-needed business to competing ports. Each mandatory inspection cost ten dollars, which amounted to an annual expense of $120 for packet vessels monthly conveying passengers and goods between Charleston and New York.[37] Shipowners complained that in addition to this inspection fee, they were required to execute a one-thousand-dollar bond—not coincidently the same amount as the New York fugitive protective law's "penal sum"—to secure compliance with the law and cover "all damages which may be assessed against them, if a slave should be found on board."[38]

Critics also protested that payment of this ten-dollar "tax" was required even if the inspector did a poor job and failed to detect a stowaway. That outcome was not improbable given the abundant nooks and crannies of a loaded ship's hold.[39] Indeed, if a fugitive slave was later discovered, the vessel's owner was fined five hundred dollars for violating the law.[40] In 1845 Charleston's shipowners asked the state legislature to repeal the act and reminded lawmakers of the city's recent economic decline relative to other southern ports: "Our aim should be, not to close our ports, but to open every avenue, and widen every channel that would lead us once again to that commercial pre-eminence which once marked our City but has so long departed from us."[41] Any hindrance to commercial trade impacted not only those merchants at the top of Charleston's waterfront hierarchy but also the enslaved laborers whose diminished employment opportunities curtailed their extraordinary autonomy. This unfree workforce had come to count on the unique access that dockside labor afforded not only to urban wage earning but to the port's porous littoral environment, which in turn made possible their regular engagement with the maritime dimension of the Underground Railroad.

Measured in terms of actual ship arrivals and departures, total tonnage, and export figures, Charleston's commercial economy impressively withstood events ranging from the Nullification Crisis of 1832–1833 and Panics of 1837 and 1839 to the passage of the Negro Seamen Acts and New York Ship Inspection Law.[42] Despite the latter piece of legislation, for instance, ship arrivals at Charleston's docks rose from 1,673 in 1841 to 1,718 in 1842, with departures increasing from 1,610 to 1,713.[43] Twenty-eight packet vessels regularly transported freight and passengers between Charleston and New York in 1848; that figure was more than double the number with any other Atlantic, Gulf, or West

Indies port.[44] In addition to the climb in overall cotton and rice exports, the number of cotton bales shipped coastwise north of Charleston, primarily to New York and New England, increased from 61,519 in 1840–1841 to 70,783 in 1841–1842; the number of rice tierces shipped, meanwhile, rose from 20,773 to 29,140.[45] In light of these rising statistics, Charleston's mercantile interests may have overstated the negative impact of controversial legislation on Charleston's commercial trade.

There is some evidence, however, of both real and relative commercial decline in Charleston and other South Carolina ports immediately following the passage of the New York Ship Inspection Law in December 1841. Whereas $1,557,431 of goods were imported to South Carolina in 1841, that figure dropped steadily to an antebellum low of $822,602 four years later. Despite the broader economic recovery from the previous decade's devastating financial panics by 1843, the total tonnage of vessels engaged in foreign commerce and calling at the state's ports declined from 25,394 in 1841 to 19,515 in 1845. Relative to other southern ports, Charleston exported 230,000 bales of cotton in 1841—roughly 90,000 fewer than Mobile and nearly 600,000 fewer than New Orleans, but 81,000 more than Savannah. Given a choice between two rival southern Atlantic ports a mere one hundred miles apart, New York shipowners and captains could punish Charleston's proslavery radicals by loading their cotton in Savannah. Many planters along the Savannah River too may have elected to float their cotton to the Georgia port rather than transport it via railroad to South Carolina's more sectionally militant entrepôt. Indeed, while Charleston exported 269,007 bales of cotton in 1842—39,000 more than the previous year—Savannah's shipment of the staple rose dramatically to 299,173 bales—150,000 more than in 1841.[46] Though such disadvantageous short-term trends cannot be attributed to the 1841 ship inspection law alone, these figures contextualize the remonstrances of the port's competing security and commercial interests.

Another controversial provision of the New York Ship Inspection Law required a search even if New Yorkers owned only a small percentage of a vessel and South Carolinians owned the remainder.[47] The law was furthermore in effect if a ship owned entirely by citizens of South Carolina was commanded by a New Yorker. Stockholders in the Charleston–New York packet lines, including wharfingers and employers of enslaved waterfront workers, reminded legislators that they too were slave-owners and were "interested in all laws tending to the security of slave property."[48] They nevertheless joined with other shipowners and merchants to ask for relief from the act's "exceedingly onerous" tax burden and argued that South Carolinians were being "made to bear all the weight of the retaliation that was intended for the people of New York" after the enactment of that state's 1840 fugitive slave law.[49]

Champions of the law answered that it was "a wise and necessary protection to [South Carolina's] citizens" from northern abolitionists, who sought "to tamper with our slaves, to seduce them from their obedience, and to protect them when fugitive."[50] In January 1860, Judge T. J. Withers sentenced Francis Michel, a young white porter aboard the New York steam packet *Marion,* who had been convicted "of aiding any [*sic*] assisting in the escape of a runaway slave" belonging to a Charleston butcher. During the hearing, Judge Withers contended, "There is a peculiar duty on the part of a Government which holds slaves to protect that description of property."[51] Blaming the abolitionist "crew such as now infests the Northern part of the United States," the judge argued that the 1754 law under which Michel was convicted was

> a wholly insufficient barrier to the multitudinous thieves who have been spawned upon this country by a fierce fanaticism on the part of some, by a cheap, hypocritical, pretensive, vagabond philanthropy, on the part of many more, inspired by the numerous Pharisees of Northern pulpits, the 'unco good and rigidly righteous,' all seized upon and moulded into a homogeneous but corrupt mass by the greedy lovers of political power and general plunder.[52]

The ease with which Charleston's slaves could stow away—"through the instrumentality of those who may come from New York or other places, tainted and corrupted by such men as the Cheevers and Beechers"—compelled the state legislature to pass a special ship-inspection law that, admittedly, "involv[ed] heavy expense and much trouble."[53] Despite such candid concessions from supporters and severe critiques from opponents, legislative committees in Columbia that were assigned the task of reviewing grievances against the New York Ship Inspection Law of 1841 repeatedly rejected calls for repeal.[54] South Carolina's Committee on Federal Relations even doubled down, calling for "the adoption of more stringent and effectual measures to protect our Citizens from the outrages of New York on our Slave property."[55]

But as time passed and Charleston's export economy continued to lose ground to rival ports such as Savannah, Mobile, and especially New Orleans, state legislators acknowledged that alterations were advisable. In 1848 the members of the Committee on Federal Relations had a temporary change of heart and agreed that the law was "only productive of injury to individuals" and failed to efficiently curtail slave stowaways.[56] As John Andrew Jackson's remarkable maritime escape aboard a Boston-bound vessel the year before attested, a steady stream of waterfront workers and other bondsmen also continued flowing to less-scrutinized northern ports. The New York Ship Inspection Law, after all, futilely omitted Boston, Philadelphia, and other destinations attractive to maritime runaways. And even if the law was an effective, though severely limited, means of deterrence and detection, slaves who were doggedly resistant to mastery nonetheless found indirect waterborne routes to New York. Reminiscent of the 1838 account in *The Emancipator*, for instance, a slave named Alick who had been hired out to a drug store in Columbia absconded in 1850 to Charleston aboard a rail car. Having safely reached the waterfront, the runaway secreted himself on a steamboat bound first for Wilmington, then New York.[57]

The legislature's Committee on the Colored Population maintained in 1851 that, if the law was fully and faithfully enforced, it was sufficient to prevent waterfront runaways but also conceded that amendments were needed.[58] And twice the Committee on Federal Relations suggested that the inspection fee be reduced—in one instance to five dollars and in the other to only one dollar—in the effort to relieve the burden on Charleston's shipowners and to increase both the number of vessels owned by South Carolinians and those trading in Charleston.[59] The 1841 act nevertheless remained on the books essentially unrevised until the Civil War engulfed the Cooper River waterfront and ultimately rendered the matter of stowaway slaves moot. But with Union forces occupying much of the South Carolina and Georgia coasts by late 1861 and with the Union naval blockade located just miles from Charleston's wharves, bondsmen, including Robert Smalls, continued until emancipation to seek freedom via the distinctive maritime conduit that formed a key component of the Underground Railroad.[60]

NOTES

1. John Andrew Jackson, *The Experience of a Slave in South Carolina* (London: Passmore & Alabaster, 1862). Jackson's account is also published in Susanna Ashton, ed., *I Belong to South Carolina: South Carolina Slave Narratives* (Columbia: University of South Carolina Press, 2010), 83–126.
2. Jackson, *Experience of a Slave*, 24–25.
3. Ibid., 26.
4. Ibid., 23–28; Ashton, *I Belong to South Carolina*, 4. See also Thomas H. Jones, *The Experience of Rev. Thomas H. Jones, Who Was a Slave for Forty-Three Years. Written by a Friend, as Related to Him by Brother Jones* (New Bedford, Mass.: E. Anthony & Sons, Printers, 1885), 42–43. Jones was an enslaved stevedore in Wilmington, North Carolina, who also successfully colluded with the steward of a vessel to stow away to New York in 1849.

5. Concerning Robert Smalls, see John W. Blassingame, ed., *Slave Testimony: Two Centuries of Letters, Speeches, Interviews, and Autobiographies* (Baton Rouge: Louisiana State University Press, 1977), 373–79; Okan Edet Uya, *From Slavery to Public Service: Robert Smalls, 1839–1915* (New York: Oxford University Press, 1971); Andrew Billingsley, *Yearning to Breathe Free: Robert Smalls of South Carolina and His Families* (Columbia: University of South Carolina Press, 2007); and Edward A. Miller Jr., *Gullah Statesman: Robert Smalls from Slavery to Congress, 1839–1915* (Columbia: University of South Carolina Press, 2008).
6. *Royal Gazette*, 25–29 August 1781, in Lathan A. Windley, comp., *Runaway Slave Advertisements: A Documentary History from the 1730s to 1790* (Westport, Conn.: Greenwood Press, 1983), 3:586.
7. *Charleston Royal South Carolina Gazette*, 22–25 May 1784, in ibid., 3:736.
8. *Royal Gazette*, 31 October-3 November 1781, in Windley, *Runaway Slave Advertisements*, 3:590. For similar ads see ibid., 3:698–99, 3:730.
9. *Charleston South Carolina Gazette and General Advertiser*, 20 March 1784, in ibid., 3:730.
10. *Charleston South Carolina Gazette and General Advertiser*, 20 May 1783, in ibid., 3:715.
11. David J. McCord, ed., *The Statutes at Large of South Carolina; Edited, under Authority of the Legislature* (Columbia, S.C.: A. S. Johnston, 1840), 7:426–27, 460–61. For a copy of the Grand Jury Presentment, see Governors' Message, 1797 #703, South Carolina Department of Archives and History, Columbia (hereafter SCDAH).
12. Governors' Message, 1797 #701, and Committee Report of the General Assembly, 1797 #59, SCDAH.
13. Petition to the General Assembly, ND #1415, SCDAH.
14. *Charleston (S.C.) Times*, 5 April 1821.
15. *Charleston (S.C.) Courier*, 1 July 1822. See also Helen Tunnicliff Catterall, ed., *Judicial Cases Concerning American Slavery and the Negro* (1926–1937; reprint, Buffalo, N.Y.: W. S. Hein, 1998), 2:274, 338, and Court of General Sessions, Charleston County, South Carolina, Indictments, 1810–55A, 1825–15A, 1826–8A, 1839–22A-19, and 1840–15A, SCDAH.
16. *Augusta (Ga.) Chronicle*, 28 July 1824. See also John Hope Franklin and Loren Schweninger, *Runaway Slaves: Rebels on the Plantation* (New York: Oxford University Press, 1999), 33, 118–19, 131, 133–34.
17. *Charleston (S.C.) Courier*, 30 January 1860.
18. *New York Emancipator*, 18 October 1838. See also Ashton, *I Belong to South Carolina*, 50. This note refers to the previous two paragraphs.
19. George P. Rawick, ed., *The American Slave: A Composite Autobiography, vol. 2, South Carolina Narratives, pt. 2* (1941; reprint, Westport, Conn.: Greenwood Publishing, 1972), 233–34.
20. *Charleston (S.C.) Courier*, 3 March 1835; *New York Emancipator*, 12 May 1836.
21. See U. B. Phillips, *American Negro Slavery* (New York: D. Appleton, 1918), 418; and

Bernard E. Powers Jr., *Black Charlestonians: A Social History, 1822–1885* (Fayetteville: University of Arkansas Press, 1994), 27.

22. Thomas C. Marshall to John W. Mitchell, 18 December 1839, John Wroughton Mitchell Papers, Southern Historical Collection, University of North Carolina, Chapel Hill.
23. Edward Pettingill to Langdon Cheves, 22 June 1837, Langdon Cheves Papers, South Carolina Historical Society, Charleston (hereafter SCHS).
24. *Savannah Georgian* quoted in *Boston Liberator*, 30 May 1845.
25. Equity Petition, Charleston District, 1846 #800, SCDAH. See also Loren Schweninger, ed., *The Southern Debate over Slavery, vol. 2, Petitions to Southern County Courts, 1775–1867* (Urbana: University of Illinois Press, 2008), 234–35.
26. Jacob Schirmer diary, 17 May 1860, Schirmer Family Journals and Registers, 1806–1929, SCHS.
27. See Rawick, *The American Slave*, vol. 3, *South Carolina Narratives*, pt. 3 (1972), 130.
28. *Charleston (S.C.) Courier*, quoted in the *Savannah (Ga.) Morning News*, 13 April 1852.
29. *Charleston (S.C.) Courier*, 27 October 1836; *Charleston (S.C.) Mercury*, 27 October 1836.
30. The principal owner and master of the New Orleans–based *Robert Center* was Joseph Shepard. For a series of documents dealing with this incident, see *Annual Report of the American Historical Association for the Year 1907, vol. 2, Diplomatic Correspondence of the Republic of Texas, pt. 1* (Washington, D.C.: Government Printing Office, 1908), 425, 432–34, 443–44.
31. Stephen J. Valone, "William Henry Seward, the Virginia Controversy, and the Anti-Slavery Movement, 1839–1841," *Afro-Americans in New York Life and History* 31 (January 2007): 65; William Seward to [Virginia Lt. Governor] Henry Hopkins, 24 October 1839, in George E. Baker, ed., *The Works of William H. Seward* (New York: Redfield, 1853), 2:468. The three free Black seamen's names were Isaac Gansey, Peter Johnson, and Edward Smith.
32. Committee Report, 1847 #237, SCDAH; Valone, "William Henry Seward," 65–66, 75. See also Luther Rawson Marsh, ed., *Writings and Speeches of Alvan Stewart, on Slavery* (New York: A. B. Burdick, 1860), 219–33.
33. Leslie M. Harris, *In the Shadow of Slavery: African Americans in New York City, 1626–1863* (Chicago: University of Chicago Press, 2003), 215.
34. Committee Report, 1847 #237, SCDAH.
35. Committee Reports, 1847 #130 and 1847 #237, SCDAH; Petition, ND #2895, SCDAH. For the text of the New York Ship Inspection Law, see *Statutes at Large of South Carolina, vol. 11, Containing the Acts from 1838, Exclusive . . .* (Columbia, S.C.: Reprinted by Republican Printing Company, State Printers, 1873), 163–66.
36. Lacy K. Ford, *Deliver Us from Evil: The Slavery Question in the Old South* (New York: Oxford University Press, 2009), 481–504; William W. Freehling, *Prelude to Civil War: The Nullification Controversy in South Carolina, 1816–1836* (New York:

Harper & Row, 1965), 340–48; Harris, *In the Shadow of Slavery*, 238–39, 223, 215, 273–74.

37. For the $120 figure, see Petitions, 1845 #30 and ND #2823, SCDAH. Various other petitions from Charleston's shipowners claimed that this "Tax" collectively cost them the "large and enormous amount" of $1,000, $1,900, or $2,000 per year. See Petitions, 1853 #58, 1845 #30, ND #2823, 1847 #90, and 1847 #91, SCDAH.
38. Committee Report, 1847 #237, SCDAH; Petitions, 1847 #90 and 1847 #91, SCDAH. See also Petitions, 1845 #30 and ND #2823, SCDAH.
39. Petitions, 1847 #90, 1847 #91, 1845 #30, and ND #2823, SCDAH.
40. Petitions, 1845 #30, ND #2823, 1847 #90, and 1847 #91, SCDAH. The captains or owners of vessels departing the state without having undergone an inspection were fined five hundred dollars. Committee Report, 1847 #237, SCDAH.
41. Quotation from Petition, 1845 #30, SCDAH. See also Petitions, ND #2823, 1847 #90, and 1847 #91, SCDAH.
42. See J. L. Dawson and H. W. DeSaussure, *Census of the City of Charleston, South Carolina, for the Year 1848* (Charleston, S.C.: J. B. Nixon, 1849), 60–79, 90–102; John G. Van Deusen, *Economic Bases of Disunion in South Carolina* (New York: Columbia University Press, 1928), 333, app. c; and Frederick Burtrumn Collins Jr., "Charleston and the Railroads: A Geographic Study of a South Atlantic Port and Its Strategies for Developing a Railroad System, 1820–1860" (master's thesis, University of South Carolina, 1977), 100, table 5.
43. Dawson and DeSaussure, *Census of Charleston for 1848*, 66–67. The number of American-flagged steamboats, those from New York included, entering and leaving Charleston Harbor also rose slightly between 1841 and 1842. See ibid., 72, 74.
44. The collective tonnage of these vessels, 11,027, was nearly equal to the combined tonnage of the Charleston packet ships calling at all other ports. Dawson and DeSaussure, *Census of Charleston for 1848*, 80.
45. Ibid., 97.
46. Van Deusen, *Economic Bases*, 332, app. b; Collins, "Charleston and the Railroads," 100, table 5; Charleston's proportion of cotton bales received for export from the four southern Atlantic states (presumably Virginia, North Carolina, South Carolina, and Georgia) dropped slightly from 46.67 percent between October 1840 and August 1841, to 42.90 percent between September 1841 and August 1842. Dawson and DeSaussure, *Census of Charleston for 1848*, 148.
47. Petitions, 1845 #30, ND #2823, 1847 #90, 1847 #91, and 1853 #58, SCDAH.
48. Petition, 1853 #58, SCDAH.
49. Petitions, 1853 #58 and ND #2895, SCDAH.
50. Committee Report, 1847 #237, SCDAH.
51. *Charleston (S.C.) Courier*, 30 January 1860. See also Schirmer diary, 6 July 1859, 28 January 1860, and 4 February 1860, SCHS; *Charleston (S.C.) Courier*, 9 July 1859; Court of General Sessions, Charleston District, Criminal Dockets, January 1860 term, SCDAH; Court of General Sessions, Charleston District, Criminal Journals,

1:475, 561, SCDAH; and Michael P. Johnson and James L. Roark, *No Chariot Let Down: Charleston's Free People of Color on the Eve of the Civil War* (Chapel Hill: University of North Carolina Press, 1984), 128–29.

52. *Charleston* (S.C.) *Courier*, 30 January 1860.
53. Ibid.
54. See Committee Reports, ND #2548, 1847 #237, 1847 #130, and 1853 #141, SCDAH.
55. Committee Report, 1847 #130, SCDAH.
56. Though the committee was "inclined to recommend" the law's repeal, this report came too late in the legislative session to take action. Committee Report, 1848 #235, SCDAH.
57. Catterall, *Judicial Cases*, 2:418.
58. Committee Report, 1851 #16, SCDAH.
59. Committee Reports, 1853 #235 and ND #2548, SCDAH.
60. Shortly after the commencement of the naval blockade, two slaves "attempted to go off in the British Ship A & A" but were discovered and returned to Charleston. And on 28 April 1862, Jacob Schirmer commented how the night before, "some 8 negroes run [*sic*] away with one of Genl Ripley's boats and gone [*sic*] out to the Fleet." Schirmer was referring to Confederate Brigadier General Roswell Sabine Ripley. Schirmer diary, 27 May 1861 and 28 April 1862, SCHS. Robert Smalls's daring escape took place on the night of 13 May 1862.

3

BLACK WATERMEN, FUGITIVES FROM SLAVERY, AND AN OLD WOMAN ON THE EDGE OF A SWAMP

Maritime Passages to Freedom from Coastal North Carolina

DAVID S. CECELSKI

> 25 DOLLARS REWARD.
>
> RAN AWAY from the subscriber, on Sunday last, a Negro man named CEASAR . . . about 20 years of age . . . it is probable that he will endeavour to get on board of some vessel at Wilmington and effect his escape to the North. Masters of vessels and all others are forewarned from harbouring, employing, or carrying him away, under the penalty of the law. WILLIAM V. BARROW. Craven County, 12 June 1833.
>
> —*New Bern (N.C.) Spectator and Literary Journal*, 14 June 1833

In the last years before the Civil War, as the oceangoing shipping trade in cotton and naval stores boomed, an enslaved man named Peter guided vessels in and out of the harbor at Wilmington, North Carolina. Merchants and planters depended on local pilots and skilled engineers like him to guide their vessels safely around the serpentine shoals on the Cape Fear River and across the narrow channel into the Atlantic.[1] But Peter navigated more than freight through those treacherous coastal passages. He also steered fugitive slaves toward freedom along furtive maritime routes that endured throughout the era of legal slaveholding in the United States. In a little-known autobiography, his son, William H. Robinson, who was also held in bondage, remembered that Peter

> enjoyed the friendship of two very distinguished Quakers, Mr. Fuller and Mr. Elliot, who owned oyster sloops and stood at the head of what is known in our

> country as the underground railroad. . . . Father was with Messrs Fuller and Elliot every day towing them in and out from the oyster bay. This gave them an opportunity to lay and devise plans for getting many [slaves] into Canada . . . and my father was an important factor in this line.[2]

The success of their conspiracy was evident in October 1849, when a correspondent to the *Wilmington Journal* complained, “It is almost an every day occurrence for our negro slaves to take passage [aboard a vessel] and go North.” Echoing a long-standing grievance against sailors and watermen, the newspaper’s editors lamented this maritime escape route as “an evil which is getting to be intolerable.”[3] Alert to the portal of opportunity offered by shipping and the maritime trades, runaway slaves regularly headed to the coast instead of attempting overland paths out of bondage.[4]

Charting that clandestine corridor up the Eastern Seaboard offers a rare glimpse into the struggle for freedom in North Carolina and the rest of the maritime South. In addition, while Peter and other Black watermen may have been the most critical link in this oceangoing route to freedom, many other tidewater people of all races and creeds helped liberate enslaved people from their bondage, sustained them in hiding, and arranged their passage to free territory. Their stories reveal a powerful, complex, and dissident undercurrent to maritime life in the slavery era—and divulge the crucial agency of enslaved men and women that was vital to successful escapes through North Carolina’s coastal waterways and swamps. Wealthy planters and merchants held the reins of power, but lowly watermen, slave stevedores, piney woods squatters, reclusive swampers, and sometimes even slaveholders’ wives and children defied those laws and sustained tenuous pathways by which fugitives might pass from land to sea.[5]

Historians are fortunate to know anything at all about this maritime passage to freedom. It was, after all, an illicit undertaking, a potentially capital crime that necessarily occurred only on the fringes of society. Few former slaves dared to leave written accounts of their involvement; most who were apprehended had no day in court, where their courage might have become part of the documentary record. Historical documents understandably yield only oblique references to these ocean-bound slave runaways and their sympathizers. “I was to escape in a vessel, but I forebear to mention any further particulars,” wrote a formerly enslaved woman who had succeeded in escaping in a schooner’s hold.[6] Fugitive and participants disclosed only enough details about the “Underground Railroad” to hint at its breadth and vitality but upheld a habitual caution against discussing specific names, routes or vessels.

Documentary sources reveal several dozen accounts of specific runaway slaves who reached vessels sailing out of North Carolina ports between 1800 and the Civil War. Given the degree of secrecy that enveloped this maritime route out of bondage and a sizable body of corroborating evidence, one may safely conclude that they represent only a small portion of those fugitives who fled the South by sea. The presence of a coastal escape route was widely known in tidewater African American communities, among merchants and planters who went to great lengths to control it, and among northern abolitionists who frequently assisted fugitive slaves after their voyage from the South. From a wide assortment of contemporary newspapers, slave narratives, personal diaries, court records, and travel accounts, it is possible to reconstruct much of the

FIGURE 6. Captain Albert Fountain, Suspected of Smuggling Fugitive Slaves. Fountain was compelled to submit to a search of his schooner, *City of Richmond*, by the police led by the mayor of Norfolk, Virginia, in November 1855. The authorities discovered none of the twenty-eight fugitives concealed in this vessel. All sailed safely to Philadelphia. Illustration in William Still, *The Underground Rail Road: A Record of Facts, Authentic Letters, Narratives, &c.* (Philadelphia: Porter & Coates, 1872); image from Digital Collections, General Research Division, The New York Public Library, https://digitalcollections.nypl.org/items/510d47df-79a9-a3d9-e040-e00a18064a99.

character and scope of this watery path that passed through North Carolina ports toward freedom in the North.

In the eastern part of North Carolina, most enslaved people who sought to escape aboard seagoing vessels attempted first to reach the busy harbors at Wilmington, New Bern, Washington, and Edenton. Relying on their own watercraft skills or on the ubiquitous Black boatmen who plied the waters, fugitive slaves often followed rivers to those ports. The majority could not risk a long canoe or flatboat trip and traveled only at night. But the enslaved escaped frequently enough by boat that when a Slocumb Creek man discovered a cypress dugout deserted near his home on Christmas Day 1828, he simply assumed that the craft "must have been last in the possession of a runaway negro."[7] If they could not commandeer a boat or make their own, runaways had to depend on sympathetic watermen, usually enslaved men or women, to transport them across rivers, creeks, and bays.

Wilmington, the largest port in antebellum North Carolina, had a special reputation, in the words of a Rocky Point planter, as "an asylum for Runaways" because of its location near the mouth of the Cape Fear River, its steady sea traffic, its strong ties to New England and its Black-majority population.[8] Fugitive slaves from rice and turpentine plantations throughout southeastern North Carolina followed the Cape Fear River to Wilmington. Stealing away from cotton and tobacco fields as far inland as Goldsboro, they fled to New Bern along the Neuse and Trent Rivers.[9] And they trailed the Tar River toward Washington and the Roanoke River to Plymouth from timber camps and herring fisheries stretching to the Virginia border. African Americans confined in the remote wetlands east of those major ports—in soggy Hyde and Tyrrell Counties, for instance—often fled west to their wharves.[10] Men and women who escaped from the Albemarle Sound vicinity more frequently headed north through the Great Dismal Swamp to rendezvous with seagoing vessels in Norfolk or Portsmouth, Virginia.[11]

The larger ports were not the only destinations for fugitive slaves. Runaways and race rebels extended this maritime escape route into fishing hamlets and seafaring villages up and down the North Carolina coast. Henry Anderson, for example, escaped by ship from a slave trader in Beaufort. Miles White, only twenty-one years old, stowed away on a vessel carrying shingles from Elizabeth City to Philadelphia. Harriet Jacobs escaped by sea from Edenton in 1842. And in July 1856 Peter Heines, Mathew Bodams, and James Morris all escaped on a schooner captained by a man named Albert Fountain, who apparently met them at one of the roughhewn villages along the Roanoke River or Albemarle

Thirty (Silver) Dollars Reward.

RUN AWAY on the 3d inſt. from the ſubſcriber, a Negro Man, named TONEY, about five feet eight or nine inches high, his breaſt a good deal projected, a very likely active fellow, about 25 years of age; has been whipped (before I had him) conſequently his back much marked; he is as black as moſt negroes, drinks hard. By information he was ſeen at the Great Swamp, paſſing as a freeman, having procured from ſome villain a free paſs to protect him, and ſaid he intended to ſhip himſelf on board the firſt veſſel going out of the country. He had on and carried with him a white negro cotton coat and breeches, a ſhort blue cloth coat and black breeches, common negro ſhoes and ſtockings, oznaburgh ſhirts, and a cocked hat. The above reward will be given to any perſon that delivers the ſaid negro to me if taken out of the counties of Norfolk or Princeſs Ann, or half the ſum if taken in either of them, or the ſame ſum if ſecured in any gaol ſo that I get him. All maſters of veſſels and others are forbid employing or carrying him off.

DENNIS DAWLEY.

Virginia, Princeſs Ann, Jan. 17. o 3

FIGURE 7. Runaway Slave Advertisement Published in the *State Gazette of North Carolina* of New Bern, 29 January 1789. Transcript:

Thirty (Silver) Dollars Reward. RUN AWAY on the 3d inst. from the subscriber, a Negro Man, named TONEY, about five feet eight or nine inches high, his breast a good deal projected, a very likely active fellow, about 25 years of age; has been whipped (before I had him) consequently his back much marked; he is as black as most negroes, drinks hard. By information he was seen at the Grant Swamp, passing as a freeman, having procured from some villain a free pass to protect him, and said he intended to ship himself on board the first vessel going out of the country. He had on and carried with him a white negro cotton coat and breeches, a short blue cloth coat and black breeches, common negro shoes and stockings, oznaburgh shirts, and a cocked hat. The above reward will be given to any person that delivers the said negro to me if taken out of the counties of Norfolk or Princess Ann, or half the sum if taken in either of them, or the same sum if secured in any gaol so that I get him. All masters of vessels and others are forbid employing or carrying him off. DENNIS DAWLEY. Virginia, Princess Ann[e], Jan. 17.

Sound.[12] Others fled from the landings at larger plantations and timber camps, where vessels that combined shallow drafts and ocean worthiness took on crops, fish, or timber and sailed for New England and the West Indies.

No matter which ports runaway slaves sought out, they faced many dangers before reaching the open sea. Bloodhounds, bounty hunters, and port inspectors stood between their first steps in flight from bondage and the safety of the Gulf Stream's warm currents flowing northward to freedom.[13] Escaping slaves risked life and liberty around every turn. Slave catchers and patrols pursued them, and anyone could turn them in for a substantial bounty. Inspectors searched many seagoing vessels and regularly fumigated ships to drive hidden runaways up onto the deck. The chance of betrayal or discovery always existed, and an extraordinarily high proportion of fugitives never reached a wharf. The exceptional ones who did, such as a slave named Anthony on board the schooner *Butler* in 1836, were occasionally caught before departure.[14] Punishments included re-enslavement, public whipping, hard duty, deportation into the Deep South, and even death.

Confronted by so many pitfalls and deterrents, most slaves could only dream of the sea. Like the young Frederick Douglass, who was once a slave in a port town, they may have mused about the "beautiful vessels, robed in white" that might "yet bear me into freedom."[15] But throughout the plantation belt of eastern North Carolina, slaves tried to fulfill that dream frequently enough that their owners viewed the ocean as a serious threat and regularly suspected that runaways would try to sail away from them. Their preoccupation with the ocean's proximity often bordered on obsessiveness. Reward posters and newspaper advertisements routinely warned masters of seagoing vessels not to harbor, employ, or carry away their departed workers.[16] State penalties for protecting fugitive slaves were harsh; ship captains after 1793 risked hanging for carrying a runaway out of North Carolina.[17] Slaveholders also threatened seamen with civil prosecution for bearing away their slaves and offered extravagant rewards for information that would identify sailors who had helped an enslaved man, woman, or child to flee. In February 1838, to mention only one of many instances, Edward Dudley, the state's governor, offered up to five hundred dollars to anyone who would identify the mariner who had allowed his runaway slave to sail from Wilmington to Boston.[18]

Coastal geography and the willingness of some local inhabitants to protect runaways compounded the threat of the open sea for slaveholders and its powerful allure for their enslaved laborers. Remote swamps and dense forests offered havens for runaway slaves who needed a long-term refuge, a point for hasty reconnaissance, or a momentary way station *en route* to a port.[19] Blackwater swamps, *pocosins* (freshwater evergreen shrub wetlands), pine savannas, or tidal marshes encroached on every settlement in coastal North Carolina. Towns were few, scattered, and small. Though drainage and foresting of the wetlands were well underway by the early nineteenth century, those areas promised a haven for fugitive slaves, many of whom had at least some schooling in how to survive in the wild.[20]

To reach the sea, fugitive slaves could not simply vanish into coastal swamps and backwoods. Even for those who had the skills necessary for wilderness survival, a hermit's life did not provide access to crucial information about sea traffic or expose them to the kinds of contacts necessary to reach a seagoing vessel. As a result, runaways usually had to rely on the complicity of men and women prepared to disregard the slave laws. All runaways, but especially those who planned to board a vessel, looked to clandestine networks of both enslaved and free persons, and they often discovered support for their journey to the sea.

Whether or not they aspired to reach a seagoing vessel, fugitive slaves found their most important backing from others held in bondage. "The slaves generally know where the runaway is secreted," remembered Nehemiah Caulkins, a white carpenter who closely observed daily life on several rice plantations near Wilmington between 1824 and 1835, "and visit him at night and on Sundays."[21] William Robinson, who was a onetime runaway, remembered the assistance that slaves gave their fugitive brethren in the Wilmington vicinity. In his autobiography, he recalled that during his youth in the 1850s, "there was always an understanding between the slaves, that if one ran away they would put something to eat at a certain place; also a mowing scythe, with the crooked handle replaced with a straight stick with which to fight the bloodhounds."[22] Over weeks, months, and even years, those enslaved laborers supplied refugees with provisions and intelligence that might help them to elude their pursuers. Fugitive slaves looked most often for this sort of help among family members who remained with their owners or who had been sold in the vicinity. The concentration of slave markets in port towns meant that runaways often had enslaved relatives at several locations on a river flowing into a port—a consequence of the otherwise tragic separation of Black families on the auction block.[23]

Runaway slaves also depended on kindred souls concealed in coastal blackwater swamps and pocosins. Maroons, communities of fugitive slaves, continued to inhabit the North Carolina coast, particularly the Great Dismal Swamp, to a degree that scholars may never fully know. Runaway slaves counted heavily on maroons to assure a successful flight. When William Robinson escaped from an abusive owner near Wilmington in 1858, he immediately sought out an old enslaved woman on the edge of town. She fed him and directed him to seek protection with a group of fugitives living in the nearby swamps. His knowledge of the woman's home and their hideout dated from his early childhood.[24] To ocean-bound fugitives, maroon camps provided temporary shelters and opportunities to learn from experienced fugitives how to navigate the many obstacles to reaching a port.[25]

Fugitive slaves with an eye to going a-sea sometimes found allies among free men and women.[26] Resorting to free collaborators was a dangerous choice but one that could not always be avoided. While runaways sought asylum most often among the poor and dispossessed, the historical record suggests a more varied picture of their free sympathizers. Thomas H. Jones conspired with free worshipers at his Methodist church to arrange his family's escape from Wilmington.[27] In Chowan County, an upper-class white woman who had long been a family friend concealed Harriet Jacobs.[28] In 1848 a Wilmington merchant named Zebulon Latimer even contrived his own slave's escape to New York, since he could not legally liberate her under North Carolina law.[29] Historians can usually only guess at motivations, but runaways recognized and exploited a variety of forbidden bonds—including romantic love, friendship, family, and faith—that connected the enslaved and the free peoples of both races. While proslavery militants drove nearly all public expression of abolitionist viewpoints underground during the antebellum era, it was far more difficult to pluck out the slender threads of collusion that remained tightly woven into the fabric of coastal society.

Blacks who aspired to flee by sea had a special need to interact with free persons in order to earn money for their ship's fare. There were good Quaker salts and militant abolitionists who would not deign to charge to stow away a slave. But most seamen demanded compensation, and it was also necessary in many cases to bribe port officials and harbor guards. Though obtaining money must have often seemed an insurmountable obstacle, some runaway slaves nevertheless found ways to finance their passage northward.[30] Even in slavery, many African Americans secretly sold products that they grew, traded for, or made after completing their other duties.[31] They also traded stolen goods to poor whites and to black market brokers. Port slaves, in particular, earned money by "hiring out" when their masters did not require their labor. Sometimes the master gave permission and shared the proceeds; other times such work was done clandestinely, increasing both the risk and the reward for the slave.[32] This hidden economy flourished despite the threat of repercussions ranging from sizable fines to extrajudicial murder—"Judge Lynch"—for slaves, their trading partners, and illicit employers.

The extensive forest products industry had a special reputation for hiring runaway slaves, "no questions asked," to cut shingles and to extract submerged timber out of swamps. Those shadowy laborers were legendary in the vicinity of Lake Phelps and the Great Alligator Swamp, and the Dismal Swamp Land Company was constantly tempted to hire runaways in the Great Dismal Swamp.[33] Often they also hired runaways to work on lighters and flatboats that carried the shingles and lumber out of the swamp.[34] Shingling, lumbering, and the naval-stores industry all employed large numbers of enslaved laborers in remote locales, where crew leaders or their enslaved workers could develop symbiotic relationships with refugee slaves without a great deal of public scrutiny. Those jobs were exploitative and risky, built around the vulnerability of desperate men and women, but for those who would try to board a seagoing vessel, they provided one of the most tempting sources of income for their fare and access to people who might help them to arrange contacts in coastal ports.

Political leaders recognized the subversive nature of illicit collusion between fugitive slaves and free persons. The North Carolina General Assembly warned in its 1846–1847 session that the numbers of free men and women sheltering and employing runaway slaves posed a serious danger, especially near the Great Dismal Swamp:

> Many slaves belong[ing] to persons residing or having plantations in the neighborhood of the great dismal swamp, and by the aid of free persons of color and of white men, have been and are enabled to elude all attempts to secure their persons. . . . Consorting with such white men and free persons of color, they remain setting at defiance the powers of their masters, corrupting and reducing their slaves, and by their evil example and evil practices, lessening the due subordination.[35]

State legislators responded to the crisis by requiring Dismal Swamp employers to register the names and descriptions of their Black workers with local clerks of court. They also obligated the officials to verify with owners that their enslaved laborers had permission to work in the swamp.[36] Legislative mandates, however, could not confer on local authorities the willingness or capability to enforce those laws. Fugitive slaves, many of them dreaming of the sea, continued to find asylum among the free citizenry of these elusive worlds.

African Americans who dared to flee bondage and made it to slavery's shore faced the formidable task of finding sympathetic seamen who could help them obtain a secret berth to freedom. Finding passage on a vessel to free territory proved a difficult, risk-laden endeavor that sometimes required months or years. A single wrong step, misplaced trust, or rash inquiry doomed a runaway. Success depended as much on patience and prudence as on daring and courage. Henry Gorham, a thirty-four-year-old slave carpenter, remained in forests for eleven months before he found a way to board a schooner sailing out of a North Carolina port in 1856. The slave Ben Dickenson waited and eavesdropped on harbor conversations for three years until the right opportunity arose to stow away. Harriet Jacobs hid in an attic in Edenton for seven years before friends and family succeeded in arranging her passage to Philadelphia. And Harry Grimes lived in swamp forests for eighteen months before contacting a ship in November 1857.[37]

Word of a vessel's master who harbored runaways spread quickly along the docks and from ports into the hinterlands. As Captain Daniel Drayton wrote of his encounters with slaves in Chesapeake Bay ports, "no sooner, indeed, does a vessel, known to come from the North, anchor in any of these waters—and the slaves are pretty adroit in ascertaining from what state a vessel comes—then she is boarded . . . by more or less of them, in hopes of obtaining a passage to a land of freedom.[38] Gossip, vain hopes, and reality mingled in precarious measure. Approaching the master of a vessel who was rumored to assist slave runaways always posed special dangers, and African Americans who had already escaped or who were planning to flee could rarely afford total confidence in any stranger.

The experience of two young slaves in Wilmington illustrates that dilemma. In 1857 Abraham Galloway and Richard Eden approached with considerable trepidation the captain of a schooner bound for Philadelphia. According to William Still, a Black leader of the Underground Railroad in Philadelphia who later helped the two men reach Canada, their conversation "had to be done in such a way, that even the captain would not really understand what they were up to, should he be found untrue."[39] By sly indirection, Galloway and Eden had found a captain willing to conceal them amid barrels of turpentine, tar, and rosin for the northward passage—but they were fortunate. He could just as well have collected a reward on them or kidnapped and sold them back into slavery in another southern port.

The dangers of soliciting a shipboard berth loomed too great for most runaways and especially for fugitives unfamiliar with the waterfront. Slaveholders posted descriptions of their runaway slaves in harbor towns and advertised in local newspapers. An unfamiliar Black man or woman making inquiries or lingering by the wharves quickly attracted attention. Wilmington and other ports required hired-out slaves and all free Black laborers to wear badges obtained for a fee from the town commissioners, and the absence of the proper badge alerted the town guards. Several ports, including Wilmington, enforced evening curfews on all Black people within town limits.[40] Local authorities often imprisoned Black strangers on the slightest suspicion. To avert capture, fugitives relied heavily on intermediaries to establish contact with masters of vessels or with other sailors.

In 1842 a free Black man named Peter helped Harriet Jacobs make her escape by schooner from Edenton. During the years when Jacobs was concealed in town, Peter continually kept in touch with her. Probably with the help of Black sailors, Peter finally identified a sea captain who would provide Jacobs passage to Philadelphia aboard his vessel. Jacobs later admitted that the obligatory bribe would have "paid for a voyage to England," but her family and Peter somehow raised enough to pay off the captain.[41] Peter had made meticulous arrangements in all respects. He met Jacobs under cover of dusk at her hideaway and escorted her through the streets of Edenton. He had a rowboat and two oarsmen waiting for her when she arrived at the wharf, and he had posted lookouts to detect any intruders. The captain set sail immediately, and Jacobs soon found herself safely in Philadelphia.[42]

In 1855 another escaped slave, William Jordan, survived in a Cape Fear forest by pilfering from local plantations and eating wild plants and animals. Jordan also depended on a trusted ally to find a seaman sympathetic or mercenary enough to secret him away on his vessel. According to William Still,

> William had a true friend, with whom he could communicate; one who was wide awake, and was on the alert to find a reliable captain from the North, who would consent to take this 'property,' or 'freight,' for a consideration. He heard at last of a certain Captain, who was then doing quite a successful business in an Underground way. This good news was conveyed to William, and afforded him a ray of hope in the wilderness.[43]

Jordan escaped by sea after hiding in forests for ten months.

Jordan's accomplice knew the Wilmington waterfront. In order to identify the "certain Captain," he must have met with sailors, watermen, or dockworkers known to be abolitionists. Though it is impossible to know precisely who those contacts were, a sizable contingent of local sea captains and shipping merchants had recently emigrated from New York and New England, lured by the city's cotton and naval-stores boom. Those men and their families continued to keep personal ties and trading interests in the North. The fact that they had moved south to share in a prosperity built on slave labor did not mean that they embraced slavery (though many did). Some held abolitionist sympathies and others, homesick for the North and resentful of unfamiliar southern folkways, came to detest the peculiar institution.[44] In any event, when northern abolitionists or enslaved southerners offered bounties to sea captains who brought runaway slaves out of the South, they doubtless spurred a stronger traffic along the Underground Railroad's maritime routes.

Few runaways had intermediaries between land and sea situated as advantageously as did the enslaved people of New Bern. According to a letter written in 1838 by a Quaker society president, the son of a local slaveholder regularly concealed slaves in timber vessels bound for Philadelphia. Described as a "most effective worker," the unnamed conspirator also provided northbound slaves with the address for the Vigilance Committee of Philadelphia or had them accompanied by its undercover agents.[45] The slaveholder's son may have been the final contact in a spur of the Underground Railroad that followed the Neuse and Trent Rivers to New Bern, or he may have operated by himself. The surviving correspondence is understandably silent on that question. Either way, this homegrown dissident affirms the unpredictable backgrounds of the men and women who supported runaway slaves bent on reaching the sea.[46]

To cross the dangerous divide between land and sea, those in bondage depended most heavily on Black maritime laborers. Their maritime culture provided runaways a complex web of informants, messengers, go-betweens, and other potential collaborators. Having one foot in the local shoreline culture and the other on board the vessels that sailed the Atlantic, slave watermen lay like a gangplank between worlds that otherwise barely touched. All the clandestine pathways funneled into seafaring villages, and only watermen could provide the final portage that fugitive slaves needed.

When runaways sought such help, they entered a distinctive maritime society that existed at the outskirts of the plantation world. African Americans stood at its center, though their prevalence in river transport, harbor watercraft, and other maritime trades has rarely been fully appreciated. In nineteenth-century North Carolina, as in other southern states, Black watermen were ever-present sights, crewing flatboats, scows, periaugers, steamers, and other cargo boats on tidewater rivers and sounds. A steady traffic of enslaved boatmen converged in ports aboard river and sound boats laden with cotton bales, cedar shingles, and turpentine barrels.[47] Awaiting fair winds or new cargo, Black seamen crowded the wharf districts. They worked as stewards and cooks on most ships that sailed out of or visited North Carolina, held skilled crew stations on many vessels, and constituted a majority of hands on more than a few vessels.[48] Slave fishermen arrived in skiffs loaded with shad and mullet destined for their masters' supper tables.[49] Other slaves brought alligator, waterfowl, and small game killed in nearby salt marshes to the waterfront to sell. Still other Black boatmen passed by on foraging excursions in search of crabs and marsh-birds' eggs for their own consumption.[50]

Ferrymen, nearly always slaves, departed from local docks to convey passengers and goods across rivers and to remote island villages. Even enslaved artisans traveled in the harbor traffic, doing the caulking, refitting, rigging, and rebuilding necessary to keep wooden vessels at sea. At the wharves, slave women peddled fish and oysters, hawked stew and cornbread to hungry sailors, and found a ready market for laundry services. Draymen waited by the score to load carts with West Indian molasses and rum, Bahamian salt, English cloth, and New England manufactures.[51] Black stevedores trundled freight on and off ships, a profitable and popular day-labor job.[52] From those wharf laborers, shipping agents hired crews for dredge boats, lighters, and other local workboats.[53]

The breadth and complexity of this African American maritime culture stands out in all seven autobiographies known to have been written by the state's former coastal slaves. This is especially true in the memoirs of former slave watermen London Ferebee, Moses Grandy, and Thomas H. Jones. Raised by Currituck Sound in the 1850s, Ferebee learned the principles of boatmanship and navigation from his father, who worked in a local shipyard, and from the enslaved crewmen on his master's sloop.[54] Grandy, as we have already seen, was indeed a maritime jack of all trades. He operated a river ferry in Camden County, captained canal boats between Elizabeth City and Norfolk, crewed an Albemarle Sound schooner, served on coastwise packets, and manned brigs and schooners that sailed as far as the Mediterranean Sea.[55] Thomas H. Jones was no less a part of maritime life. He loaded and unloaded cargo on the Wilmington waterfront, where he encountered sailors and boatmen from places far and wide. Jones ultimately found a master of a vessel who was prepared to carry his wife, Mary, and their three children to New York and later negotiated his own escape with a Black sailor bound for the same city.[56]

While Ferebee, Grandy, and Jones all indicate slave watermen's potential for assisting runaways, another North Carolina memoirist, William H. Robinson, whose father, Peter, was a slave pilot, provided the greatest insight into how the enslaved drew on contacts in that Black maritime culture to escape by sea. The experience of Peter and the two Quaker oystermen who were his accomplices also illustrates the intricate planning required to reach a seagoing vessel.

Piloting oyster sloops and other vessels in and out of Wilmington Harbor around 1850, Peter belonged to an elite corps of Black pilots on whom much of coastal transport had relied since the colonial era.[57]

Despite the risks, Peter put his watercraft skills and independence at the disposal of enslaved African Americans who hoped to escape north. He worked closely with the two Quaker abolitionists, Samuel Fuller and "Mr. Elliot," piloting their oyster sloop through local bays and sounds. Deeply enmeshed in harbor life, the three watermen were well positioned to identify mariners who might convey escaping slaves away from Wilmington. Those sailors also kept them in touch with potential benefactors in New England and Canada. Runaways contacted them through Peter, who was well known among local Blacks and was readily approached in the wharf district, or through other Black watermen, stevedores, tradesmen, or hawkers with whom they dealt in their oyster business.[58] Even from plantations well inland and remote swamps, fugitive slaves may have communicated with Peter and his colleagues with the aid of slave boatmen and draymen who delivered inland products into port towns.

Their regular interaction in the far reaches of coastal waters, well distant from public scrutiny, gave the three conspirators an "opportunity to lay and devise plans" for helping enslaved souls to secure passage on a seagoing vessel. They also knew many seamen, observed efforts to catch slaves headed to sea and cultivated local abolitionists on whom they might call to hide fugitive slaves temporarily or to raise funds for their passage.[59] Aspiring runaways must have found their collective knowledge indispensable. The trio may even have carried Black Carolinians from the wharf to seagoing vessels waiting either on the Cape Fear River or farther south beyond the bar at the two local inlets into the Atlantic.

The success of Peter and his collaborators hinged less on their own unique skills than on the general characteristics of maritime slavery. The harsh restrictions enforced on plantation labor gangs broke down in a maritime economy so thoroughly reliant on slave watermen for travel, trade, and communication.[60] Close supervision or regular surveillance proved impractical: too many enslaved watermen performed too many important jobs over too wide and remote a coastline. Marshy shores and poor roads meant that the simplest chores, such as communicating with neighbors or sending produce to market, revolved around African American boatmen. Work routines used to exact slave productivity and regulate slave behavior on plantations did not stand up well before the forces of wind and tide. Even charting the length of a slave waterman's journey could not be done reliably.

Except on steamers, which only began appearing locally about 1840, traveling from Beaufort to Currituck could take one day or two weeks. Poling a Cape Fear flatboat between Hallsville and Wilmington could require two weeks or a month.[61] Inlets and shoals changed constantly and could delay a vessel further. Storm damage and fallen trees rendered smaller creeks and rivers impassable for months. Confronted with that uncertainty and dependent on African American maritime skills, merchants and planters generally conceded slave watermen the unusual degree of mobility and independence that was necessary to conduct their business.

Most significant to runaways headed to sea was that many slave boatmen enjoyed an exceptional amount of privacy and autonomy. Many traveled for days and weeks without overseers on board their vessels. Even those obligated to return to their masters' households every evening had uncommon liberty during the day. They cooked, slept, and socialized in boatmen's camps, which sprang up nightly on isolated beaches and riverbanks. They mingled with Black stevedores and other enslaved maritime workers in busy seaports, and they fraternized with the solitary residents, free and enslaved, at fishing camps and piloting stations.[62] Their work afforded slave watermen the best opportunity to meet runaways, glean information useful to them, and connect them with seagoing vessels.

Black watermen also had opportunities to build relationships with white boatmen and sailors who might assist runaways. These kinds of encounters took place especially on remote islands like the Outer Banks. In small windswept settlements sitting on marshy atolls and sandbanks, enslaved laborers associated with their white counterparts, within bounds, on far more equal terms than on the mainland. Certainly the high proportion of watermen in the slave population, their autonomy, and the premium placed on their maritime skills stretched the conventional boundaries of slavery. Many of the Outer Banks slaves were also mulattos, descended from enslaved mothers and free white sailors or from Indian watermen, and their mixed-race heritage and extended family lines contributed in some cases to a certain ambiguity in race relations.[63] Their distance from the seats of power was also significant. Not having plantation slaveholders or slave patrols looking over their shoulders, white islanders seem to have taken a greater latitude in their public relationships with enslaved men and women.

No less importantly, the islanders lived on the edge of an Atlantic seafaring culture renowned for a crude egalitarianism among Black and white seamen.[64] Since the colonial era, Atlantic shipping had been characterized by an unusual degree of racial equality in seamen's wages, social status, and duty assignments.[65] In port towns, slaveholders might viably confine such heresies at least to the taverns and sailors' boarding houses in the wharf district, but at isolated outposts like Ocracoke, Portsmouth, or Davis Ridge, those shipboard customs eroded the stricter racial barriers on shore. Island residents had more contact with northern and foreign sailors than with mainland slave patrols. Oftentimes in fact, they seemed to have deeper commercial and cultural ties to the ports of New England than to mainland North Carolina. Because white watermen mingled so extensively with northern seamen, owned few slaves, and dealt so often with Black boatmen, their loyalties had long been suspect in the eyes of North Carolina slaveholders. It was no wonder that, at the outbreak of the Civil War, the state's planters so quickly and deeply doubted the loyalties of coastal watermen of both races.[66]

Race relations in seaports were not as wide-open as on some of the state's more remote islands, but Black and white maritime laborers still lived and worked together in ways quite different from the practices of inland towns. A snapshot of New Bern's wharf district in 1850, for instance, would have shown a veritable ethnic melting pot. The waterfront district was majority Black, and of the three sailors' boardinghouses, free Blacks shared living quarters with white sailors in two.[67] This was obviously not the plantation South, and for enslaved Black men and women determined to reach a ship, it presented one of their most promising chances to escape.

Whether or not they sheltered fugitive slaves, African American seamen had regular contact with a broader world and were fonts of information to Blacks confined to shore. Coastal ports like Bath, Ocracoke and New Bern may have outwardly resembled backwater outposts on minor trade routes, but a tour of those harbor districts would have belied any notion of provincialism. There a visitor would have met Black sailors from many nations, swapping the latest scuttlebutt from Boston, San Juan, and Port-au-Prince in a half-dozen languages. By disseminating news, those sailors united African American seaboard communities throughout the Atlantic.[68] The scope of their maritime fraternity could be glimpsed in 1859, when one plot to assist a single Wilmington slave to escape by sea involved Black seamen from the West Indies, Sierra Leone, the Sandwich (later the Hawaiian) Islands and New England.[69] Even if they refused such risks, Black sailors still kept coastal slaves informed about the political climate beyond the South and offered practical details about coastal geography, sea traffic, and sympathetic captains. Black seamen were also known to carry letters between slaves in the Carolinas and family, friends, and church leaders in the North.[70] Planters inland may have more successfully stanched its flow, but at the coast, slaveholders tried in vain to dam a torrent of forbidden knowledge, from which even the smallest droplets could prove invaluable to the enslaved men and women trying to flee.

The attributes of maritime work also gave enslaved watermen their own opportunities to escape. This trend had emerged even in the colonial era; slave watermen were the skilled occupational group most likely to run away.[71] Not surprisingly, enslaved sailors most readily fled during voyages to ports outside the South.[72] However, slaveholders routinely anticipated that all fugitive slaves in maritime industries, even those confined to North Carolina, would employ their skills and contacts to escape by sea. Reward announcements published in port newspapers reflected that suspicion.[73] In 1803 Benjamin Smith warned that his enslaved laborer Bristol, who had briefly been a stevedore in Wilmington, would surely try to reach a ship. Outraged that Bristol enticed two other slaves to go with him, Smith offered fifty dollars for "his head, severed from his body."[74] In 1820 the seaman Sam allegedly masqueraded as a free sailor and "has, no doubt, already gone or will attempt to go to some of the Northern seaports."[75] When an enslaved man named Jim escaped in 1832, his master warned that "he was raised to the water" and was likely to try to board a ship for the North.[76] Captain James Wallace believed in 1838 that Rodney, an enslaved man "accustomed to a seafaring life," would naturally try to flee by ship.[77] And that spring, Sam Potter of Wilmington also expressed confidence that Caesar, whom he described as "well acquainted with all sorts of vessel work," would seek employment on a northbound vessel.[78] Slaveholders recognized that runaways had to be intercepted before they headed out to sea, or they could disappear without a trace into the maritime underworld.

To thwart runaways, political leaders tried to circumscribe Black watermen's duties and influence. The maritime economy depended so extensively on Black laborers, however, that many shipping agents and business leaders were reluctant to place any restrictions their activities, much less ban them from working on the water altogether. In 1800 the General Assembly did compel merchants who employed enslaved pilots to apply for licenses and post bonds of five hundred dollars to assure their good conduct.[79] But when state legislators introduced a bill outlawing slave pilots completely in 1816, merchants in Wilmington and Fayetteville defeated the measure.[80] The persistence of Blacks' escaping by sea finally prompted the state legislature to prohibit enslaved watermen from piloting vessels over bars or inlets and to ban slaves from traveling on steamboats or schooners without written permission.[81] But even if enforced strictly, which was certainly not feasible, those restrictions left slave pilots and other Black watermen a very strong presence on the North Carolina coast.

Port authorities tried similarly to control Black shore workers. Stevedoring, in particular, provided Blacks with openings to conceal their escaping brethren on vessels and to prevent the detection of slaves already stowed away. Because Black stevedores had regular contact with seamen, they also heard about persons with reputations for aiding runaways and could have introduced them to slaves hoping to reach the North. A citizen writing in the *Wilmington Journal* echoed a popular white sentiment when he argued that "we must have *White* men in the place of *negroes* engaged in that business," because they "shall be under the obligations to inspect the stowage [of] vessels."[82] Shipping agents and harbor authorities found it impractical to outlaw Black stevedores, but concerns over slave smuggling eventually led the Commissioners of Navigation and Pilotage on the Cape Fear River to contract with private agents to board, search, and fumigate ships in order to force hidden runaways above deck.[83]

Political leaders viewed Black sailors with the greatest wariness. "They are of course," wrote the *Wilmington Aurora*'s editor, "all of them, from the very nature of their position, abolitionists, and have the best opportunity to inculcate the slaves with their notions."[84] Slaveholders went to great lengths to limit the influence of Black sailors. The General Assembly passed a law in 1830 that quarantined ships employing free Black sailors and prohibited, under penalty of up to thirty-nine lashes, all African Americans from visiting those vessels. The law also made it illegal for those sailors even to "communicat[e] with the coloured people" of North Carolina. The General Assembly also prohibited free Blacks not employed on a ship from visiting a vessel at night or on a Sunday, presumably after the quarantine period of thirty days. The reliance of commerce on Black watermen and sailors, however, again conflicted with the spirit of restriction. Coastal merchants harmed by the penalties against northern vessels and local boats with Black crewmen had the measure overturned during the next legislative session.[85]

Recognizing their critical link in aiding slave runaways, political leaders also sought through municipal ordinances to separate Black sailors and the enslaved. Wilmington, for instance, finally outlawed its slaves from piloting or stevedoring on seagoing vessels manned by free Blacks.[86] White citizens also discouraged free Black sailors from coming ashore by harassing them in a number of ways. Slave patrols were known to flog and jail Black seamen for the most minor infractions of racial decorum.[87] Sheriffs quickly jailed any Black sailor whose seaman's papers had been lost or were of questionable authenticity, and sailors who failed to prove their free status were sold into slavery.[88] Ports also took the firmest stands in requiring all free Blacks to register with town clerks and wear badges emblazoned with "FREE" on their shoulders.[89]

As a further deterrent, white authorities severely punished free Black sailors caught aiding runaways, as illustrated by three cases from the 1850s. In 1855 the Bertie County Superior Court sentenced Alfred Wooby to hang for concealing an enslaved man on a schooner headed down the Roanoke River. In rejecting a petition for pardon, Governor Thomas Bragg reminded Wooby's former employer that "our lawmakers . . . have deemed such punishment necessary to put a stop if possible to the practice of enticing away slaves from the northern states."[90] That same year, Dawson Wiggins faced the hangman's noose for stowing away an enslaved man named Bill on a voyage from New Bern to New York City. His attorney, Thomas Sparrow, worried that "the public appetite is whetted for the sacrifice of a victim" because so many local people held in bondage had recently escaped by sea. Sparrow argued that Wiggins had been blamed solely because he was the only Black hand on the vessel, and that any crewman could have been the culprit.[91] No wonder that, in 1859, Wilmington abolitionists frantically raised funds to secure a prominent lawyer for Black seamen accused of concealing slaves aboard a ship. They not only secretly financed legal counsel for the four sailors but also somehow arranged for a sympathetic judge to preside over the trail. The high stakes were incontestable. "There would be but little danger of hanging if they were slaves," wrote a Quaker ally to a colleague, for "it would be an unjustifiable waste of *property* [but] it is none too good for a free negro in Carolina."[92]

Even after they had successfully embarked on the sea voyage for the North, runaway slaves encountered many dangers. Betrayal or exposure lurked constantly. A schooner is a small vessel, and fugitives who had hidden themselves or had only the protection of a single seaman crouched in steady fear. Often stowaways were not so lucky. On a voyage from New Bern to New York in 1847, sailors discovered an enslaved young man named Ned concealed in the forecastle of the schooner *Dolphin*. He had apparently been sheltered by two Black seamen, Thomas Fortune and Furney Moore. None of the three made it out of the South.[93] Two years later, while sailing to New York City, Captain Smith of the schooner *Minerva Wright* found two Wilmington slaves concealed on board. He abandoned the two men in port at Norfolk, where the sheriff oversaw their return to North Carolina.[94]

A sudden storm, a damaged rudder or any unexpected delay exposed the frailty of this maritime passage out of bondage. One can scarcely imagine the disappointment of Mary Smith, a stowaway captured only because the *Mary of Duxbury* wrecked on Ocracoke Island.[95] Indeed, the threat of shipwreck loomed in the back of every mind when passing the Outer Banks. The skeletons of wrecked vessels littered the beaches from Cape Lookout to Currituck Banks, a constant reminder to all, regardless of race, of mortality and the precariousness of sea travel. But for a runaway slave or a free Black, a shipwreck meant something additionally ominous: slave castaways such as Mary Smith might be re-enslaved, while free Black sailors might find themselves in bondage for the first time.[96]

Other stowaways found that a seagoing vessel did not always afford true asylum, even on the threshold of freedom. After passage of the Fugitive Slave Law in 1850, inspectors searched arriving vessels for runaways in several northern seaports.[97] Antislavery sentiment often prevented the law's strict enforcement, but local officials did capture fugitive slaves from Wilmington in Boston harbor on board the brigantine *Florence* in July 1853 and on the schooner *Sally Ann* in September 1854.[98] Once exposed, stowaways could find little aid from the maritime underworld that had sheltered them.

From colonial days onward, the shores of North Carolina had frustrated slaveholders. Small, ill-protected harbors had prevented the development of a major port and inhibited growth in the state's plantation economy. Outer Banks inlets posed a constant threat to shipping. Frying Pan Shoals and Diamond Shoals inspired fear in sailors throughout the world. The coastline that seemed so inhospitable to slaveholding merchants and planters, however, provided their Black workers with hope of passage to freedom. It was a tenuous hope, dampened by what must have seemed an endless number of futile attempts and bitter reprisals for every triumph. Yet coastal slaves still dreamed of freedom and continued to dare the high seas all the way up to the Civil War. When war broke out, some of those who had braved the sea's escape route returned to guide Union naval vessels through those dangerous waters. Beyond teaching historians about that unquenchable thirst for freedom, their struggles compel us to look beyond the relatively few enslaved African Americans who managed to escape by sea, to the broader aspects of maritime and tidewater culture that sustained their clandestine current out of the South. The boundaries of slavery and freedom may have been more complicated than we have ever imagined.

NOTES

1. William Tatham, "Survey on the Coast of North Carolina from Cape Hatteras to Cape Fear," 1806, North Carolina Collection, Wilson Library, University of North Carolina, Chapel Hill.

2. Reverend W. H. Robinson, *From Log Cabin to the Pulpit; or, Fifteen Years in Slavery*, 3d ed. (Eau Claire, Wisc.: James H. Tifft, 1913), 13.
3. *Wilmington (N.C.) Journal*, 9 November 1849.
4. John Hope Franklin and Loren Schweninger, *Runaway Slaves: Rebels on the Plantation, 1790–1860* (New York: Oxford University Press, 1999), 26–27, 127–28, 143–44; William Wells Brown, *The Black Man: His Antecedents, His Genius, and His Achievements* (New York: T. Hamilton, 1863), 23–26.
5. Loren Schweninger, "The Underside of Slavery: The Internal Economy, Self-Hire, and Quasi-Freedom in Virginia, 1780–1865," *Slavery and Abolition* 12 (September 1991): 1–22.
6. Harriet Jacobs, *Incidents in the Life of a Slave Girl, Written by Herself*, ed. L. Maria Child, ed. and annot. Jean Fagan Yellin (Cambridge, Mass.: Harvard University Press, 1987), 151.
7. *New Bern Carolina Sentinel (New Bern, N.C.)*, 17 January 1829.
8. *Wilmington (N.C.) True Republican*, 23 May 1809.
9. *New Bern Carolina Centinel* (New Bern, N.C.), 4 April, 16 May, 30 May, and 13 June 1818.
10. Runaway slave advertisements appeared regularly in North Carolina newspapers. See, for example, the *Washington (N.C.) American Recorder*, 4 May and 7 September 1821.
11. William Still, *The Underground Rail Road: A Record of Facts, Authentic Letters, Narratives, &c.* (Philadelphia: Porter & Coates, 1872), 137–38.
12. Ibid, 137–38, 234, 316–17.
13. Sir Charles Lyell, *A Second Visit to the United States of North America*, vol. 1 (New York: Harper and Bros., 1849), 219; Rufus W. Bunnell, untitled manuscript, 1858, Writings, 1832–1950, Series 4, Bunnell Family Papers, 1772–1958, Manuscripts and Archives, Yale University Library, New Haven, Connecticut.
14. *Wilmington (N.C.) Advertiser*, 25 March 1836.
15. Frederick Douglass, *Life and Times of Frederick Douglass* (Hartford, Conn.: Park, 1881), 125, 196.
16. *Edenton (N.C.) Gazette*, 19 January 1819; *Wilmington (N.C). Journal*, 24 October 1851.
17. Marion Gleason McDougall, *Fugitive Slaves (1619–1865)* (Boston: Ginn and Co., 1891), 102; and John Spencer Bassett, *Slavery in the State of North Carolina* (Baltimore, Md.: Johns Hopkins University Press, 1899), 15.
18. *Wilmington (N.C.) Advertiser*, 2 February 1838.
19. Peter H. Wood, "Nat Turner: The Unknown Slave as Visionary Leader," in *Black Leaders of the Nineteenth Century*, ed. Leon Litwack and August Meier (Urbana: University of Illinois Press, 1988), 21–40.
20. Allen Parker, *Recollections of Slavery Times* (Worcester, Mass.: Chas. W. Burbank and Co., 1895), 43–62.

21. "Narrative of Mr. Caulkins," in *American Slavery As It Is: Testimony of a Thousand Witnesses* (New York: American Anti-Slavery Society, 1839), 11.
22. Robinson, *From Log Cabin to the Pulpit*, 30–32.
23. *Carolina Centinel* (New Bern, N.C.), 1 December 1821.
24. Mortimer DeMott, "Sojourn in Wilmington and the Lower Cape Fear, 1837," *Lower Cape Fear Historical Society Bulletin* 22 (May 1979).
25. *Carolina Sentinel* (New Bern, N.C.), 8 April 1826; *New Bern (N.C.) Spectator*, 7 March and 2 May 1829; and *Newbernian* (New Bern, N.C.), 16 May 1848.
26. Gerald Mullin, *Flight and Rebellion: Slave Resistance in Eighteenth-Century Virginia* (London: Oxford University Press, 1972), 110–13.
27. Jones, *Experience of Thomas H. Jones, Who Was a Slave for Forty-Three Years. Written by a Friend, as Related to Him by Brother Jones* (New Bedford, Mass.: E. Anthony & Sons, Printers, 1885), 17–35. See also Curtis, Personal Diary (1830–1836), 3 December 1831, Moses Ashley Curtis Papers, 1720–1952, Wilson Library, Southern History Collection, University of North Carolina, Chapel Hill.
28. Jacobs, *Incidents in the Life of a Slave Girl*, 99–100.
29. "Juble Cain" to Zebulon Latimer, 13 October 1848, Lower Cape Fear Historical Society Archives, Wilmington, North Carolina.
30. See Parker, *Recollections of Slavery Times*, 56–59, 76–77, and articles by John Campbell, John J. Schlotterbeck, Roderick A. McDonald, and Ira Berlin and Philip D. Morgan in *Slavery and Abolition* 12 (May 1991): 1–208.
31. Robinson, *From Log Cabin to the Pulpit*, 12; Jones, *Experience of Thomas H. Jones*, 33; and James Battle Avirett, *The Old Plantation: How We Lived in Great House and Cabin before the War* (New York: F. Tennyson Neely, 1901), 88.
32. Avirett, *The Old Plantation*, 118–19; Guion Griffis Johnson, *Ante-Bellum North Carolina: A Social History* (Chapel Hill: University of North Carolina Press, 1937), 670.
33. C. H. Wiley, *Roanoke; or "Where Is Utopia?"* (Philadelphia: T. B. Peterson and Bros., 1866), 77; Porte Crayon [David Hunter Strother], *The Old South Illustrated* (Chapel Hill: University of North Carolina Press, 1959), 145–50; *Edenton (N.C.) Gazette*, 7 January 1822. See also items in the David M. Rubenstein Rare Book and Manuscript Library, William R. Perkins Library, Duke University, Durham, North Carolina: John Driver to [?], 2 May 1790, Letters and Papers, 1783–1791; and Memorandum from Thomas Swepson, 31 December 1810, and Frederick Hall to James Henderson, 10 June 1817 and 20 January 1818, Dismal Swamp Land Company Papers.
34. *Edenton (N.C.) Gazette*, 1 February 1811; *Carolina Centinel* (New Bern, N.C.), 13 June 1818.
35. North Carolina General Assembly, *Laws of North Carolina*, Passed by the General Assembly, at the Session, 1846–1847 (Raleigh, N.C.: Thomas J. Lemay), chap. 46 (hereafter *Laws of North Carolina*).

36. Ibid.
37. Still, *The Underground Rail Road*, 381, 382, 422–27; Jacobs, *Incidents in the Life of a Slave Girl*, 95–155.
38. Daniel Drayton, *Personal Memoir of Daniel Drayton, for Four Years and Four Months a Prisoner (for Charity's Sake) in Washington Jail: Including a Narrative of the Voyage and Capture of the Schooner Pearl* (Boston: Bela Marsh; New York: American and Foreign Anti-Slavery Society, 1855), 20.
39. Still, *The Underground Rail Road*, 150–52; Larry Gara, *The Liberty Line: The Legend of the Underground Railroad* (Lexington: University of Kentucky, 1961), 175–78.
40. Bunnell manuscript, Bunnell Family Papers.
41. Jacobs, *Incidents in the Life of a Slave Girl*, 230.
42. Ibid., 236–38.
43. Still, *The Underground Rail Road*, 129–31.
44. Bunnell manuscript, Bunnell Family Papers.
45. R. C. Smedley, *History of the Underground Railroad in Chester and the Neighboring Counties of Pennsylvania* (Lancaster, Pa.: Office of the Journal, 1883), 335–36; *Wilmington (N.C.) Advertiser*, 19 October 1838 and 18 January 1839.
46. D. Worth to Lewis Tappan, 2 October 1859, and George Mendenhall to Lewis Tappan, 20 December 1859, American Missionary Association Archives, Dillard University, New Orleans, Louisiana.
47. References to Black boatmen appeared frequently in contemporary newspapers and travel accounts. See *Fayetteville (North) Carolina Observer*, 27 February 1817 and 30 April 1818; *Carolina Centinel* (New Bern, N.C.), 3 October 1818; *Carolina Sentinel* (New Bern, N.C.), 23 March 1836; *New Bern (N.C.) Spectator*, 18 December 1830; *Tarboro (N.C.) Free Press*, 27 August 1824; and *Wilmington's Weekly Chronicle (North Carolina)*, 9 December 1840.
48. John Hope Franklin, "The Free Negro in the Economic Life of Ante-Bellum North Carolina," part 1, *North Carolina Historical Review* 19 (July 1942): 254; *Newbern (N.C.) Herald*, 17 November 1809.
49. William H. Singleton, *Recollections of My Slavery Days*, ed. Katherine Mellen Charron and David S. Cecelski (Raleigh, N.C.: Department of Cultural Resources, Division of Archives and History, 1999), 37; Mark T. Taylor, "Seiners and Tongers: North Carolina Fisheries in the Old and New South," *North Carolina Historical Review* 69 (January 1992): 4–10.
50. Curtis Diary, 5 October and 24 October 1830, Curtis Papers; Michael Luster, "'Help to Raise Them': The Menhaden Chanteymen of Beaufort, North Carolina" (Ph.D. diss., University of Pennsylvania, 1993), 3–6.
51. See the description of the Wilmington wharf district in the Bunnell manuscript, Bunnell Family Papers.
52. Johnson, *Ante-Bellum North Carolina*, 606.
53. Abraham Rencher, "Report of Meeting of Cape Fear and Deep River Navigation Company to Governor Bragg," 24 April 1855, Thomas Bragg, Governors Papers,

North Carolina State Archives, Raleigh; Edward B. Dudley to Governor Graham, 23 February 1846, William A. Graham, Governors Letter Books, North Carolina State Archives; and "Rates of Lighterage for the Port of Wilmington," *Wilmington (N.C.) Gazette*, 26 February 1801.

54. London R. Ferebee, *A Brief History of the Slave Life of. Rev. L. R. Ferebee* (Raleigh, N.C.: Edwards, Broughton, & Co., 1882), 8–9; James H. Craig, *The Arts and Crafts in North Carolina, 1699–1840* (Winston-Salem, N.C.: Museum of Early Southern Decorative Arts, 1965), 251–66.
55. Moses Grandy, *Narrative of the Life of Moses Grandy, Late a Slave in the United States of America* (London: Gilpin, 1843), 14, 18–19, 21–22, 41–42.
56. Jones, *Experience of Thomas H. Jones*, 35–36; John Andrew Jackson, *The Experience of a Slave in South Carolina* (London: Passmore & Alabaster, 1862), 24–28.
57. William L. Saunders, ed., *Colonial Records of North Carolina*, vol. 9 (Raleigh: State of North Carolina, 1890), 803–4; J. Gilpin to John Gray Blount, 18 August 1802, in *The John Gray Blount Papers*, vol. 3, *1796–1802*, ed. William H. Masterson (Raleigh: North Carolina State Department of Archives and History, 1965), 532–33; Josiah Bradley to John Gray Blount, 30 November 1810, in *Blount Papers*, vol. 4, *1803–1833*, ed. David T. Morgan, (Raleigh: North Carolina State Department of Archives and History, 1982), 136; William Blount to John Gray Blount, 30 August 1813, John Gray Blount Correspondence, William Blount Rodman Papers, Manuscript Collection, J. Y. Joyner Library, East Carolina University, Greenville, North Carolina; James Howard Brewer, "Legislation Designed to Control Slavery in Wilmington and Fayetteville," *North Carolina Historical Review* 30 (April 1953): 163–64.
58. Stephen B. Weeks, *Southern Quakers and Slavery* (Baltimore, Md.: Johns Hopkins University Press, 1896), 224–44.
59. Robinson, *From Log Cabin to the Pulpit*, 13.
60. Grandy, *Narrative of the Life of Moses Grandy*, 26–31.
61. Benjamin F. Hall Paper, 1924, 13–15, Private Collections, North Carolina State Archives.
62. Frederick Law Olmsted, *A Journey in the Seaboard Slave States, with Remarks on Their Economy* (New York: Dix & Edwards, 1856), 359–60.
63. Nannie Davis Ward, interview by Michael and Debbie Luster, tape recording, 1988, North Carolina Coastal Folklife Collection, North Carolina Maritime Museum, Beaufort.
64. W. Jeffrey Bolster, "'To Feel like a Man': Black Seamen in the Northern States, 1800–1860," *Journal of American History* 76 (March 1990): 1173–99.
65. J. S. Buckingham, *The Slave States of America* (London: Fisher, Son, and Co., 1842), 2:471–72.
66. Beth Gilbert Crabtree and James W. Patton, eds., *Journal of a Secesh Lady: The Diary of Catherine Ann Devereux Edmondston, 1860–1866* (Raleigh, N.C.: Division of Archives and History, Department of Cultural Resources, 1979), 86–87.

67. Seventh Census of the United States, 1850, Craven County, North Carolina, Population and Slave Schedule, United States National Archives, Washington, D.C.
68. Julius S. Scott, *The Common Wind: Afro-American Currents in the Age of the Haitian Revolution* (London: Verso Press, 2018), 38–54.
69. George Mendenhall to Lewis Tappan, 20 December 1859, American Missionary Association Archives.
70. Jacobs, *Incidents in the Life of a Slave Girl*, 128; Jones, *Experience of Thomas H. Jones*, 36–43; Singleton, *Recollections of My Slavery Days*, 26–27, 69; Daniel Williams to Amos Wade, 16 August 1857, in John W. Blassingame, ed., *Slave Testimony: Two Centuries of Letters, Speeches, Interviews, and Autobiographies* (Baton Rouge: Louisiana State University Press, 1977), 110–11; James W. Hood, *One Hundred Years of the African Methodist Episcopal Zion Church* (New York: A.M.E. Zion Book Concern, 1895), 290–93.
71. Marvin L. Michael Kay and Lorin Lee Cary, "Slave Runaways in Colonial North Carolina," *North Carolina Historical Review* 63 (January 1986): 18–19.
72. For a good illustration of the ties that bound slave sailors to their southern homes and of their propensity to escape in distant ports when those ties had been severed, see Jacobs, *Incidents in the Life of a Slave Girl*, 276.
73. See slave hiring contracts in the Roberts Papers, 1806–1814, and in the Miscellaneous Papers, 1729–1868, Cupola House Papers, Shepherd-Pruden Memorial Library, Edenton, N.C.
74. *Wilmington (N.C.) Gazette*, 4 May 1803.
75. *Carolina Sentinel* (New Bern, N.C.), 3 June 1820.
76. *North Carolina Sentinel* (New Bern, N.C.), 5 October 1832.
77. *New Bern (N.C.) Spectator*, 23 January 1838.
78. *Wilmington (N.C.) Advertiser*, 25 May 1838.
79. Brewer, "Legislation Designed to Control Slavery," 163.
80. Ibid., 163–64; *Laws of North Carolina*, 1817, chap. 135, and 1828–1829, chap. 112; and "Petition of B. E. Thorpe," 5 April 1845, Civil Action Papers concerning Slaves and Free Persons of Color, Craven County Miscellaneous Records, North Carolina State Archives.
81. *Laws of North Carolina*, 1836–1847, chap. 35, and 1840–1841, chap. 58.
82. *Wilmington (N.C.) Journal*, 19 October 1849.
83. "List of Vessels Searched and Fumigated, 1858–1862" and "Account Records with Wm. J. Love," Board of Commissioners of Navigation and Pilotage for the Cape Fear River and Bar Papers, Rubenstein Rare Books and Manuscript Library, Perkins Library.
84. *Aurora* quoted in Johnson, *Ante-Bellum North Carolina*, 577–78.
85. *Laws of North Carolina*, 1830–1831, chapter 30; Franklin, 253–54; Bassett, 35; and Bolster, "'To Feel like a Man,'" 1192–99.
86. Minutes of the Town Commissioners of Wilmington, 6 March 1847, Cape Fear Museum Archives, Wilmington, N.C.

87. Johnson, *Ante-Bellum North Carolina*, 577–78.
88. "Plea for a writ of *Habeas Corpus* by Abraham Carpenter," 4 February 1830, Slaves and Free Negroes, Craven County Miscellaneous Records, North Carolina State Archives; *Wilmington (N.C.) Gazette*, 17 and 24 April 1804; John Kollock to Henry Vanneter, 19 October 1815, Henry Vanmeter Papers, Historical Society of Pennsylvania, Philadelphia; *Carolina Sentinel* (New Bern, N.C.), 11 October 1823; *First Annual Report of the New York Committee of Vigilance* (New York: Piercy and Reed, 1837), 50; "Plea for a writ of *Habeas Corpus* by Francis A. Golding," 1835, Slaves and Free Negroes, Craven County Miscellaneous Records, North Carolina State Archives; *Wilmington (N.C.) Journal*, 10 January 1851 and 22 August 1851; George Aaron to Governor Reid, 22 October 1851, David. S. Reid, Governors Papers, North Carolina State Archives.
89. Johnson, *Ante-Bellum North Carolina*, 128.
90. Governor Bragg to J. H. Crowdrey, 5 April 1855, and related correspondence for 9 April 1855 and 25 June 1855, Thomas Bragg, Governors Letter Books, North Carolina State Archives.
91. Thomas Sparrow, file, State v. Dawson Wiggins, 1853–1856, Thomas Sparrow Papers, Southern History Collection, Wilson Library, University of North Carolina, Chapel Hill.
92. D. Worth to Lewis Tappan, 2 October 1859, and George Mendenhall to Lewis Tappan, 20 December 1859, American Missionary Association Archives.
93. Thomas S. Singleton to John S. Hawks, 18 July 1847, and Samuel Salyer and Caldwell Jones to Governor Graham, 23 July 1847, and Governor Graham to the governor of Virginia, 5 August 1847, William A. Graham, Governors Letter Books, North Carolina State Archives.
94. Minutes of the Town Commissioners of Wilmington, 9 January 1850, Museum of the Lower Cape Fear Archives, Wilmington, North Carolina.
95. Edward Everett, governor of Massachusetts, to Governor Spaight, 22 February 1836; John Pike to Governor Spaight, 30 April 1836; and Governor Spaight to Edward Everett, 24 May 1836, Richard Dobbs Spaight Jr., Governors Letter Books, North Carolina State Archives.
96. *Wilmington (N.C.) Gazette*, 24 April 1804.
97. Stanley Campbell, *The Slave Catchers: Enforcement of the Fugitive Slave Law, 1850–1860* (Chapel Hill: University of North Carolina Press, 1968), 110–69.
98. Austin Bearse, *Reminiscences of Fugitive-Slave Law Days in Boston* (Boston: Warren Richardson, 1880), 34–39.

4

HAMPTON ROADS AND NORFOLK, VIRGINIA, AS A WAYPOINT AND GATEWAY FOR ENSLAVED PERSONS SEEKING FREEDOM

CASSANDRA NEWBY-ALEXANDER

ISAAC FORMAN, WILLIAM DAVIS, AND WILLIS REDICK.
HEARTS FULL OF JOY FOR FREEDOM—VERY ANXIOUS FOR WIVES IN SLAVERY.

These passengers all arrived together, concealed, per steamship *City of Richmond*, December, 1853. Isaac Forman, the youngest of the party—twenty-three years of age and a dark mulatto—would be considered by a Southerner capable of judging as "very likely." He fled from a widow by the name of Mrs. Sanders. . . . He stated that he had a wife living in Richmond, and that she was confined the morning he took the U. G. R. R. Of course he could not see her. The privilege of living in Richmond with his wife "had been denied him." Thus, fearing to render her unhappy, he was obliged to conceal from her his intention to escape.

—William Still, *The Underground Rail Road*

Such was the beginning of an account recorded by Philadelphia stationmaster William Still about Isaac Forman, a former Norfolk resident and freedom seeker. The proximity of Forman, like thousands of other slaves, to the waterways, helped his successful escape. Hired as a steward aboard the steamship *Augusta*, which traveled from Richmond and Norfolk, Virginia, to Philadelphia, Forman used his mobility to flee aboard another steamship, the *City of*

Richmond. Although Forman and his wife, Fanny, were not allowed to live together as husband and wife, they were parted when he escaped. According to Forman, he did not inform Fanny of his imminent departure because he feared she would convince him to stay. Indeed, his excuse was that "he was only allowed, once or twice in the year to visit her."[1]

It was in December 1853 that Forman and fellow freedom seekers William Davis and Willis Redick escaped, with the assistance of Underground Railroad conductors William Bagnall and John Minkins. Fellow escapee, thirty-two-year-old Willis Redick, was, like Isaac Forman, a slave for hire. Redick's owner, Portsmouth merchant S. J. Wilson, hired him out to labor for others, and, like Forman, Redick was forced to leave his wife of five months, Lydia, without consulting her. He suspected that his owner was planning to sell him, and if he and his wife had children, he would have no means to protect them. Redick said, "Slavery existed expressly for the purpose of crushing souls and breaking tender hearts." Armed with these fears, Redick left.[2]

Similarly, there was thirty-one-year-old William Davis from Portsmouth, Virginia. Davis apparently had no complaints to lodge against his owner, Joseph Reynolds, except that on occasion Reynolds threatened to sell him. Davis found unbearable this constant anxiety over possibly being put on the auction block, prompting him to flee to Philadelphia. In doing so, Davis regrettably left behind his wife, Catharine, daughter, Louisa, and infant son. Apparently, after word spread that he had fled, his owner, fearing that Davis would depart with them, placed Catharine and her son in Norfolk's slave jail. Davis left aboard a ship, without saying a word.[3]

Once they arrived in Philadelphia, Forman, Redick, and Davis temporarily stayed in a home in the city's free Black community, which supported abolitionist efforts to undermine slavery, before they departed for Toronto, Canada. Each of the three men, propelled by desperation, fear, and hope for a better life, left wives and families in their quest for freedom.

As is evident in these and many other accounts recorded by William Still, American slavery created and enforced a system of despair, abuse, and exploitation. Yet, while the watery sea lanes of the Atlantic Ocean enabled the transport and delivery of Africans to bondage to the New World and African Americans to the Lower South as part of the domestic slave trade, they also offered them and their descendants pathways of hope to possible freedom, especially for those enslaved people located in or near a port. Norfolk was the site of the Virginia's harbor and the center of the Hampton Roads region that stretched from Williamsburg to Suffolk and included the cities of Norfolk, Portsmouth, and

Hampton. This region of Virginia, with its complex and interwoven waterways, provided a starting point for thousands of slaves fleeing bondage to freedom in the North.[4]

My discussion focuses on the accounts of freedom seekers who successfully escaped from Virginia's Hampton Road region by using waterborne means to convey themselves to the North. Considered the center of the southern Underground Railroad network, this region had a relatively successful yet locally autonomous underground network that worked in concert with northern operations to transport fugitives via steamships, schooners, and other coastal vessels to freedom. What earmarked this region as an important departure point on the Underground Railroad was the dominance of the maritime industry in the local economy, which provided enslaved people with access to the numerous mercantile ships plying the seas between southern and northern harbors. Because Norfolk served as Virginia's main port, many enslaved men were hired there to work in the maritime industry or aboard ships that often traveled to northern ports. Moreover, because thousands of ships traveled into and out of the port, even women and children were able to use ships as vehicles for gaining freedom. Most fugitives who successfully escaped their masters settled in northern places where communities of color thrived. These centers of support included New Bedford, Massachusetts, Philadelphia, Pennsylvania, and numerous cities and towns throughout the Ontario Province in Canada, including Toronto.[5]

Although no records were uncovered to explain what happened to William Davis and Willis Redick, Isaac Forman's activities were detailed in the Canadian records. Forman was fortunate because shortly after his arrival and with freedom guaranteed by Canadian law, he secured work as a porter at Russell's Hotel in Toronto. But before long, Forman sank into a deep depression when he realized that freedom had no meaning without Fanny, the love of his life. He wrote to Still that he was "very gloomy and his heart is almost breaking about his wife." In his second letter, he said: "My soul is vexed, my troubles are inexpressible. I often feel as if I were willing to die. I must see my wife in short, if not, I will die. What would I not give no tongue can utter. Just to gaze on her sweet lips one moment I would be willing to die the next. I am determined to see her some time or other."[6]

Amazingly, Forman secured the escape of his beloved wife, Fanny, within a year or two after his departure, bringing her to Canada. His work at one of Toronto's first hotels, located near the center of town at the northeast corner of Church and Colborne streets, probably positioned Forman to make enough money to pay for his wife's passage aboard a steamship or schooner. John Hill, a freedom seeker who was assisted by John Minkins in his escape from Petersburg, Virginia, discussed Forman in one of his letters to William Still.[7] According to Hill, Forman received a letter from his wife in February 1854 explaining how she was ready to join him whenever arrangements were made for her escape. Apparently, the presence of Fanny and Isaac's young child complicated Minkins's efforts to secret Fanny aboard the *City of Richmond*. Using his contacts, he sent a letter to Fanny alerting her that he had secured passage for her and her son aboard a ship traveling to Boston.[8]

By 1861, census records listed the couple living in Brantford, Canada, where numerous other freedom seekers lived, despite rampant prejudice among the white populace against these Black arrivals. Eventually the couple had another child, William, sometime in 1857. (No mention was made in the records of the older child who escaped with Fanny.) Listed in the records, as early as 1861 as a hotel porter, Forman became a milk dealer by the 1870s, living with his family in a lovely frame house. They also became members of the local Baptist Church, an affiliation common among most southern African Americans. Forman would live the rest of his life in Brant, Ontario, eventually succumbing to a stomach and bladder disease at the age of sixty-five on 24 September 1897.[9]

Another interesting dimension of the story of Isaac Forman is that his brother, James H. Forman, also managed a seaborne escape in June 1855, two years after his brother. Like his older brother, James was about twenty-three years old when he fled from his owner, James Saunders, Esq., in Norfolk. James told William Still that he did not have a particular issue with his Saunders. Rather, he was compelled to depart because of his desire to be free. James left Hampton Roads, Virginia, by ship with a group of seven freedom seekers, arriving at William Still's station in Philadelphia. So active was this maritime component of the Underground Railroad at the time James arrived in June that he was one of twenty-six men, women, and children fugitives recorded by Still. Yet, his escape was not without sadness. He left his parents and two sisters as well as his sweetheart, Mariah Moore, still in bondage in Norfolk. His longing to be reunited with his fiancé, however, led to the successful arrangement of Mariah's escape aboard a steamship in 1856.[10]

James's letter to William Still provided important information about the Underground Railroad routes, the information network, and the supportive communities in the North and in Canada. James asked Still to forward Mariah to him via a train to Niagara Falls. She probably carried forged documents to hide her fugitive status. He also asked Still to tell his fiancé to telegraph him at the International Hotel in Niagara Falls, New York, upon her arrival in Philadelphia. Similar to that of many recent arrivals by other fugitives, the plan was that James would meet Mariah at the Suspension Bridge that connected the U.S. and Canadian sides of Niagara Falls. Mariah's train pulled in on 30 June, and, by 22 July, the couple were married in the English Church in Canada. Though somewhat rare in the movement's history, this family affair of freedom seekers was made possible by an active maritime Underground Railroad network in Hampton Roads. What remained unknown was the fate of the parents and sisters of the Forman brothers.[11]

Oftentimes, as detailed in the accounts of the Forman brothers, Davis, and Redick, the decision to escape resulted from events transpiring in the lives of slaveholders (debt, death, or relocation) or slaves (sale, brutality, opportunity, family, or desire for freedom). In the cities and towns in Hampton Roads where the maritime industry dominated, the Underground Railroad flourished because thousands of small vessels and steamships frequented an extraordinary regional confluence of busy waterways. These included the James, Elizabeth, York, Nansemond, Susquehanna, Rappahannock, and Potomac Rivers. Yet, escape was not without risk and occasional capture. Those slaves who attempted to flee or successfully escaped enjoyed an advantage that many other more closely supervised slaves did not have: they either hired out their own time or were allowed relative freedom of movement through maritime-oriented labor. Even more importantly, through their maritime work, they developed connections with those employees who worked aboard ships and had abolitionist contacts.[12]

Historian Wilbur Siebert's account of an Underground Railroad station keeper at Valley Falls, Rhode Island, supports the perspective that the waterways were the primary vehicle of escape from Hampton Roads. This station keeper said that slaves in Virginia in the 1850s secured, either secretly or with the consent of captains, transit on small trading boats coming from Portsmouth and Norfolk.[13]

While the majority of fugitives departing aboard ships came from the contiguous cities and counties of Hampton Roads, some did not. The area around Norfolk County (the Dismal Swamp) linked regions as far away as Florida and as close as eastern North Carolina through a continuous line of swamps that offered a refuge and passage for those seeking liberty and freedom. By the 1850s, with an average of a thousand to fifteen hundred ships annually sailing into the Hampton Roads harbor, it was difficult for authorities to ascertain where most freedom seekers originated. So concerned were authorities about the steady stream of escapes that U.S. Senator James Mason of Virginia ventured an estimate that Virginia lost an average of one hundred thousand dollars in slave property each year throughout the 1850s. Initially proposed by Mason as an amendment to the Fugitive Slave Act of 1793, Mason's bill, which became the 1850 Fugitive Slave Act, gave federal officials the power to hold "rendition hearings."[14] As a result, those accused of being fugitives were denied the right to trial or appeal or the option to be heard in another court.[15] Based on the Hampton Roads newspapers figures, Mason's dollar amount was a rather low estimate, given that the region was the largest Underground Railroad embarkation point in Virginia.

An examination of fugitives who left aboard the same ships traveling from Hampton Roads to points north revealed that they hired out their time, lived near the waterways, worked in maritime industries, or were employed in jobs that provided them with special labor passes, which they used as their proverbial tickets to freedom. Beginning in 1782, Virginia's legislature attempted to curtail the number of slaves being hired out for semiautonomous maritime labor; the lack of owner supervision created flight risks. Those concerns were addressed three years later when the legislature established rewards for the capture of fugitives.[16] By 1795, however, the state officially recognized what were shadows of a secret network formed to assist in the absconding of slaves. Virginia's authorities were so concerned about the escape of fugitives in large numbers from the Old Dominion that starting in 1820, the state legislature passed countless statutes granting local authorities the power to search and seize vessels, especially those from the North, that entered Virginia's waterways.[17]

As early as 1827, local newspapers published accounts reporting freedom seekers absconding on steamships to seek freedom in the north. For example, in a September 1827 issue of *Norfolk and Portsmouth Herald*, the writer complained about the "transportation of persons of color, more particularly by the Baltimore and Philadelphia [steamship] lines. There is every reason to believe that several slaves, who within a short time past, have been enticed away, or have eloped of their own accord, from their owners, have escaped by the boats of one of these lines. It is known that slaves have been carried off by these boats, for they have been apprehended abroad, and brought back in the boat that took them out of the State."[18]

In December 1833, a number of influential citizens from Richmond and the County of Henrico formed a committee whose efforts would lay the groundwork for the 1856 fugitive slave fund, an endowment intended to prevent the flight of slaves from that area.[19] By rewarding those who would "lead to the detection and punishment of evil disposed persons, who, it is believed, are aiding and abetting in attempts to destroy all security to that kind of property," the committee, and later the state legislators, were certain that they could prevent the departure of slaves and thereby protect their investments.[20] Despite these efforts, slaveholding was vulnerable to the practical realities of access to waterways and the frequent visitation of ships to the area.

Slavery in the coastal or tidewater South was a double-edged sword for slaveholders. They used enslaved people in every industry. At the same time, some industries created a potentially advantageous situation for the enslaved. The practice of employing slaves to do much of the loading and unloading of boats and ships and to perform waterborne-transport work on riverside plantations and in port areas afforded Black men and women easy access to the numerous ferries, sloops, and other ships that plied the waterways throughout Hampton Roads. African Americans crowded the shipyards, wharves, and docks as part of the throng of laborers. The area's shipyards, more than any others, produced numerous ships, providing Blacks and whites, free and enslaved, with skilled and unskilled jobs. Among the most popular trades were those of sail makers, caulkers, cordwainers, riggers, ship's carpenters, and blacksmiths. Visitors to the area may have been surprised to see canal boats, scows, flatboats, and skiffs commanded by Black men and operated by all-Black crews.[21]

Virginia slaveholders and officials reacted to the loss of enslaved property through escapes in newspaper editorials and public laws. In 1854 the Virginia legislature passed a law restricting slaves from hiring out their time. Not surprisingly, this act had little impact on the departure of fugitives. Editorialists wrote that, according to slaveholders, too many slaves were disappearing, especially from the ports of Norfolk, Portsmouth, Richmond, and Petersburg. With over a thousand ships annually coming into these ports, maintaining security was impossible. It seemed that maritime Underground Railroad activities in Hampton Roads had reached a pinnacle. The historical record demonstrates that numerous enslaved Portsmouth residents succeeded in their quest for freedom—all using northbound seagoing coastal craft to do so.[22]

Moses Wines, in particular, was quite familiar with the Hampton Roads port. As a slave who hired out his time probably to do a number of odd jobs in and around the docks, he knew about the steamships and schooners that came in and out of the area every week. Although Wines was not mistreated by his owner, Abigail Wheeler, he lived in constant fear that she would sell him. As a member of the African Society Methodist Church, Wines came in contact with many other African Americans who either had escaped or were secretly involved with the Underground Railroad. Indeed, Wines eventually escaped aboard the vessel, *City of Richmond,* with the assistance, no doubt, of John Minkins.[23]

Despite increased efforts launched by slaveholders and public notices offering rewards, the decade of the 1850s witnessed the steady flow of slave escapes by sea from Virginia. However, unlike the earlier notices that offered clues about their slave's whereabouts in the region, most of these alerts suggested that in the owners' view, the fugitives had left the area with assistance from the Underground Railroad on board northbound merchant vessels. Contemporary fugitive advertisements offered rewards for their return and descriptions of the men and women who had departed. In 1852 a Norfolk newspaper warned of a growing restiveness among its enslaved population that, the editor believed, was the result of leniency among slaveholders and the hiring-out practices.[24]

This position, however, belied the realities of slavery, especially in the port towns of Portsmouth and Norfolk. Hampton Roads at this time was in the midst of economic transformation, which was partly driven by new railroad lines and heavy shipping traffic coming into its ports. They brought external economic, social, and cultural forces from the North and from Western Europe that challenged and conflicted with the southern provincialism of many of its white residents. For those Blacks working in the maritime industries, contact with free Black sailors and with people from beyond the southern regions informed them of an outside world—a free society—very different from their slave society in the Hampton Roads region.[25] Many free and enslaved Black residents, especially those who subscribed to the abolitionist newspapers of the day, were familiar with abolitionism. Slaveholding Virginians and their supporters were concerned enough over this issue that a July 1835 session in the hustings (county) court pronounced that the "circulation of the [abolitionist] papers would 'produce a spirit of disobedience and dissatisfaction among the free negroes and slaves.'" Therefore, the court directed the mayor to request that the postmaster stop delivering abolitionist newspapers to Norfolk's free and enslaved populace.[26]

An article in the *American Beacon* proclaimed that between $40,000 and $50,000 worth of slave property left the Hampton Roads port in 1853 alone. In 1854, the *American Beacon* exclaimed that slaves escaped "almost daily," with leaders from both Portsmouth and Norfolk fearing that their cities' losses annually totaled as much as $500,000. These losses caused lawmakers to step up efforts to deter escapes with the increased deployment of night watchmen, the imposition of laws penalizing those who assisted fugitives, and the threat of severe prison terms. Civil authorities also arrested or detained numerous ship captains, stewards, and crewmen for assisting runaways, although only a few violators received prison terms. Virginia officials were desperate to respond firmly and decisively to stop these slave flights, with some recommending extreme measures to capture, prosecute, and punish those persons assisting fugitives. Some state authorities even advocated allowing enslaved people to testify in court and establishing an inspection system for all ships leaving Virginia ports. In fact, despite these efforts by local and state officials, the Virginia Penitentiary records between 1842 and 1860 registered only twenty-seven men who were imprisoned for assisting fugitive slaves in the state.[27]

An 1854 notice that appeared in the *American Beacon* stated that five slaves, who had somehow escaped from William Hall, Sigourney, and Mrs. Shepherd, left the area aboard a charter ship.[28] A year later, W. W. Parsons of Cabin Point posted a one-hundred-dollar reward for the return of his slave, Reuben, who was twenty-seven years old, black-complexioned, and five feet tall. From the Isle of Wight in Smithfield, Reuben had last been seen six weeks before near Deep Creek—suggesting that he was attempting to secure passage aboard a ship. In that same year, Norfolk resident and merchant Peter W. Hinton posted a two-hundred-dollar reward for Jeffry, a twenty-six-year-old dark-complexioned slave who, if caught, was to be confined to the Norfolk jail.[29]

These ads suggest that authorities tried to create a more organized form of retrieving slaves because most requested that the fugitives, if captured, be delivered to William W. Hall's jail in Norfolk. Despite the frequent fugitive slave advertisements and the maritime activity of the Underground Railroad operatives, not all of the enslaved successfully absconded. On 9 March 1855, Hall caught four runaways who had been missing for a month; they were two women and one boy owned by Alex M. Pennock, a commander in the U.S. Navy, and one woman owned by Hall. Apparently, their efforts had been so elaborate that Hall did not recognize his own slave, who was dressed like a man.[30]

The constant stream of runaway incidents in the Hampton Roads region triggered two letters to the editor of the *American Beacon* from men signed, "A Citizen" and "A Slaveholder," who complained about the seaborne fugitive problem. The Citizen believed that the daily "and even hourly" arrival of vessels—especially northern ships—to the area's ports invited Underground Railroad activities. In an letter published on 22 April 1854, he noted that Portsmouth's citizens, unlike their counterparts in Norfolk, were proactively addressing their dilemma of runaways by creating a vigilance committee.[31] What the letter revealed was an inkling of how effective the maritime Underground Railroad

FIGURE 8. Fifteen Freedom Seekers Arriving at League Island, Philadelphia Harbor, in July 1854 Aboard an Unnamed Schooner from Norfolk, Virginia. The group included Portsmouth resident Isaac Forman and Rebecca Lewey, who were met by abolitionists with carriages that took the fugitives to Philadelphia's Underground Railroad Stationmaster, William Still. Illustration in William Still, *The Underground Rail Road: A Record of Facts, Authentic Letters, Narratives, &c.* (Philadelphia: Porter & Coates, 1872); image from Digital Collections, General Research Division, The New York Public Library, https://digitalcollections.nypl.org/items/510d47df-79d2-a3d9-e040-e00a18064a99.

network methods were at the time and how important the slaves were to providing monies to families without fathers. From Portsmouth, Citizen wrote:

> We have said that our slaves are stolen from us almost daily—we may add hourly—and the question arises, how do they escape?—in what manner do they elude us with so much impunity? Some believe that they are spirited off in vessels from our harbor; that they are secreted on board in such a manner as to escape the scrutinizing eye of the officer in search of them. . . .
>
> No slaves we believe escape in vessels from our harbor, or rather few secrete themselves on board while in our harbor. But it is our firm belief that they are taken on board after the vessels have left our port. . . . We believe [it] is the great Underground Railroad, through whose channel our slaves are escaping from us. But if such is the case, how are we to remedy the great evil? how secure the offenders and preserve our property?—There is only one way, and that is to have a law passed thro' the Governor, that all outward bound vessels should be obliged, under a heavy penalty to heave to off Fort Monroe, and there undergo a rigid examination by officers appointed for the purpose.[32]

Two significant points come to light from Citizen's editorial and Slaveholder's letter published three days later in the Norfolk *American Beacon*, which was known for its vehemently proslavery stance. First, Citizen was convinced—wrongly it turned out—that fugitives were finding departure points in places other than the established wharves and docks located along the Elizabeth River between Norfolk and Portsmouth. The writer charged that schooners and oystering vessels, which regularly plied the main waterways and inlets throughout Hampton Roads, were responsible for spiriting away fugitive slaves. Second, the writer believed that abolitionist agents were secretly working in the region with the assistance of local Blacks and whites as well as African American churches and other secret societies. Citizen argued that unless action was taken to disband all Black churches and to closely monitor the docks, the area would lose many more of its valuable slaves. Three days later, Slaveholder further suggested:

> No negro, slave or free, should be permitted to pass after ten o'clock, without special permission in writing for that night only, and the object for the permit stated on the pass. Passes written by children should be disregarded. . . . All negro oyster boats to be prohibited under severe penalties from leaving the harbor after dark and be anchored above Town Point in the night. A watch should be located on Town Point to stop all vessels and boats leaving during the night. They should be armed, have a swift boat and power to search and detain suspicious crafts. Free negroes from other places should be prevented from gaining a residence in the city, and those from States north of Virginia coming here in vessels, steamers or otherwise to be [confined] as in Charleston. . . . A secret police to be organized by the Mayor and liberal rewards allowed for all discoveries of attempts to violate the police.[33]

Not until 1856 did the state of Virginia agree with and act on such opinions by enacting an overarching inspection law known as the Inspection of Vessels Act. Slaveholders from the Hampton Roads area successfully pressured the legislature to pass a comprehensive program that involved boarding and searching all vessels coming into and sailing from Virginia's ports. They vainly hoped that this policy would deter slave escapes. A reward of one hundred dollars would be given to anyone who apprehended fugitives found aboard vessels.[34] The law stipulated a five-to-ten-year imprisonment of free persons found guilty of assisting fugitives and the payment of five hundred dollars as a reward to those who provided information that led to the "conviction of a free white person engaged in carrying off a slave, or in any manner concerned in helping an escape."[35]

Most of the people convicted of assisting enslaved people to escape were skilled artisans whose work was often conducted in conjunction with the maritime industry. Among them were men such as H. Charous, a mulatto wheelwright, Cato Ricketts, a Black wheelwright, John A. Blevins, a white shoemaker, S. Brooks, a white blacksmith, and A. Ewing, a white carpenter. For instance, in July 1858, Portsmouth slaveholders James Murdaugh, William H. Wilson, Joseph Carter, and James Hodges turned Edward Lee into the authorities and presented evidence of his guilt. Lee was later convicted under section twenty-seven of the 1856 Act because he had assisted slaves to escape in April 1858.[36]

Evidence abounds to illustrate that useful information to facilitate escapes by sea was transmitted throughout this clandestine regional network in the Virginia waterfront and tidal-hinterland waterways. For instance, Jefferson Pipkins, a slave who escaped from Baltimore with his wife and five others in April 1853, wrote to William Still three years later requesting that he arrange for the escape of his children, who lived in North Carolina and Virginia. How could a slave living in Maryland know the location of his children—unless they had been sold to his owner's relatives or friends? It was possible that Pipkins tapped into a coordinated network replete with detailed information about individuals and their whereabouts.[37]

Local newspaper editorials bemoaned the impact of what they termed a conspiracy to steal slaves away by sea orchestrated by agents and willing participants.[38] In Norfolk's *Southern Argus* newspaper, the editor intoned that the frequent escapes "have become such an intolerable evil, that it behooves our citizens and municipal rules to adopt such stringent measures as will be most likely to put a stop to the heavy losses which the holders of slaves are continually incurring."[39] With slave-owners desperate to find a solution, the editor recommended strengthening the police force and the ship inspections, increasing surveillance of the harbors and waterways, and flooding each ship prior to departure with *Phillip's fire annihilator,* a device to extinguish fire using gasses and vapor, to force anyone hidden on board to flee the ship. Even with these rather extreme remedies to thwart escapes, the editor would not admit that slavery was a horrendous institution from which its victims wanted to flee voluntarily. Instead, he claimed that the freedom seekers were "enticed from their owners" by criminal covert actors, even leaving behind their wives and children.[40]

The challenge for slaveholders was twofold: first, combating the passion of enslaved people to gain freedom; and second, contending with the financial incentives for ships' captains and others to transport freedom seekers to northern ports in exchange for a fee. William Still also opined throughout his account that, while some ship captains were committed abolitionists, the majority were motivated by the prospect of monetary rewards, charging up to one hundred dollars per passenger, an amount that translates to thirty-two hundred dollars today.[41] Of course, this meant that many fugitives whose contacts with ship captains were independent of Underground Railroad conductors in the area, risked betrayal, as historian Larry Gara cites in his book, *The Liberty Line*. Isaac Forman, however, was fortunate, for his work as a steamship steward helped him to find other individuals to assist him when he escaped.[42]

In another seaborne fugitive narrative, Portsmouth native John Atkinson declared his slaveholder to be "a worthless sot" with a character that was "too disgusting for record." "For some years before escaping [Atkinson] had been in the habit of hiring his time. Daily toiling to support his drunken and brutal master was a hardship that [Atkinson] felt keenly, but was compelled to submit to up to the day of his escape." Throughout John's life he had "suffered many abuses" from his owner, James Ray, a twenty-six-year-old sailor who lived at the U.S. Navy Yard in Gosport, Virginia (located just outside the city of Portsmouth). According to Still's narrative, Atkinson contacted John Minkins, a Black steward aboard the *City of Richmond,* who, it seemed, frequently arranged transit for fugitives within the bowels of that steamer. Leaving Portsmouth without informing his wife, Mary, Atkinson arrived in Philadelphia in 1854. Afterward, the Vigilance Committee arranged his transportation to St. Catharines, a city just across the border near Niagara Falls in Ontario, Canada, and home to numerous fugitives, including Harriet Tubman.[43] Like many men who were forced to leave their families behind, it is unknown whether Atkinson was ever able to reunite with his wife.

Similarly, Robert Irving, alias Sheridan Ford, regretted leaving his wife and three sons in 1855. Born in Portsmouth, Virginia, in 1827, Sheridan married Julia Ann Gregory in 1845 and lived his life as best he could, hiring out his time at the Portsmouth Naval Hospital and giving a portion of his earnings to his slaveholder, Elizabeth Brown. Like many men who escaped without their families, Sheridan got wind that his owner was going to sell him. So, in November 1854 he fled, hiding in the woods just beyond the borders of the small city of Portsmouth, hoping to eventually get to his wife and children. But Julia's owner was wise to this scheme and placed them in Hall's slave jail in Norfolk, far from the reach of Sheridan or anyone who might assist. For months, Sheridan tried to reach his family, but, fearing he would be captured, he got aboard a steamship and fled north, eventually settling in New Bedford, Massachusetts.[44]

Ford's neighbor, Clarissa Davis and her brothers, thirty-year-old William and twenty-eight-year-old Charles, also attempted to make their escape from Portsmouth in 1854. William and Charles successfully secured transit aboard the *Ellen Barnes* from Wareham, Massachusetts, in May while Clarissa did not. Instead, she hid in "a miserable coop," praying that Providence would allow her a chance to join her brothers. Eventually word was conveyed to her that the steamship *City of Richmond* had arrived from Philadelphia and that the steward, John Minkins, would hide her while William Bagnall, a white agent, would assist by storing her in a box once she got aboard.[45]

The challenge for Davis, however, was getting from the coop to the ship. The docks were closely monitored because of the large numbers of fugitives who had left from Hampton Roads in the 1850s. Moreover, authorities had been alerted to her disappearance. A one-thousand-dollar reward had been posted by their slaveholders for the return of Clarissa and her two brothers. For that reason, she prayed that a heavy rain would reduce the numbers of people monitoring the docks. Fortunately for her, torrential rains did fall by midnight on the date chosen for her attempt, allowing Clarissa, dressed in male attire, to embark the ship at the appointed time of 3:00 A.M. Once there, Bagnall hid her in a box while Minkins made sure that the box was delivered to the Vigilance Committee upon arrival in Philadelphia. Renamed Mary D. Armstead, Clarissa was furnished with a passport and then forwarded to New Bedford, Massachusetts, at which point she was reunited with her brothers and eventually connected with Sheridan Ford.[46]

In 1863, about eight years after Clarissa Davis and Sheridan Ford lived in proximity to one another in New Bedford, they married. Perhaps Ford, like many who had to leave their families, buried his wife and children in his mind, never expecting to see them again. In a remarkable twist of fate, two years later after the end of the Civil War, Ford was contacted by a friend who still lived in Portsmouth to alert him that his wife, Julia, had returned with her new husband. In so many ways, Ford's story typified those slaves who were forced to leave their family in an effort to better secure the well-being of their loved ones as free people. While reconnecting with his family eleven years after his escape, the circumstances of his and his former wife's personal lives would prevent them from reassembling as a family because both had married other people, believing they would never reunite.[47]

Ironically, it was the waterways in Hampton Roads that provided pathways to freedom and avenues to reunite, even though the reconnections were sometimes bittersweet. Still chronicled that 120 men from Hampton Roads, out of the 242 fugitive men, left their wives and families when they went aboard ships to flee to freedom. Their reasons were often like Ford's cause: They fled because sale to the Lower South was imminent. Many hoped to reconnect with their wives later, while others expected to be reunited in the near term. According to Still, some of these men left because their wives and families had been sold away; others left with their wives joining them a short time later. In some cases, the women left first. Furthermore, some of the men who escaped their bondage mentioned that their free Black wives would later join them in the North or in Canada. Of those listed by William Still, only a small percentage were women who traveled alone, and children escaping with their parents made up only about ten percent.

It was fortunate that William Still collected and preserved his notes of freedom seekers and his correspondence with the hundreds who passed through his Philadelphia station. Unlike the majority of other stationmasters who discarded their records during or after the Civil War, Still's records provide historians with a roadmap for the countless men, women, and children who traveled the dangerous waterways and pathways to freedom. And while many of the accounts of those freedom seekers who fled prior to Still's involvement and note taking are now lost to historians, those experiences that were preserved by Still and others provide significant details on the opportunities, means, and methods of their dangerous journey from slavery in the South to freedom in the North.

These heart-wrenching accounts of separation, loss, and escapes by waterways are part of the real stories of the Underground Railroad. Their lives highlight how those freedom seekers risked everything for a chance freedom, but not without a cruel cost. Many slaves who escaped from the ports of Hampton Roads never reconnected with their families; and even those who did were not able to reassemble them, as with Sheridan Ford, because they had remarried and made new families. Perhaps this circumstance explains why the nation witnessed the emergence of Negro Spirituals. Emotions of "joy and sadness, rage and love, tranquility and anxiety" are ever-present in spirituals, with these conflicting emotions expressed simultaneously. What is most interesting in the context of this essay and volume is the use of water as an important image of the road to freedom, which is found, for instance, in the song "Wade in the Water." Even as whites set up barriers to freedom, Blacks constructed both a metaphorical and a very real river of resistance, as historian Vincent Harding eloquently discusses in his book, *There Is a River.*[48] In Hampton Roads, rivers were both metaphors for autonomy and actual pathways to liberty for hundreds of freedom seekers, whose idea of happiness flowed like a river to the land of freedom.

NOTES

1. Austin Bearse, *Reminiscences of Fugitive-Slave Law Days in Boston* (Boston: Printed by Warren Richardson, 1880), 54–55; Journal C of Station No. 2 of the Underground Railroad, Agent William Still, 1852–1857, p. 41, Pennsylvania Abolition Society Papers, ed. Peter P. Hinks, Historical Society of Pennsylvania, Philadelphia (hereafter Still, Journal C), https://hsp.org/history-online/digital-history-projects/pennsylvania-abolition-society-papers/journal-c-of-station-no-2-william-still-1852-1857-0.
2. William Still, *Underground Railroad: A Record of Facts, Authentic Narratives, Letters, & C., Narrating Hardships, Hairbreadth Escapes and Death Struggles of the Slaves in Their Efforts of Freedom, As Related by Themselves and Others, or Witnessed by the Author Together with Sketches of Some of the Largest Stockholders, and Most Liberal Aiders and Advisors of the Road, rev. ed. (1878; reprint, Oxford, Eng.: Benediction Classics, 2008)*, 54, 56–57; Still, Journal C, 40.
3. Joseph Reynolds, a wealthy and influential Portsmouth merchant, was originally from Ireland. The 1850 slave schedule listed him as owning twelve slaves, ranging in age from two to fifty-four. According to the census, William Davis was the older of the two males owned by Reynolds. Still, *Underground Railroad*, 54, 56–57; 1850 U.S. Census (Free Schedule), Portsmouth, Norfolk, Virginia; 185A, digital image s.v. "Joseph Reynolds," Ancestry.com.
4. Cassandra Newby-Alexander, *Virginia Waterways and the Underground Railroad* (Charleston, S.C.: The History Press, 2017), 57–58.
5. Larry Gara, *The Liberty Line: The Legend of the Underground Railroad* (1961; reprint, with a new preface, Lexington: University Press of Kentucky, 1996), 51.
6. Still, *Underground Railroad*, 54–55.
7. Fugitive accounts from Richmond/Petersburg and Norfolk/Portsmouth indicated that a man named Minkins assisted them with securing passage aboard steamships bound for Philadelphia. The Norfolk Minkins family was the only free Black family recorded in the U.S. census schedules. The oldest son, John Minkins, was likely the steward identified by Philadelphia stationmaster William Still. According to the 1850 U.S. Census records for the City of Norfolk, John Minkins worked as an omnibus driver, an occupation that would have familiarized him with passenger ships, mariners, taverns, hotels, and the city at large. When Norfolk restricted omnibus driving to whites only in the early 1850s, Minkins undoubtedly had to find another job. By 1853, he began appearing in William Still's accounts as responsible for assisting numerous freedom seekers traveling by ship from Virginia to northern ports. Still, *Underground Railroad*, 60–61, 64, 67–68, 81, 163, 191, 202, 228, 230–31, 268–70, 299–300, 308, 316–17; Tommy Bogger, *The Darker Side of Freedom*

(Charlottesville: University Press of Virginia, 1997), 61, 78–79; 1850 U.S. Census (Free Schedule), Norfolk, Virginia, digital image s.v. "John Minkins," *Ancestry.com.*

8. J. Ross Robertson, *Robertson's Landmarks of Toronto: A Collection of Historical Sketches of the Old Town of York from 1792 until 1833 and of Toronto from 1834 to 1893* (Toronto: J. Ross Robertson, 1894), 50; Still, *Underground Railroad,* 194.
9. 1861 Canada Census (Free Schedule), Ottawa, Ontario, Canada, digital image s.v. "Isaac Foreman," Ancestry.com.
10. Still, *Underground Railroad,* 267–68,
11. Ibid., 268; Tom Calarco et. al., *Places of the Underground Railroad: A Geographical Guide* (Santa Barbara, Calif.: ABC-CLIO, 2011), 225.
12. Still, *Underground Railroad,* 29, 57; Gary Collinson, *Shadrick Minkins: From Fugitive Slave to Citizen* (Cambridge: Harvard University Press, 1997), 46; Gerald Mullin, *Flight and Rebellion: Slave Resistance in Eighteenth Century Virginia* (New York: Oxford University Press, 1972), 4, 6.
13. Wilbur Siebert, *The Underground Railroad from Slavery to Freedom* (New York: Macmillan, 1898), 81, 144.
14. Statistics for Hampton Roads are in the Virginia state quarterly reports from 1856 to 1860. Although the first half of the decade is not included, references are made in these reports about the early 1850s. "Quarterly Report of the Chief Inspector under the Law for the Better Protection of Slave Property in the Commonwealth of Virginia Passed March 17, 1856 for the Quarter ending September 30, 1858," Quarterly Reports, 1856–1861, Virginia Chief of Inspector of Vessels, Manuscript Division, Library of Virginia, Richmond. Siebert, *Underground Railroad from Slavery to Freedom,* 25; Collinson, *Shadrick Minkins,* 44–45; David G. Smith, *On the Edge of Freedom: The Fugitive Slave Issue in South Central Pennsylvania, 1820 -1870* (New York: Fordham University Press, 2013), 119.
15. Steven Lubet, *Fugitive Justice: Runaways, Rescuers, and Slavery on Trial* (Cambridge, Mass.: Belknap Press of Harvard University Press, 2010), 42.
16. "Minutes of the Society for the Prevention of the Absconding and Abducting of Slaves, 1833–1849," Accession no. 9272, Special Collections, University of Virginia Library, Charlottesville; "Fugitive Slave Fund: Claims for Payment, 1857–1860," box 1801, APA 689, Auditor of Public Accounts, Record Group 48, Manuscript Division, Library of Virginia, Richmond.
17. Bogger, *Darker Side of Freedom,* 165; June Purcell Guild, *Black Laws of Virginia: A Summary of the Legislative Acts of Virginia Concerning Negroes from Earliest Times to the Present* (New York: Negro Universities Press, 1936), 61, 63, 67–68.
18. "Steamboats Seen as Agencies of 'Underground Railway,'" *Norfolk and Portsmouth (Va.) Herald,* 28 September 1827.
19. "Minutes of the Society for the Prevention of the Absconding and Abducting of Slaves, 1833–1849," University of Virginia Library.
20. Ibid.; "Fugitive Slave Fund: Claims for payment, 1857–1860," Library of Virginia.

21. Mullin, *Flight and Rebellion*, 94–96, 106, 119.
22. Still, *Underground Railroad*, 50, 52, 223, 230, 297; Eric Foner, *Gateway to Freedom: The Hidden History of the Underground Railroad* (New York: W. W. Norton, 2015), 152.
23. 1850 U.S. Census (Free Schedule), Portsmouth, Norfolk, Virginia, digital image s.v. "Abigail Wheeler," *Ancestry.com*; Still, 230–31.
24. William Link, "The Jordan Hatcher Case," *Journal of Southern History* 64 (November 1998): 620.
25. Ibid., 620.
26. Bogger, *Darker Side of Freedom*, 138.
27. "Quarterly Report of the Chief Inspector under the Law for the Better Protection of Slave Property in the Commonwealth of Virginia, Passed March 17, 1856 for the Quarter ending September 30, 1858;" Manuscript Division, Library of Virginia; Collinson, *Shadrick Minkins*, 86; Schwartz, *Slave Laws in Virginia*, 139–40.
28. *Norfolk (Va.) American Beacon*, 19 April 1854, 2.
29. *Norfolk (Va.) Southern Argus*, 4 April 1855, 2–3.
30. Ibid., 19 December 1854, 3, and 10 March 1855, 2; Still, *Underground Railroad*, 273, 325; 1860 U.S. Census (Free Schedule), Norfolk, Virginia, digital image s.v. "William W. Hall," *Ancestry.com.*
31. *Norfolk (Va.) American Beacon* (Norfolk, VA), 22 April 1854.
32. Ibid., 22 April 1854.
33. Ibid., 25 April 1854.
34. James Matthews, *Digest of the Laws of Virginia of a Civil Nature*, vol. 2 (Richmond: C. H. Wynne, 1857), 324–25; Virginia Statutes (1856), chaps. 47–49; Guild, *Black Laws of Virginia*, 86, 89–90.
35. Philip Schwarz and the Virginia State Penitentiary records include a comprehensive list of those imprisoned under this criminal statute. State of Virginia Penitentiary Inmates, in 1860 US Census Records, County of Henrico, City of Richmond, Manuscript Division, Library of Virginia, Richmond; Year, 1860, Census Place, Richmond Ward 3, Henrico, Virginia, pp. 472–76, 478, 481, Family History Library Film, 805353; Philip Schwarz, *Slave Laws in Virginia* (Athens: University of Georgia Press, 1996), 137, 145.
36. State officials hoped that threats of imprisonment in the State Penitentiary, located at the western terminus of Byrd Street, would be a deterrent for whites and free Blacks because incarceration there was seen as a death sentence (few convicts survived more than three years). Between 1842 and 1860, the state of Virginia imprisoned twenty-seven men convicted of aiding fugitive slaves. Virginia toughened the penalties by 1860 and increased the sentence to twenty years, hoping to strengthen the law as a legal deterrence. Collinson, *Shadrick Minkins*, 45; Schwarz, *Slave Laws in Virginia*, 127–28, 134, 137, 145; Siebert, "The Underground Railroad in Massachusetts," *New England Quarterly* 9 (September 1936): 447. State of Virginia

Penitentiary Inmates, in 1860 U.S. Census, County of Henrico, City of Richmond; "Fugitive Slave Fund: Claims for Payment, 1857–1860," State Library of Virginia; Virginia Statutes (1860), chap. 42; Guild, *Black Laws of Virginia*, 91.

37. Still, *Underground Railroad*, 66, 136–37. According to Still, Jefferson Pipkins asked him to locate his daughter, Susan, by contacting Dr. George Collins or Dr. William Collins at the ferryboat in Portsmouth, or Rose who worked at the Crawford House. Although Still's account only identified a Dr. Collins, the 1860–1861 Portsmouth Directory listed one person with the last name Collins as a physician practicing in the city. George W. Collins resided on Washington between County and King Streets. His brother, John Collins, was listed in the 1850 census as residing at the Crawford House. E. M. Coffield & Co., compiler, *Directory for the City of Portsmouth, to Which Is Added Business Directory for 1860–1861* (Portsmouth: Hume & Brown, Booksellers and Stationers, 1861), 116.
38. Collinson, *Shadrick Minkins*, 50–51.
39. *Norfolk (Va.) Southern Argus*, 23 June 1855, 2.
40. Ibid.
41. Still, *Underground Railroad*, 65, 160–61, 436.
42. Gara, *The Liberty Line*, 51–52, 54.
43. Still, *Underground Railroad*, 297–98.
44. Ibid., 57–58.
45. Ibid., 50–51; Kathryn Grover, *The Fugitive's Gibraltar: Escaping Slaves and Abolitionism in New Bedford, Massachusetts* (Amherst: University of Massachusetts Press, 2001), 242–43.
46. Still, *Underground Railroad*, 61; Grover, *The Fugitive's Gibraltar*, 242–43. Margaret Berkley, one of two owners of Clarissa Davis, was listed as a Portsmouth resident. Interestingly, in the 1840 census she was listed as Burkley and in the 1850 census as Berkley. 1840 U.S. Census (Free Schedule), Portsmouth and Norfolk, Virginia, digital image s.v. "William Bagnall," *Ancestry.com*.
47. Deposition of Mary Ann Hodges, 12 October 1899, Commonwealth of Massachusetts, Probate Court, Chelsea, Massachusetts, 17 April 1899, 758/276. Mary Ann Hodges was the sister of Sheridan Ford.
48. Vincent Harding, *There Is a River: The Black Struggle for Freedom in America* (New York: Vintage Books, 1983), xix, 27.

5

THE UNDERGROUND RAILROAD IN MARYLAND'S PORTS, BAYS, AND HARBORS

Maritime Strategies for Freedom

CHERYL JANIFER LAROCHE

> It cannot be that I shall live and die a slave. I will take to the water. This very bay shall yet bear me into freedom . . . and when I get to the head of the bay, I will turn my canoe adrift, and walk straight through Delaware into Pennsylvania.
>
> —Frederick Douglass, *Narrative of the Life of Frederick Douglass*

Escape by water differed from land-based escapes; at a minimum, a boat was required, in addition to sheer physical determination, to realize the goal of freedom. Before invention of the railroad in the 1830s, boats, be they skiffs, schooners or steamers, were the fastest form of transportation that allowed escapes of large or small groups. Historically, the Underground Railroad implied overland escape routes. The broadened definition by the National Park Service Network to Freedom encompasses all time periods and all forms of escape, on land and by sea, individual or assisted, from the inception of slavery to the close of the Civil War.

The extensive waterway system in Maryland shaped the state's unique, waterborne Underground Railroad history. Although generally not discussed as a discrete topic within the Underground Railroad narrative, waterways have always been crucial arteries of escape from slavery. Maryland's distinctive geography played a significant role in the maritime freedom journeys.

The Chesapeake Bay, Maryland's defining waterway, touches nine counties, Fells Point, Annapolis, Havre de Grace, in addition to Baltimore Harbor, the

Patapsco, Potomac, Choptank and Susquehanna Rivers, as well as the Chesapeake and Delaware Canal. The Bay and its tributaries seem to crawl up the spine of the state, separating Maryland into the western shore and its famed Eastern Shore. The Bay and the Eastern Shore, combined with Delaware and a small slice of Virginia, form the Delmarva Peninsula, historically considered a major navigational obstruction between Boston, New York, and Philadelphia seaports and Maryland and Virginia. The Chesapeake and Delaware Canal was designed to alleviate the problem. As a result, the foremost method of travel and trade in the mid-1800s was by water. Streams, creeks, and rivers that flowed to the Bay and beyond to the Atlantic Ocean, shaped the routes of Delmarva's Underground Railroad, often called the Chesapeake Station or Chesapeake Underground. These bodies of water unlocked escape routes, both maritime and inland.[1]

The Chesapeake Bay, an avenue of escape throughout Maryland's involvement with slavery, had an intimate impact on individuals living in small communities and plantations along its tributaries during the War of 1812. The Chesapeake, a vital trade route and transportation highway, became a pathway for the marauding British Royal Navy. Blockades, privateering, attacks, escapes, and raids were wartime realities for the Chesapeake's population. In two years during the British blockade, ordinary people transformed into heroes, slaves found freedom, captains became legal pirates, and shipbuilders created wooden weapons of war. The Chesapeake Pilot Bay Schooner, invented in Fells Point, could outrun any sailing vessel in the British naval fleet.[2]

For African Americans, the War of 1812 on the Chesapeake went beyond large-scale battles, naval flotillas, and international conflict. Escaping slaves increasingly appeared as spies, guides, messengers, and laborers for the British, leaving White Americans to contend with "two enemies." Blacks provided information and services that greatly enhanced British military effectiveness, which only increased the ire of White Americans.[3]

The National Intelligencer reported that enslaved laborers on Kent Island in the Bay abandoned their work and acted as pilots for British parties out for plunder. Along the shores near Norfolk, Virginia, the British fleet routinely sent small boats to intercept groups of Blacks fleeing slavery, hoping to employ them in the British cause. When the fleet failed to pick them up, freedom seekers stole small boats and made their way to the English nonetheless. Others escaped to the Chesapeake's heavily wooded shores, waiting for opportunities to seize freedom. Armed patrols of local Whites routinely scoured coastal areas looking for suspected escapees, whom they shot on sight.

Between the summers of 1813 and 1814, between four to five thousand freedom seekers in the Chesapeake region fled enslavement, frequently by water,

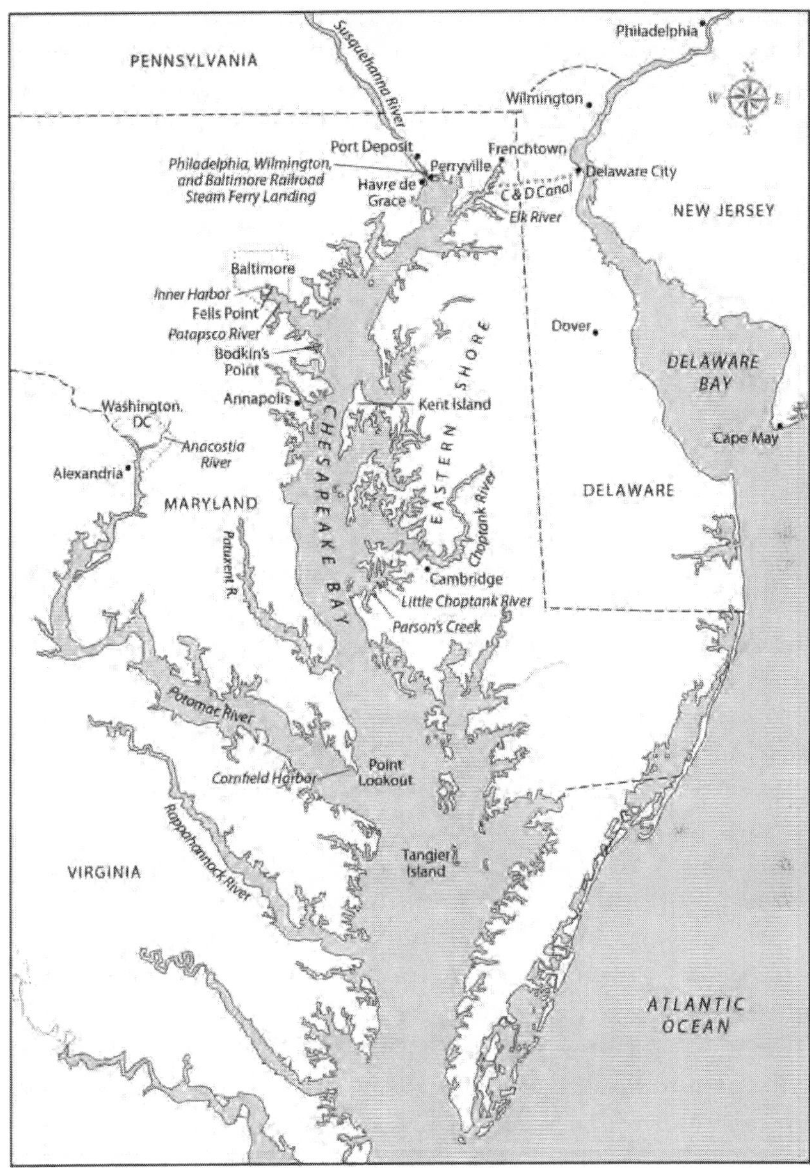

FIGURE 9. Coastal Geography Map of the Mid-Atlantic Seaboard, with Chesapeake Bay and Delaware Bay. Map by Bill Nelson. Used by permission of the author.

to join the side of the British. The large numbers of escapees led the British to establish a semipermanent refugee camp at Fort Albion on Tangier Island near the mouth of the Potomac River. Nearly a thousand escapees found refuge there. From this place, the British recruited "a Corps of Colonial Marines from the People of Colour who escape to us from the enemy's shores in this Neighborhood to be formed, drilled, and brought forward for service."[4] These soldiers' familiarity with Chesapeake water routes made them excellent scouts and allowed them to participate in raids stretching the full length of the Chesapeake Bay. The British commander, Rear Admiral George Cockburn, described them as "the best skirmishers possible for . . . this country"; he came to appreciate their "extraordinary steadiness and good conduct" in action.[5] Problems of fleeing bondsmen and -women, and the resulting economic losses, became so acute during the 1812 conflict that states exerted pressure on the national government to provide compensation.[6]

After the War of 1812, Maryland continued its ambiguous policies and attitudes toward slavery. Baltimore's excellent harbor brought both employment and misery. The City, which had the largest free Black population in the country, also exploited opportunities to profit from human capital. Throughout the first half of the nineteenth century, more than a dozen slave traders operated from harborside storefronts along Pratt and adjacent streets, affording domestic coast interstate slave traders a central location within a developing "selling market." They built notorious slave pens near Pratt Street, the major east-west connection to wharves in the Inner Harbor and Fells Point. Between 1815 and 1860, slave traders in Baltimore made the port a leading point of disembarkation for ships carrying enslaved laborers to New Orleans and other Deep South ports. Maryland's enslaved population was literally being "sold down the river." Between 1790 and 1859, more than one million among the enslaved were "sold south." Most came originally from Virginia and Maryland, where the slave economy was shrinking.[7]

Between 1790 and 1820, the free Black community in Baltimore grew from a few hundred to more than ten thousand. Within this large concentration of African Americans, anonymity, work, safety, and danger coexisted along the wharfs, among the Black caulkers, sailors, and seamen, who coexisted in-between the blurred lines separating slavery from freedom. Whether it was a clandestine community of enslaved watermen and dock workers who directed freedom seekers to ships or Black crewmen who secreted them on board, they constituted what historian and mariner W. Jeffrey Bolster has called a "seafaring pipeline to freedom" testing "porous boundaries."[8]

Ferryboat workers carried and received messages affecting day-to-day Underground Railroad operations. In seafaring Maryland, sailors garnered high respect and elicited a kind and sympathetic feeling toward "those who go down to the sea in ships"; free trade and sailor's rights expressed national sentiments.

According to historian David Cecelski, author of *The Waterman's Song: Slavery and Freedom in Maritime North Carolina*, African American maritime communities used shipping along coastal trading routes to maintain contact with the larger Black community, both in the United States and neighboring regions, and with distant family, friends, and religious and fraternal leaders.[9]

Baltimore Harbor sat at a pivotal point along the East Coast as ships worked their way from Boston to Norfolk. By 1850, Baltimore had grown to become one of the nation's largest cities, rivaled in size only by New York and Philadelphia. Earlier in the century, Baltimore's shipbuilding prowess helped establish the city's urban and maritime preeminence. Design and construction of the Baltimore clipper, "the fastest cargo vessel yet introduced," only added to the city's growing economy. Its commodious harbor accommodated trading vessels to and from the West Indies and Europe as well as the Atlantic Seaboard. Because the city functioned as the principal port for exports for most of the upper Chesapeake and western Maryland, Blacks and Whites flooded Baltimore to take advantage of its economic offerings.[10]

Enslaved boatmen found ready sea access, although often working at the lowest rungs of the maritime industry. Navigation of sloops did provide basic training in fundamental seafaring skills as the century progressed. Bolster observes that in the Chesapeake, enslaved sailors "took charge of vessels, managing their crews, their navigation, and their lading." He noted that as early as 1770, "it was already common to refer to runaway slaves' considerable experience as watermen; one such slave had 'gone [as] Skipper of the Sloop for some Years past, and is well acquainted with the Bay' and most Virginia and Maryland rivers."[11]

FREE BLACK COMMUNITIES AND MARYLAND'S MARITIME ESCAPES

Many free and enslaved African Americans sometimes remained in Baltimore rather than traveling farther north for a number of reasons: employment opportunities, family, and perhaps most important, the feeling that no matter the hardships, as Frederick Douglass recalled, "life in Baltimore, when most oppressive, was a paradise" when compared to plantation life.[12] Freedom seekers who escaped to Baltimore in the late eighteenth century appeared to have shared a number of characteristics with their free African American counterparts already living there. Between 1747 and 1790, 80 percent of Baltimore escapees were young males and 75 percent were between the ages of fifteen and thirty-four. Women who escaped were not as heavily advertised and thought less capable of long-term escape. They are well represented among freedom seekers, nonetheless. About one-quarter of the men listed had skills such as ship carpentry or blacksmithing. In the 1770s and 1780s, most slaveholders thought Pennsylvania or other distant locations were as likely a destination for escapees as Baltimore. Advertisements for freedom seekers in Maryland newspapers suggest that escapes climbed in the years following the American Revolution. One historian of Baltimore estimates that from 1773 to 1819 nearly 20 percent of freedom seekers in the region escaped to Baltimore, that number increasing to nearly 30 percent in the 1810s. A mere 7 percent went to Pennsylvania. Sliding-scale cash rewards were typically calculated by the distance the escapee had traveled before he or she was captured and returned.[13]

Constituting a majority of Baltimore's African Americans after 1810, free people of color could ally with escapees, shelter them or meet other needs. Active religious and abolitionist groups also provided support. "Explosive growth of Baltimore's free African American community from a few hundred in 1790 to more than ten thousand by 1820 played a role in evolving patterns of runaway destinations."[14]

After a young boy from New York named James Emerson had been lured on board a Petersburg-bound vessel, he was not permitted to go ashore with the crew when the ship docked in Baltimore. The captain let the youngster know, "You are not in New York now, but in Baltimore" and then threatened to sell him. A Black man, Gideon Gross, who overheard the conversation, managed to bring the boy ashore, conceal him, and find him shelter and safety, apparently within the city's Black community.[15]

From 1822 into the 1840s, southern legislatures, particularly that of South Carolina, became convinced that freedom seekers regularly escaped aboard northern vessels and passed numerous Negro Seamen Acts as a result. The statutes subjected free Black sailors to detention in southern ports and potential arrest and sale into slavery. In South Carolina, the law stipulated that free Black sailors had to be jailed while their vessels docked at Charleston ports. The laws, intended to limit the movement of free Black and "mulatto" crewmen in southern ports, had interstate and international repercussions, particularly for Black sailors on foreign vessels. Thought of as a "moral contagion" and a "catalyst for racial unrest" intent on "undermining the Southern slave system," at least ten thousand free Black sailors were directly affected by these southern regulations. Free Black mariners were particularly dangerous in the minds of slaveholders and lawmakers. These "Atlantic-savvy" sailors of color were believed to spread poisonous ideas about freedom and undermine an erroneous but general assumption that the enslaved were happy with their lot in life. They fled, southerners argued, because free Black sailors and other outsiders were enticing them to escape.[16] Insurrections, such as the one on board the *Decatur,* contradicted that assumption.

In 1826, slave trader Austin Woolfolk, who owned one of the largest slave-holding pens in Baltimore, led thirty-one enslaved captives down Pratt Street, many shackled and bound in chains. Once they reached the wharves at Fells Point, the captives were placed aboard the schooner *Decatur*. They sailed down the Chesapeake, destined to be sold at New Orleans. After five days at sea, the captives overwhelmed the crew, threw the captain and another crewman overboard, and restrained another crew member. With the two most-experienced seamen dead and the remaining crew unable to navigate the ship, the *Decatur* drifted off the Eastern Seaboard for five more days before seventeen of the insurrectionists were captured by a passing New England whaling ship. Days later, the brig *Rooke* took on the remaining fourteen rebels, transporting them to New York, where they promptly escaped into the city. Only one was recaptured. New York, like Baltimore, offered freedom seekers concealment within a large and free Black community.[17]

By 1831, the very large free Black community in Baltimore guaranteed that someone escaping slavery might blend in almost unseen. Sizeable numbers of watermen, sailors, caulkers, and pilots were able to quickly transmit information around ports and harbors and along coastal and inland waterways. Escape by water was also far less taxing on the body than land-based escapes, although drowning presented a hazardous possibility. On foot, an escapee might exert maximum physical effort to travel twenty-five miles, mostly at night if conditions were conducive. By water a fast ship could average nine miles in an hour.

THE CHESAPEAKE AND DELAWARE CANAL

One unanticipated outcome of the research undertaken for this project is a newfound appreciation for the importance of the Chesapeake and Delaware Canal to escapees. Completed in 1829, the short waterway—only fourteen miles in length—known as the C & D Canal served as a vital link between two great bays. Ships entered the canal through Elk River and Back Creek in Cecil County, Maryland, and exited into the Delaware River a few miles north of Reedy Point in New Castle County, Delaware.[18] The C & D Canal reduced the water route between Philadelphia and Baltimore by nearly three hundred nautical miles.

Regional shipping that passed through the Port of Baltimore used the canal, which functioned as a major transportation route in the antebellum period. Freedom seekers quickly realized that the canal also provided a route out of slavery aboard steamboats, schooners, and small watercraft. Although the canal provided an attractive escape route along the Chesapeake Bay, civil authorities also recognized its advantages and carefully policed it, making flight along the route risky at the minimum.[19]

A little-known but dramatic maritime escape involving the C & D Canal occurred on 4 (or possibly 6) April 1831 from the southeastern shore of the Chesapeake. Joseph Keene and his wife, Nelly, "far advanced in pregnancy," stole a small boat and sailed their seven children, ages three to fifteen years old, to freedom from Parson's Creek in Dorchester County. Enslaved by Levin Woolford, the Keene family took an unusual and perilous step to liberate themselves. The escape of entire families—particularly one as large as the Keenes—was extraordinary but not unprecedented in the annals of the Underground Railroad.

In the escape ad, Woolford noted that Joseph, a sailor of "experience and notoriety," used his skill to rescue his wife and children, sailing from Parson's Creek out the Little Choptank River and into the Chesapeake Bay. Woolford speculated that they would probably "pass up the bay and through the C & D Canal," which had been completed eighteen months earlier. The southern entrance to the Canal lay about seventy-five miles to the north up the Bay from Parson's Creek. From the Canal terminus in Delaware Bay at Delaware City, it was less than forty miles to the Pennsylvania border, then a few short miles to Philadelphia. Keene could have sailed his family to freedom in less than three days. According to Woolford, the Keenes fled in a twenty-three-foot "sail canoe," also known as a "log canoe," a common coastal vessel in the Chesapeake Bay. A shipyard was not necessary for building and launching such a shallow-draft boat, which was useful in the marshy and sandy bays and creeks. Joe stripped the boat of all sails with the exception of one "gaff-sail."[20]

Joseph exploited his sailing skills to elude Levin Woolford's numerous attempts to recapture the family. Similar to land-based escapes, the Keene family's carefully planned flight yielded maximum escape time, taking advantage of days when the slaveholder would be most distracted. Holidays, birthdays, and the death of the slaveholder were prime times for successful escapes. The Keene family most likely fled on Good Friday, 1 April. Woolford either discovered them missing on Easter Monday the fourth or later on 6 April. Analysis of his runaway ads reveals that the slave-owner had no idea when the Keenes actually left. Nor did he accurately understand the ages of the family members. Most likely the Keenes's well-designed escape allowed them to enjoy a four- to six-day head start over the Easter holiday before the runaway ads were printed. That timing, coupled with use of a small boat to transport the family, made a near-impossible escape conceivable. The family's final destination remains speculative, but when Levin Woolford died the following year, he had not recovered this family of nine.[21]

Black sailors such as Joseph Keene were central to African American struggles for freedom. Although he did not intend it as a compliment, slaveholder Woolford observed that Keene was "shrewd and crafty." In other words, Keene had mastered nautical and sailing skills and could utilize them to both secure freedom for his family and evade recapture by Woolford. Likewise, free men of color, politically astute and worldly, became independent wage earners through seafaring and challenged southern stereotypes of the happy, content, and childlike African American. As a result, in 1836 the Maryland Assembly again tackled the problem of sailing vessels being comprised entirely of Black sailors and navigators. Because Black seamen carried slaves to freedom, the majority concluded, no Black man could navigate a ship without having at least one White man over the age of eighteen on board.[22]

Maritime research has exposed Underground Railroad routes as vital for potentially thousands of freedom seekers who escaped slavery by stowing away, impersonating free Black mariners, buying passenger tickets, or, like Harriet Tubman or the escapees on the *Pearl*, enlisting the aid of sympathetic captains and crewmembers. Runaways relied on maritime Blacks as part of their strategies. With good reason, the editor of *The Southern Argus* charged that free Black crewmen on those ships gave slaves "notions of freedom, and afterwards afford them the means of transportation to free soil." The editor believed "virtually the entire coasting trade" lay "in the hands of Northern abolitionists" and grumbled that slaves repeatedly escaped on northern vessels.[23]

Critical points of escape existed at the confluence of rivers and the Chesapeake Bay, at port towns and crossing points—ferry crossings chief among them. Careful study reveals the maritime "geography of resistance," where important stories remain untold. A representative example in Maryland was the Philadelphia, Wilmington, and Baltimore Railroad Steam Ferry Landing site, which connected Havre de Grace with Perryville at the mouth of Susquehanna River at the northernmost point of the Bay. The ferry company may not have known that it was an accomplice in clandestine Underground Railroad operations. Because there was no bridge crossing before the Civil War, trains stopped at Havre de Grace. Passengers got off, the engine was detached, cars were rolled onto the rails and loaded on top of the railroad ferry *Susquehanna*, or the larger *Maryland* after 1854, to cross the river. The overland train journey resumed on the other side at Perryville, where the cars were attached to another engine and the passengers reboarded. The whole process was fraught with the opportunity for recapture, but freedom seekers found the route effective.[24] Famed escapees William and Ellen Craft spent their most-dramatic and -harrowing moments at this ferry crossing in 1848 during their train escape out of slavery from Macon, Georgia, to Philadelphia.[25]

In 1856, Charlotte Giles and Harriet Eglin, dressed in billowing black clothes and the heavy veils of mourning, escaped from Baltimore on this railroad. While seated in the train car before leaving Baltimore, one owner actually caught up with the pair at the depot but failed to recognize them. Even after he peered under the bonnets of the distraught and weeping women and demanded that they identify themselves, their disguise held up under the effective ruse.[26]

In 1859, Underground Railroad icon, Henry "Box" Brown, legendary among the freighted escapes, had himself boxed up and shipped via Adams Express, a new company that advertised reliability and confidentiality and to never look inside the boxes it carried. One leg of the journey to freedom was on the Philadelphia, Wilmington, and Baltimore Railroad Steam Ferry. But the earliest, most well-known, if not the most dramatic, escape at Perryville belonged to Frederick Douglass.[27]

Douglass escaped slavery in Baltimore on 3 September 1838. With great "internal excitement and anxiety," he boarded a train at President Street Station, a few blocks from the City Dock, headed to Havre de Grace. Dressed in a sailor's uniform made by his future wife, Anna Murray, his "full sailor style" appearance and his ability to "talk sailor talk like an 'old salt'" matched the impressive looking identification papers loaned to him by a free Black seaman. Douglass later quipped that, armed with a train ticket, he escaped using his "symbolic fare . . . on the underground railroad." Douglass wrote that as the train neared Havre de Grace, the conductor came through the Negro car checking the tickets and papers of free African Americans. Douglass described the process as a most anxious moment although he handled the conductor perfectly. After crossing the Susquehanna River by ferry boat at Havre de Grace, Douglass continued by train to Wilmington, Delaware, and eventually to freedom in New Bedford, Massachusetts.[28]

Escapees turned to railroads and steamships for less arduous passage north. Recognizing this pattern, the Maryland Assembly made it illegal for the enslaved to use any means of transportation without the express permission of slaveholders. The penalty for violating this law was five hundred dollars. By 1838, however, the Underground Railroad was using the new forms of transportation, which made escapes such as Douglass's possible.[29]

After 1844, escapees began using the new ships built expressly for the C & D Canal. The Ericsson Line built and operated a fleet of steam-driven packet ships tailored to the canal's dimensions and soon began moving freight and cargo with these vessels, rather than towing freight, passenger barges, schooners, and sloops through the canal with teams of horses and mules. The original steamers made scheduled runs between Philadelphia and Baltimore's Light Street wharves. The route covered important steamboat ports, towns, bridges, railroads, and landmarks along the way, and the canal quickly became the preferred shipping route for coastal barge and schooner traffic. Predictably, Underground Railroad transit soon followed the canal from the tidewater region of Maryland and Virginia on the Chesapeake Bay to freedom in Philadelphia.[30]

Subterfuge worked because Black workers, both men and women, were ordinary sights along waterfronts of all coastal cities in the North and South, as were Black mariners. Renowned Underground Railroad chronicler, William Still, provided insight into Baltimore's maritime operations. He recorded escapes on steamboats and schooners that used the Ericsson Line, although he did not connect the steamships with the canal.[31]

Twenty-five-year-old William Peel Jones decided that, rather than be sold at market, he would take command of his fate. In April 1859, helped by relatives and friends, Jones had himself boxed as freight and forwarded to Philadelphia by via the Ericsson Line. As Still explained, "He preferred the box to the auction block." Free Blacks often helped their enslaved loved ones flee. William Adams, a free Black barber, convinced his mother to help with the escape of Lear Green, the enslaved woman from Baltimore with whom he had fallen in love. The family traveled to Philadelphia aboard the Ericsson Steamer Line, the mother as a passenger, Lear as cargo. Mother and son helped Lear pack herself and provisions inside a wooden chest that sailors commonly used. Still reports, "She was safely stowed amongst the ordinary freight on one of the Erricson line of steamers." Mother Adams, Lear Green's future mother-in-law, risked her own freedom to accompany the chest during the eighteen-hour trek to Philadelphia; both arrived safely some time in 1854.[32]

During the winter, from December to March, navigation of the Chesapeake Bay often proved treacherous. Baltimore relatives and friends alerted Harriet Tubman in December 1850 that her favorite niece, Kessiah "Kizzy"

Jolley Bowley and her two children—six-year-old James Alfred and infant Araminta, who had been named for Tubman—were about to be auctioned at the courthouse in Cambridge, Maryland, on the Eastern Shore. Tubman, Kessiah's free husband, John Bowley, and other Baltimore relatives quickly pulled together a plan, despite the roiling waters of the wintertime Bay.

The year's end often brought financial reckoning to white slave-owning families. Consequently, for the enslaved, the end and beginning of the year always carried the threat of being sold at auction. In nineteenth-century Maryland, slave auctions were popular spectacles—the free entertainment of human misery. People traveled great distances to watch and follow the bidding; curiosity seekers mingled with serious buyers; liquor flowed freely.[33]

This heart-wrenching possibility compelled Tubman toward one of her first important rescues. Immediately, she traveled to Baltimore, lodging among friends and relatives who lived along the city's busy and diverse waterfront. John Tubman, Harriet's first husband, had two brothers living in Fells Point, as did several Bowley family members. Harriet's brother-in-law Tom Tubman, a waterfront stevedore, concealed her until all was ready. Baltimore's waterfront became an ideal location for Harriet's operations. Friends and family members were also perfectly positioned to receive and convey news about threats to her family.[34]

On auction day, a small crowd of buyers assembled at Cambridge courthouse, a little before lunchtime. In front of them stood Kessiah and her two young children. Maryland law did not prohibit a free Black man from buying his family, so Bowley cast his own bids. He met and increased every challenge until he won the bid at six hundred dollars, the equivalent of twenty thousand today. With a buyer finally secured, seller John Brodess, acting for his slaveholding mother, was satisfied by the sale. Kessiah and her children were removed from the courthouse steps and set aside; the auctioneer went for his meal.[35]

When he returned and called for payment, no buyer appeared—no one stepped forward. Recognizing a ruse, the auctioneer restarted the bidding only to discover that Kessiah and the children had vanished. Unbeknownst to the crowd or the auctioneer, John Bowley had used the dinner break to smuggle Kizzy and their two children to the home of a nearby White abolitionist woman, a five-minute walk away. Later, under the invisibility that darkness ensured, the father and husband loaded his family into a small boat, some say a log canoe. A skilled sailor and ship carpenter with contacts throughout the Eastern Shore and Baltimore, Bowley knew the water offered the best chance for escape. It was an audacious waterborne flight that probably launched from the waters behind the Dorchester County Courthouse.[36]

The perilous journey to Baltimore would have taken a full day's sailing up the Chesapeake but, given the time of year, perhaps longer. With unpredictable weather, often cold and snowy, the journey to Baltimore was incredibly hazardous, even more so with two small children aboard. Bowley ferried his family out across the wintry Bay to Bodkin's Point on the Chesapeake's western shore near Baltimore. In Fells Point, they may have connected with Tom Tubman and found safety with Harriet, who hid them among friends. After a few days' recuperation, Harriet safely brought the Bowleys overland to Philadelphia, but one of the first dramatic rescues of her legendary Underground Railroad career—one that she had planned—was accomplished on the Chesapeake Bay.[37]

William Still observed: "Baltimore used to be in the days of Slavery one of the most difficult places in the South for even free colored people to get away from, much more for slaves." Local regulations forbade any person of color leaving the city by railroad or steamboat, without such applicant being "weighted, measured, and then given a bond signed by unquestionable signatures. Baltimore was rigid in the extreme, and was a never-failing source of annoyance, trouble and expense" to people of color generally but also to slaveholders who were forbidden to travel with those they enslaved until they had complied with the law.[38] But such laws, while making escape much more difficult, did not deter escapees or their accomplices.

Black sailors carried the latest news and information up and down the Atlantic Seaboard, connecting Blacks they encountered throughout the hemisphere. Working as pilots for ocean-going vessels, captains of sloops and schooners, and specialized maritime laborers, they "used their considerable responsibility to subvert slavery."[39] Charles Blockson, a longstanding advocate of "self-liberation" theory for Blacks and the Underground Railroad, observed: "A serious distortion . . . tended to make the people whom the Railroad was designed to aid—fugitive slaves—seem either invisible or passive and helpless without aid from others. Slaves did not sit passively waiting to be led out of slavery, however. Once free, they often reached back to help others escape to freedom. . . . The most assiduous organizers of networks to freedom were Black freemen."[40] The intent of the Negro Seaman's Act, both to curtail escapes and limit Black agency, is an unspoken acknowledgment of the extent to which Blacks participated in the cause of their own freedom.

PORT DEPOSIT

Port Deposit sits on the east bank of the Susquehanna River about five miles north of Perryville in western Cecil County at the northern tip of Maryland. The town became a trading hub between the Chesapeake Bay and Philadelphia. Howard Methodist Episcopal Church, also known as Howard Chapel, was built on the banks of the Susquehanna River by freed African Americans a decade before the Civil War. The church stood just north of Main Street, which ran parallel to the river. Black Methodist churches provided a critical spiritual lifeline for rural communities, a significant shelter for freedom seekers, and waypoints necessary to Underground Railroad success.

Howard Chapel occupied an important crossing point along a key waterborne pathway on the eastern banks of the Susquehanna. Church members worked to free other Blacks, and the church operated a station on the Underground Railroad in pre–Civil War years. Local historians found that, during the time of the Underground Railroad, freedom seekers would travel from the South up the Susquehanna, looking for refuge along the way. Port Deposit was a stop. According to historian Charles Blockson, many of the enslaved found asylum in vessels sailing from Annapolis and Baltimore ports, while others were transported in small boats on the Chesapeake Bay into the Susquehanna River and delivered to waiting conductors in Pennsylvania. Numerous stories, escape advertisements, and slave narratives support Blockson's observations and deeper research into places such as Port Deposit, Havre de Grace, and Perryville would prove Blockson's assertions correct.[41]

Eighteen-year-old Henry Fields reaped the benefit of the Underground Railroad when he fled from the neighborhood of Port Deposit.[42] When heirs of Henry Summerville posted an escape ad for "Bill," they were careful to add that he had "holes in his ears"—the sure mark of a sailor—and he had been "going by water, in a bay craft and has made acquaintances at Port Deposit, Baltimore, and other places up the bay; where it is supposed he has gone." Several escape ads described a crossing thought to be regularly used by fugitives between Port Deposit and the Columbia Bridge a little farther up the Susquehanna in Pennsylvania. Underground Railroad historian Wilbur Siebert observed that freedom seekers from the Chesapeake passed northward to Havre de Grace, where they usually crossed the Susquehanna, and, with others from the Eastern Shore, found their way to established stations in the southern part of Lancaster and Chester Counties in Pennsylvania.[43] Similar narratives could be uncovered for Maryland port towns not mentioned here.

THE POTOMAC RIVER

The Potomac, one of Maryland's longest rivers, arises in the west and runs southeast, creating a natural border between Maryland and Virginia. James Curry's narrative illuminates the river's role in many escape accounts:

> At Alexandria, I crossed the Potomac River and came to Washington, where I made friends with a colored family, with whom I rested eight days. I then took the Montgomery road [*sic*], but, wishing to escape . . . and it being cloudy, I lost my course, and fell back again along the Potomac River, and traveled on the towpath of the canal from Friday night until Sunday morning. . . . I soon entered a colored person's house on the side of the canal, where they gave me breakfast and treated me very kindly. . . .[44]

With several features of the Potomac riverscape hidden from view, many creeks, points, and lookouts presented clandestine opportunities for freedom. Attention to the waterway as a means of escaping slavery has been minimal, however. Research has shown that the enslaved used absolutely any and all measures to free themselves, and the Potomac River was a part of such efforts. The Potomac was both deep enough for boats to cross and, in places, shallow enough for crossing on horseback or by wagon.

The most-popular and well-documented escape attempt from the nation's capital occurred on 15 April 1848, when seventy-seven enslaved persons fled their quarters in Washington City, Georgetown, and Alexandria. The *Pearl*, a fifty-four-ton bay-craft schooner anchored in the Anacostia River at the Seventh Street Wharf in southeast, was waiting to deliver them to freedom.

Daniel Drayton, a White ship's captain who helped make the escape aboard the *Pearl* possible, reported that his trading up and down the bay brought him "a good deal into contact" with the enslaved population. He observed, "No sooner . . . does a vessel, known to be from the north, anchor in any of these waters—and the slaves are pretty adroit in ascertaining from what state a vessel comes—than she is boarded, if she remains any length of time, and especially overnight, in hopes of obtaining a passage to a land of freedom."[45] Drayton, continued:

> There is not a waterman who ever sailed in Chesapeake Bay who will not tell you that, so far from the slaves needing any prompting to run away, the difficulty is, when they ask you to assist them, to make them take no for an answer. I have known instances where men have lain in the woods for a year or two, waiting for an opportunity to escape on board some vessel. On one of my voyages up the

MARY AND EMILY EDMONSON

FIGURE 10. Sisters Mary and Emily Edmonson, two of the seventy-seven people captured while trying to escape to freedom aboard the schooner *Pearl*. At the time of the *Pearl* incident on 15 April 1848, Mary (1832–1853) was fifteen years old and Emily (1835–1895), thirteen. They and four of their brothers, along with additional families and individuals, comprised the freedom seekers apprehended on board the schooner. Illustration from John H. Paynter, *Fugitives of the Pearl* (Washington, D.C.: The Associated Publishers, 1930), photo opposite page 64. Original photographic image taken between 1850 and 1853. Prints and Photographs Division, Library of Congress, Washington, D.C., LC-USZ62-104364.

> Potomac, an application was made to me on behalf of such a runaway; and I was so much moved by his story, that, had it been practicable for me at that time, I should certainly have helped him off.[46]

Captain Drayton already knew the way; his first successful rescue of a woman, five children and a niece, at the behest of her husband, followed the proposed route. Ten days later, the husband met Drayton and the liberated family at Frenchtown, Maryland. After Captain Drayton had successfully helped the family flee slavery from Washington, D.C., to Frenchtown, Daniel Bell, a free Black ironmonger who worked at the Navy Yard, told him of a family of two whose sales were at hand and who needed help escaping. Bell asked for Drayton's assistance. Drayton refused, explaining that he had no ship and that "the season was too early for navigation through the canal." He made one or two other attempts to help those who sought his assistance, but none met with success until the summer of 1847.[47]

Earlier in March 1848, Paul Jennings, enslaved by Senator Daniel Webster, had approached Drayton about chartering the *Pearl*. By spring, Bell and Thomas Ducker had planned another rescue. Drayton and his mate, Sayres, proceeded down the Delaware by the C & D canal into the Chesapeake to the mouth of the Potomac onward to the Anacostia River. With help from Washington's free Black community, enslaved men, women, and children who had been laboring in the best homes and hotels in Washington, quietly slipped away from their places of work or residence. Making their way in twos and threes from Georgetown and some from Alexandria, Virginia, across the Mall, they headed to a small, secluded wharf somewhere around Buzzard's Point on the Anacostia River, where they boarded the *Pearl*.[48]

The small, now very crowded 65-to-80-foot two-masted vessel was designed for the currents and winds of the semiprotected Delaware and Chesapeake Bays. Escapees anticipated that the next time they walked on land, freedom would be close at hand at their destination, Frenchtown, Maryland, on the Elk River, a few miles from the entrance of the C & D canal.[49] Among the escapees on the *Pearl* were thirteen children, six of them from the Edmonson family, including Emily and Mary Edmonson and their brother, Samuel, of Rockville, Maryland. After boarding, they were met, as planned, by three more of their siblings.[50]

The rickety schooner departed about 10:00 p.m., but there was no wind that night and they made little headway. They sailed from the Anacostia downriver to the Potomac in Alexandria, where they spent the day. The next day the *Pearl* set a northward course for the Chesapeake Bay. After enduring no wind at the beginning of the journey, the wind was now against the schooner, forcing it to anchor for the night in Cornfield Harbor. The windstorm interruption forced the ship to take refuge at Point Lookout at the confluence of the Potomac River and the Chesapeake Bay. But Drayton was convinced the freedom seekers on the schooner were safely out of reach of Washington slaveholders.[51]

Among the seventy-seven aboard, owned by forty-one different slaveholders, were fifteen-year-old Mary Ellen Steward, enslaved by former First Lady Dolly Madison, as well as a coachman for the secretary of the U.S. Treasury and the slave of a South Carolina congressman. The next morning, numerous powerful Washington, D.C., slaveholders quickly missed their customary labor. Realizing their captives and the *Pearl* were missing, they sent an armed posse of thirty-five men on the steamboat *Salem,* which churned 140 miles down the Potomac River in pursuit of the wind-powered schooner. When the *Salem* overtook the *Pearl* near Point Lookout, the posse boarded the vessel. All escapees and crew on board, including the Edmonson sisters, were towed back to nation's capital and imprisoned. In less than a week, according to the laws of the District of Columbia and the state Maryland, the majority of the freedom seekers were sold to traders to be transported south to endure much harsher labor in Georgia and New Orleans. Some were eventually held in Baltimore slave pens.[52] The Edmonson sisters were sold to slaveholders from New Orleans, a market known for "fancy girls," destined for a life of sexual exploitation, often the fate of Black women thought to be attractive and highly valued for their fair skin.

Ultimately, after the entreaties of their father, Paul, two of the Edmonson children, Mary and Emily, were purchased and freed with funds raised by Henry Ward Beecher's Plymouth Congregational Church in Brooklyn, New York.[53] The sisters eventually returned to Alexandria after the campaign to free them in 1848 and became instant celebrities. They united with fellow Marylander Frederick Douglass in the abolitionist cause. Ship captain Drayton, however, did not fare well. He was tried, found guilty, and initially received an unprecedented twenty-year prison sentence. He was later resentenced in 1849, fined more than ten thousand dollars, and served four years and four months in prison. He ultimately took his own life in a New Bedford, Massachusetts, hotel in 1857. Unexpected consequences of the *Pearl* escape attempt deepened divisions between influential slave-owners and abolitionists. Washington was swept by controversy that changed the course of history. A provision of the Compromise of 1850 enacted by Congress ended the slave trading in the District of Columbia, although it did not abolish slavery there.[54]

FIGURES 11. Tombstone Memorial of Daniel Drayton, Captain of the schooner *Pearl*, Rural Cemetery, New Bedford, Massachusetts. On 15 April 1848, Drayton (*inset portrait*) attempted to carry seventy-seven enslaved persons aboard the *Pearl* from Washington, D.C., to eventual freedom in the North. This was the largest such escape attempt in U.S. history, but the vessel, plagued by foul winds, was apprehended near the mouth of the Potomac River. Photograph of tombstone by Timothy D. Walker. Portrait in Personal Memoir of Daniel Drayton . . . (Boston: Bela Marsh; New York: American and Foreign Anti-Slavery Society, 1855); image from Prints and Photographs Division, Library of Congress, Washington, D.C., LC-USZ62–65805.

The *Pearl* ranked as the most prominent example of using the Potomac River as an Underground Railroad route to freedom. During the 1830s and continuing late into the next decade, Washington, D.C., operated one of the most aggressive Underground Railroad networks because of its location and its artful leadership. The mass-escape attempt is said to have inspired Harriet Beecher Stowe in her writing of *Uncle Tom's Cabin*, published in 1852.[55]

CONCLUSION

Some Underground Railroad stories recounted here are not new. Placing freedom journeys in a geographic context, however, allows a new interpretation of the importance of water routes and waterborne pathways to freedom. Connecting the C & D Canal with the Ericsson Line or discussing the relationship of the Susquehanna Ferry to Havre de Grace and Perryville situates escapees and their journeys in a new light. Understanding relationships between the Elk River at the head of the canal and escape routes places other escape narratives inside the Underground Railroad realm.

Nautical escapes, significant forms of resistance, spanned the duration of slavery in Maryland. The state's unique geography, combined with its large free Black community and proximity to the long border with a free state, Pennsylvania, yielded a unique Underground Railroad history. Although some ship's captains appear to have consistently lent their vessels and service in the cause of the Underground Railroad, escapes by water were more often singular events rather than recurring efforts of organized Underground Railroad conductors. Waterborne modes of transportation, whether by sloop, ferry, or canal boat, and the locations were the repeating factors. Family groups attempted to escape together on seafaring vessels. When weather cooperated and the plan was sound, water escapes rewarded escapees with expedient release from slavery. Harriet Tubman, known almost exclusively as a land-based Underground Railroad conductor, proved that she could outmaneuver her pursuers at sea as well as on land.

Blacks plied the waters of the Chesapeake Bay and the state's many rivers and streams to quench their thirst for freedom. With waterways as their conduit, "dangerous" free Black sailors were thought "to introduce a moral pestilence" and a "contagion of liberty" that destroyed "subordination in the slave."[56] Knowing the heavy work of ubiquitous free Blacks and enslaved maritime laborers along Baltimore's wharfs and docks and up and down Maryland's rivers adds a new appreciation to an understudied dimension of pre–Civil War escapes from bondage. While seemingly less systematic or organized than the traditional Underground Railroad networks, escape on canals, steamship lines, and other vessels were the vehicles of deliverance for maritime journeys to freedom.

NOTES

1. Johnathon E. Briggs, "Signs of the Bay's Role in Underground Railroad," *Baltimore* (Md.) *Sun*, 6 February 2001.
2. "How Fell's Point Helped Turn the Tide of the War of 1812," The Preservation Society: Society for the Preservation of Federal Hill and Fell's Point, accessed 20 August 2019, www.preservationsociety.com/history/1812.html.
3. Frank A. Cassell, "Slaves of the Chesapeake Bay Area and the War of 1812," *Journal of Negro History* 57, no. 2 (1972): 144–55.
4. Ibid., 151.
5. James A. Percoco, "The British Corps of Colonial Marines: African Americans Fight for Their Freedom," American Battlefield Trust, accessed 20 August 2019, https://www.battlefields.org/learn/articles/british-corps-colonial-marines.
6. Cassell, "Slaves of the Chesapeake Bay Area," 146.
7. Ralph Clayton, "A Bitter Inner Harbor Legacy: The Slave Trade," *Baltimore (Md.) Sun*, 12 July 2000; Scott Shane, "The Secret History of City Slave Trade; . . . Jails That Played a Key Role in the U.S. Slave Trade of the 1800s," *Baltimore (Md.) Sun*, 20 June 1999.
8. W. Jeffrey Bolster, *Black Jacks: African American Seamen in the Age of Sail* (Cambridge, Mass.: Harvard University Press, 1997), 4, 17.
9. Eric Foner, *Gateway to Freedom: The Hidden History of the Underground Railroad* (New York: W. W. Norton, 2015), 152; David S. Cecelski, *Waterman's Song: Slavery and Freedom in Maritime North Carolina* (Chapel Hill: University of North Carolina Press, 2001), 123, 127, 136, 141.
10. Christopher Phillips, *Freedom's Port: The African American Community of Baltimore, 1790–1860* (Urbana: University of Illinois Press, 1997), 29.
11. Bolster, *Black Jacks*, 24–25.
12. Frederick Douglass, *My Bondage and My Freedom* (1855; reprint, with introduction and notes by Brent Hayes Edwards, New York: Barnes & Noble, 2005), 179.
13. "Slavery: The Role of Baltimore," Mont Clare Museum House, accessed 28 August 2019, https://www.mountclare.org/history/slave_roleofbalt.html.
14. Ibid.
15. C. Peter Ripley, ed., *The Black Abolitionist Papers, vol. 3, The United States, 1830–1846* (Chapel Hill: The University of North Carolina Press, 1991), 173.
16. Michael Schoeppner, "Peculiar Quarantines: The Seamen Acts and Regulatory Authority in the Antebellum South," *Law and History Review* 31, no. 3 (August 2012): 559–86.
17. Ralph Clayton, *Cash for Blood: The Baltimore to New Orleans Domestic Slave Trade* (Westminster, Md.: Heritage Books, 2007), 73.
18. Since then, the canal has been slightly altered by the Army Corps of Engineers. Chesapeake & Delaware Canal, Canal History, Philadelphia District and Marine Design Center Website, U.S. Army Corps of Engineers, accessed 5 August 2020,

https://www.nap.usace.army.mil/Missions/Civil-Works/Chesapeake-Delaware-Canal/Canal-History.

19. Milt Diggins, "Chesapeake and Delaware Canal (C & D Canal)," National Underground Railroad Network to Freedom Application, National Park Service, 2 July 2014.
20. Levin Woolford's ads for the return of the Keene family ran in the *American and Commercial Daily Advertiser* (Baltimore, Md.), 9 and 13 April 1831, and *Easton (Md.) Gazette*, 16 April 1831, Legacy of Slavery in Maryland, Maryland State Archives, accessed 16 August 2020, slavery2.msa.maryland.gov/pages/Search.aspx. Woolford was so unsure about the specific details of the family that he ran eight separate ads—one for each member of the escape party, except for the youngest child—some even under the wrong name, Crane, and with incorrect ages.
21. See Woolford's newspaper ads for the Keene Family, 9, 13, and 16 April 1831 cited in note 20.
22. See also *An Act to Prohibit the Owners of Vessels, and Others from Navigating the Same by and under the Sole Command of Negroes or Mulattoes* (2 March 1837), in *Laws Made and Passed by the General Assembly, of the State of Maryland, at a Session Begun and Held at Annapolis, on Monday the 26th Day of December,* 1836, chap. 150, vol. 537 (Annapolis: Printed by Jeremiah Hughes, 1837), 144–45, *Maryland Session Laws*, Archives of Maryland Online, http://aomol.msa.maryland.gov/000001/000537/html/am537--144.html.
23. "From the Southern Argus, Free Negro Sailors," *Washington (D.C.) Southern Press*, 14 November 1850, Chronicling America: Historic American Newspapers, Library of Congress, accessed 6 August 2020, https://chroniclingamerica.loc.gov/lccn/sn82014764/1850-11-14/ed-1/seq-3/.
24. Milt Diggins, "Site of Perryville Railroad Ferry and Station," National Underground Railroad Network to Freedom Application, National Park Service, 18 May 2014. This document is accessible online at https://dixonhistory.com/reports/perryvilleugrr.pdf, accessed 16 August 2020.
25. William Craft, *Running a Thousand Miles to Freedom* (London: William Tweedie, 1860), 71.
26. William Still, *Underground Rail Road: A Record of Facts, Authentic Letters, Narratives, &c.* (Philadelphia: Porter & Coates, 1872), 214–15.
27. Hollis Robbins, "Fugitive Mail: The Deliverance of Henry 'Box' Brown and Antebellum Postal Politics," *American Studies* 50, no. 1/2 (Spring/Summer 2009): 6; Diggins, "Site of Perryville Railroad Ferry and Station."
28. Frederick Douglass, *Life and Times of Frederick Douglass: His Early Life as a Slave, His Escape from Bondage, and His Complete History to the Present Time* (Hartford, Conn.: Park Publishing Co., 1881), 198–99; David W. Blight, *Frederick Douglass: Prophet of Freedom* (New York: Simon & Schuster, 2018), 81.

29. *An Act to Encourage the More Effectual Apprehending of Runaway Servants and Slaves*, in *Maryland Session Laws*, 1833, chap. 111, vol. 210, pp. 130–31, Archives of Maryland Online, https://msa.maryland.gov/megafile/msa/speccol/sc2900/sc2908/000001/000210/html/am210--130.html.
30. Diggins, "Chesapeake and Delaware Canal (C & D Canal)."
31. Still, *Underground Rail Road*, 46.
32. Still, *Underground Rail Road*, 28. Still refers to the steamer company as the Ericsson Line but does not make the connection to the C & D Canal. See ibid., 46.
33. James McGowan and William C. Kashatus, *Harriet Tubman: A Biography* (Santa Barbara, Calif.: Greenwood, 2011), 29.
34. Kate Clifford Larson, *Bound for the Promised Land: Harriet Tubman, Portrait of an American Hero* (New York: Ballantine Books, 2004), 89–90.
35. McGowan and Kashatus, *Harriet Tubman*, 29; Catherine Clinton, *Harriet Tubman: The Road to Freedom* (New York: Little, Brown & Company, 2004), 81.
36. McGowan and Kashatus, *Harriet Tubman*, 29–30; Clinton, *Harriet Tubman, 81.*
37. McGowan and Kashatus, 30; Clinton, *Harriet Tubman*, 81; Larson, *Bound for the Promised Land,* 88–90.
38. Still, *Underground Railroad*, 136.
39. Bolster, *Black Jacks*, 23.
40. Charles L. Blockson, *The Underground Railroad: Dramatic Firsthand Accounts of Daring Escapes to Freedom* (New York: Prentice-Hall Press, 1987), 3–4.
41. Ibid.; Museums and Historic Sites, Central Maryland, Pathways to Freedom: Maryland and the Underground Railroad, Maryland Public Television, accessed 10 June 2019, https://pathways.thinkport.org/library/sites4.cfm.
42. Still, *Underground Railroad*, 509.
43. "Howard Methodist Episcopal Church Site," Cecil County, Central Maryland, Pathways to Freedom: Maryland and the Underground Railroad, Maryland Public Television, accessed 6 June 2019, https://pathways.thinkport.org/library/sites4.cfm. "Port Deposit Historic District, [Maryland]," 12 September 2018, Nomination Form, CE-1291, National Register of Historic Places, National Park Service, U.S. Department of the Interior, Washington, D.C., https://mht.maryland.gov/secure/medusa/PDF/Cecil/CE-1291.pdf, accessed 16 August 2020.
44. James Curry, "Narrative of James Curry, a Fugitive Slave," *Boston (Mass.) Liberator*, 10 January 1840, 1. This piece refers to the Chesapeake and Ohio Canal.
45. Daniel Drayton, *Personal Memoir of Daniel Drayton* (Boston: Bela Marsh, 1855), 20.
46. Ibid., 20.
47. Ibid., 22.
48. Mary Kay Ricks, *Escape on the Pearl: The Heroic Bid for Freedom on the Underground Railroad* (New York: Harper Collins, 2007), 16.
49. Within the grounds former Washington Navy Yard grounds in southeast Washington.

50. The escapees were thirty-eight men and boys, twenty-six women and girls, and thirteen children. *Washington (D.C.) Daily Union*, 19 April 1848.
51. "The Pearl Affairs and Riot," D.C. Emancipation Day, DC.Gov, https://emancipation.dc.gov/page/pearl-affairs-and-riot, accessed 28 May 2019.
52. Ricks, *Escape on the Pearl*, 131–32; Clayton, *Cash for Blood*, 95–97.
53. Harriet Beecher Stowe, *A Key to Uncle Tom's Cabin* (Boston: Jewett, 1854). Henry Ward Beecher was the author's brother.
54. Fergus Bordewich, *Bound for Canaan: The Underground Railroad and the War for the Soul of America* (New York: HarperCollins, 2005), 303; Ricks, *Escape on the Pearl*, 288; Library of Congress, Research Guides, "Compromise of 1850: Primary Documents in American History," accessed 14 August 2019, https://guides.loc.gov/compromise-1850.
55. Ricks, *Escape on the Pearl*, 232; Josephine F. Pacheco, *The Pearl: A Failed Slave Escape on the Potomac* (Chapel Hill: University of North Carolina Press, 2005), 218–19.
56. *Charleston (S.C.) Mercury*, 6 and 13 September 1823, cited in Schoeppner, "Peculiar Quarantines," 565, 567.

6

CLAIMING LIBERTY BY SEA

The Port of New York as a Fugitive's Gateway from Enslavement

MIRELLE LUECKE

> TEN DOLLARS REWARD. RUN away . . . a Negro man, named POMP. . . . It is supposed he has procured a forged pass, and will endeavor to get on board some vessel to go to the West Indies.
>
> —*New-York Packet*, 21 July 1791

In early May 1800, an enslaved man named Ned donned a sailor's jacket and made his way from New Rochelle to Manhattan, New York, where he disappeared into the bustling streets. Ned knew the area well. Before a forcible move to New Rochelle, he had "belonged to Aaron Pell, in Broad Street, in the city of New York."[1] Perhaps in returning to the city, he sought to reunite with friends and family from whom he had been separated, or maybe he hoped that the anonymity of the large city would enable him to successfully claim his freedom. It is likely that his previous familiarity with the city had prompted him to make use of a sailor's jacket in his escape. Ned was actually a hackney carriage driver by trade, but having spent time in the city, he likely knew that the prevalence of Black sailors in the waterfront neighborhoods surrounding Broad Street would help him pass through the streets unnoticed. Indeed, Ned managed to evade capture for at least a month; the advertisement noting his escape continued to appear in the *Daily Advertiser* throughout May.[2] Ned's story is not unique. His experiences are similar to those of countless other African Americans who attempted to escape enslavement during the era of the Early Republic. Using their knowledge of the maritime world, they sought freedom by traveling along coastal and river routes and stowing away on ships, impersonating sailors, and deserting the moment their ship arrived in a friendly port.

Throughout the Early Republic from the 1790s to the 1820s, hundreds of runaway slave advertisements such as Ned's appeared in New York newspapers. These notices called attention to escaped and missing servants, enslaved laborers, and bonded workers. But notices for runaway slaves were the most prevalent. The advertisements chronicle the escape routes of enslaved men, women, and children throughout the nation. Because of New York's role as a growing international seaport and its sizable population of both free and enslaved African Americans, the city was a destination for escaped slaves from throughout the country.[3] The many ships daily coming and going from the docks and the rapidly expanding population of the city created community ties and communication networks that extended well beyond the city itself. This chapter explores how enslaved African Americans took advantage of New York City's position as a burgeoning port city to chart their routes to freedom.

A rich body of scholarship examines the lived experience of enslaved and free Blacks in New York City. In recent years, scholars have explored the contrasts and connections between slavery and freedom in New York City and the surrounding countryside. For instance, Graham Russell Hodges shows that the social and economic institutions of New York City—and indeed, the entire state—were shaped by slavery. David Gellman looks at the politics of slavery in New York City, examining how the actions of African American residents shaped the debate surrounding the abolition of slavery. In tracing the history of slavery from the seventeenth century to the Draft Riots in 1863, Leslie Harris emphasizes the essential role of African Americans in shaping politics and class in the city.[4]

The definitive study of African Americans in New York City is Shane White's *Somewhat More Independent*. Looking at thousands of runaway advertisements placed in New York and the surrounding regions from 1770 to 1810, White compiled invaluable information about the ages, genders, occupations, destinations, and motivations of escaped slaves.[5] In this study, I focus on 313 runaway slave advertisements placed in Manhattan newspapers from 1790 to 1819.[6] Concentrating on the advertisements that appeared in city newspapers underlines the maritime dimensions of the road to freedom: Runaways' escape routes, employment opportunities, and communication networks were all shaped by New York's position as a port for both coastwise and international transoceanic shipping.

As a busy national and international port, new vessels and unknown crews came into New York City on a daily basis. Runaways took advantage of New York's position as the center of African American culture in the region, the common presence of Black sailors along the waterfront, and the city's high population of free African Americans to avoid detection. The runaway slave advertisements in New York newspapers reveal that both men and women escaped by water in some manner, making use of informal networks that spanned port cities from north to south. Because gradual emancipation laws in many northern states meant that slavery was not fully abolished in the region until the mid-1800s, these maritime escapees traveled not only from the Deep South but from New Jersey and upstate New York.[7] This chapter charts the existence of maritime routes to freedom created by the movement of ships, sailors, and enslaved people, well before the more famous Underground Railroad routes existed.[8] The porous nature of the port city and the unchecked and unregulated ways that people entered the city enabled fugitive slaves to disappear into the city on their paths to freedom.

A MARITIME CITY

Of the advertisements examined here, 39 percent mention maritime networks in some way.[9] Some enslaved men, such as Ned, dressed as sailors to aid their escape. Others traveled to New York City along coastal trading routes, working as sailors, stowing away on vessels, or enlisting the help of sympathetic boatmen. For many, New York City was just one in a series of destinations on a long, complicated, and dangerous journey of self-emancipation. Upon arriving in the city, these former slaves continued to seek further transportation to New England or Canada, places where emancipation was not gradual. For those who remained in New York, the port shaped their employment opportunities. Men could find work as sailors in coastal or international vessels, or as laborers or dockworkers loading and unloading ships, repairing wharves, and generally ensuring that the city's robust trade continued. The availability of work for unskilled and semiskilled laborers made New York an attractive destination for migrants of all kinds.

Indeed, maritime networks impacted life for everyone in New York during the Early Republic. In the 1790s, the city itself barely extended past modern-day Houston Street. Bounded by the Hudson on one side and the East River on the other, the city was effectively an island. Visitors, migrants, and runaways all entered the city via water routes. There was no formal ferry system until

FIGURE 12. Fugitive Slave Thomas H. Jones, Escaping on a Raft from the Brig ship *Bell*, offshore from New York City. Jones's escape in 1849 drew on the knowledge of maritime routes to freedom that he had developed over decades while loading and unloading vessels as a longshoreman at the harbor of Wilmington, North Carolina. Illustration in *The Experience of Thomas H. Jones, Who Was a Slave for Forty-Three Years* (Boston: Bazin & Chandler, 1862); image from Digital Collections, General Research Division, The New York Public Library, https://digitalcollections.nypl.org/items/510d47da-7484-a3d9-e040-e00a18064a99.

the early 1800s. Until that time, anyone who wanted to enter the city had to rely on the goodwill of local boat owners who—for a price—might offer space on their rowboats or small fishing vessels. Some enslaved people stole skiffs and other small vessels to escape to Manhattan, while others figured out which informal ferries might be sympathetic to their escape.[10] By the time that city officials began to oversee ferry operations in 1800, these informal networks of entry were already firmly in place. While the rivers could prove difficult to cross, the necessity of water-based entry into the city also made the city borders permeable.

Although ships had to register upon entering the port and submit their cargo manifests and passenger lists to the Custom House, the lengthy, unguarded coastline meant that there were countless places for unnoticed and clandestine entries. Furthermore, in a fast-growing city reliant on trade with many entry points and permeable borders, the faces of city residents were constantly changing. The more-permanent working-class inhabitants of the city changed residences frequently, and migrants arrived on the city wharves almost daily, especially in the spring and summer months.[11] While enslaved people ran away throughout the year, the majority also took flight in these warm months. Some made their home in New York; others quickly moved on to employment opportunities in other port cities or in New York's hinterland. For example, when a man named Pomp escaped slavery in the city in July 1791, the *New-York Packet* "supposed he has produced a forged pass and will endeavor to get on board some vessel."[12] Similarly, when a woman named Rose, her husband, Mink, and their five children all escaped from New Jersey in 1797, they made their way to Staten Island and were suspected of trying to reach New York.[13] Once runaways arrived in New York, it was "supposed they have taken the road to New-England," presumably to make their new home in a state where slavery was fully abolished. Sailors were also a constant presence, noticeable with their rolling gait and distinctive dress while walking along the city streets and in waterfront taverns. A runaway could easily pass undetected through this constant flow of strangers.

NETWORKS OF ESCAPE

In addition to a constantly shifting population of transient workers, both Black and white, New York City was home to a sizable Black community, with roots stretching back to seventeenth-century Dutch Manhattan. New York had been a slave society since the arrival of the first enslaved Africans, brought to New Amsterdam by the Dutch West India Company in 1626. This community continued to grow under British control of the city in the colonial period. Black New Yorkers developed a vibrant cultural community. For example, throughout the colonial period, "Pinkster" celebrations combined African and Dutch cultural traditions in a celebration in which African American communities throughout New York socialized and enjoyed a brief inversion of the usual social order, electing an enslaved person to play the role of "king" for the festivities.[14] Additionally, African Americans in New York created aid organizations for members of the community in need of support. They included churches and societies, such as the African Marine Fund, which was launched in 1810 to aid Black sailors.[15] These deep community roots helped to create in place a network of support for runaways.[16]

By the Revolutionary War, New York City had the highest population of enslaved people in the northern colonies. During British occupation of the city, the population decreased as patriots fled the city and vulnerable workers moved elsewhere when the blockaded port caused their livelihoods to vanish. Despite this general depopulation of the city, its Black population remained steady, as enslaved African Americans arrived in British-occupied New York City in search of freedom. Many of these African Americans, previously enslaved in the surrounding colonies, had emancipated themselves and made their way to New York following Dunmore's Proclamation, which in 1775 promised freedom to all enslaved Americans who joined the British forces. One enslaved person who attempted to run to the British was a man named Scipio. He tried to escape to British lines in 1776 but was captured by his master, Andrew Bostwick. Despite that setback, Scipio made another bid for freedom in 1784.[17] After the war, many of these new residents to New York fled the city alongside white Loyalists and settled in the freedom of the maritime provinces of Canada.[18] Even with this exodus following Evacuation Day, free and self-emancipated migrants continued to make their way to the port city.

In the Early Republic, Manhattan and its environs, including Brooklyn, Staten Island, Long Island, and New Jersey, had the highest concentration of enslaved African Americans in the northern United States.[19] In 1790, nonwhite people made up 10.6 percent of the population, with slaves making up 7.6 percent of the population. The term *nonwhite* in these census records would have predominantly referred to people of African descent. In the 1800 census, nonwhite people made up 5.8 percent of the city's population, with slaves accounting for 4.7 percent of the population. It is important to remember, however, the city's massive population growth in these years: From 1790 to 1800, the population of the city nearly doubled from 33,000 to over 60,000 residents.[20] While the percentage of nonwhite residents decreased in the census records, the actual number of nonwhite people—both free and enslaved—remained roughly the same as it had been in 1790.

The state of New York had passed a Gradual Emancipation Act in 1799, granting enslaved people freedom in stages. The act freed children who were born after 4 July 1799 but indentured them until they were young adults. In fact, some of the "runaway slave" newspaper advertisements were for young Black people who were technically indentured servants, although this official designation was not, in practical terms, significantly different from that of enslavement. This process sought to mitigate the labor losses that slave-owners would face with a wholesale emancipation of the state's enslaved population. The slow process towards freedom meant that slavery remained strong in the state throughout the period, until all slaves were officially emancipated in 1827. Many white New Yorkers maintained proslavery sentiments. The majority of Manumission Society members were slave-owners who hoped to "reform," rather than abolish, slavery in the state, and New York City remained a center for merchant firms that organized and financed slaving voyages well into the 1860s.[21]

One result of the gradual emancipation law was that white New Yorkers could not immediately discern which African Americans they encountered on the city streets were enslaved and which were free, making New York an attractive destination for runaways.[22] By 1810, gradual emancipation had begun to have some impact on the official status of Black residents of the city. Nonwhites made up 10.2 percent of the population, and the number of slaves had decreased dramatically to 1.8 percent. However, it is important to note that many of these "free" Blacks still worked in slavery-like conditions, as indentured or bonded laborers. In 1820, the census had changed the term "nonwhite" to "colored," and this group made up 8.8 percent of the population. Slaves were only 0.4 percent of the population.[23] The continually high concentration of African Americans in New York City meant that it was the center of African American culture in the region, the place where both free and enslaved Blacks from the city and the outlying areas of Brooklyn, Long Island, and New Jersey could congregate.[24]

White visitors to New York frequently commented on the conspicuous presence of African Americans throughout the city. One English visitor described the "greater number of Blacks, particularly women and children in the streets" than he had seen elsewhere in his travels. New York's free Black community lived predominantly near the shipyards along the Hudson and East Rivers. Enslaved Blacks, who in 1790 made up two-thirds of the city's Black population, lived in white households scattered around the city.[25] The jobs held by Black New Yorkers were similar whether they were enslaved or free. African American women predominantly worked in white households, while some worked as washerwomen, prostitutes, and street peddlers. Visitors described how these women called out "Hot corn, hot corn, here's your lily white hot corn / Hot corn all hot, just come out of the boiling pot."[26] Men might work as dockworkers, day laborers, servants, artisans, or sailors.[27] The lives of urban slaves, working long days alone indoors, were frequently more isolated than those of enslaved African Americans on large plantations. However, the daily labor required to keep a household running also took enslaved people into the city's marketplaces and along its streets. While running errands, hauling water, and interacting with Black peddlers and street vendors, enslaved Blacks made connections with other African Americans in the city. Access to this thriving Black community provided crucial support and camouflage when enslaved New Yorkers sought to escape from bondage.

The importance of African American community networks in aiding escapes was apparent in the runaway advertisements that appeared in the city newspapers. For example, Phillis escaped enslavement in New Utrecht, New York, in 1799.[28] Although her exact route to New York City is unknown, she likely traveled by foot about seven miles to the Brooklyn waterfront, where she would have had to convince a boat operator to ferry her across the East River. It seems that, like so many other freedom seekers, Phillis suspected that the large and bustling city would offer her both anonymity and employment. Shortly after her escape, it was reported that she had been seen in Fly Market, where she was perhaps hawking goods as an informal seller, or huckster, or hoping to find other employment or aid by making use of the networks of African Americans who regularly used the market.

Phillis's choice to go to Fly Market made sense. It and the other city markets were informal gathering spaces for the city's poor residents, both Black and white. They daily came in search of work and sustenance. Markets were places of commerce, performance, and community. In addition to city-sanctioned stalls occupied by vendors and merchants, hucksters set up informal stalls or displayed items on blankets on the margins of the market, and itinerant sellers clustered just outside market entrances to sell their wares. Visitors to New York marveled at the "eel dance" traditionally performed by enslaved African Americans at Catherine Market. As a chronicler of the city later recalled, "They would be hired by some joking butcher or individual to engage in a jig of break-down, as that was one of their pastimes at home on the barn-floor, or in a frolic, and those that could and would dance soon raised a collection. . . ."[29] Slaves from New Jersey also visited New York markets to sell wares and socialize before boarding boats back to New Jersey—or disappearing into the city.[30] Phillis's ultimate fate is unknown. Despite her initial sighting in Fly Market, it is possible that she, like so many other African Americans who sought freedom, managed to blend into the city's free Black population and permanently evade detection.

While the majority of runaway advertisements that appeared in New York newspapers were for runways who were from the city or the surrounding region, others came to the city from farther afield.[31] Historian Leslie Harris notes, "The presence of a large, active port gave New York City a heightened visibility among the Atlantic World community of Blacks."[32] In practical terms, New York's role as the nation's largest port meant that its ships, crewed by a cosmopolitan mixture of sailors, traveled the globe. New York proved to be an essential point in a complex network of travel to freedom. Historian Julius Sherrard Scott has shown how the "webs of commerce" that linked Caribbean ports also provided enslaved people routes for communication, movement, and escape.[33] Southern ports such as Charleston, New Orleans, Savannah, and Mobile shipped their cotton through New York before the final leg of the voyage to European textile mills.[34] The constant movement of ships between northern and southern ports made the decision of enslaved African American sailors to jump ship in New York the culmination of complex flows of information between people. Fugitives from slavery in the South knew to seek out New York City, perhaps having heard about it from sailors who passed through Charleston, Wilmington, Hampton Roads, New Orleans, and other southern ports.[35] Thus, before an "official" underground railroad existed, fugitives relied on more-informal networks to enact their escapes.

Women were less likely than men to be able to make long sea journeys to New York, although there were exceptions. In one particularly complex journey, an enslaved woman named Mary successfully hid herself and her young daughter Nancy on board a ship bound from Charleston to New York. It is likely that Mary and Nancy would have stowed away for the 627-mile voyage on a ship filled with bales of cotton.[36] Frustratingly, the only record of Mary's experience is through the advertisements noting her escape. The newspaper suggested that New York City was only a stopping point and speculated that Mary would try to take her daughter to Newport, Rhode Island, where she had family. In order to successfully make the journey from Charleston to New York City as stowaways, Mary and her daughter probably had help along the way. These networks have been obscured by time, so historians do not know whether abolitionists in Charleston, crew members, or even the ship's master helped them escape slavery. The cotton trade firmly cemented New York City as the hub of a network of seaborne communication, through which enslaved and free people could exchange knowledge of conditions conducive to escape, news of friendly ports, and the name of sympathetic captains.

Scholars have shown that enslaved people used running away as one of many forms of everyday resistance to their bondage.[37] By slowing down work, stealing, and running away, the enslaved reclaimed control over goods they produced, their time, and their lives. Others intended their escape to be permanent. Historian Shane White concluded that 74 percent of runaways in the New York area intended to "pass as free" and permanently escape slavery. Furthermore, he notes that 22 percent of runaways from New York and New Jersey intended to travel to the countryside, 36.7 intended to make a home in New York City, and 28.3 percent had a supposed destination outside the region.[38] Additionally, 19 percent of runaway advertisements from 1790–1819 warned "masters of vessels" in New York Harbor that they would "harbor or carry off" runaways "at their peril."[39] Unsurprisingly, this entreaty appears predominantly in notices for men, pointing to the fact that Black males could find work as sailors on ships destined for ports throughout the Atlantic and world. Indeed, in the port of New York, work as a sailor was an attractive escape for all sorts of bonded laborers: in addition to runaway slave advertisements, the warning to ship captains also appeared in notices for runaway servants and apprentices, both Black and white. At the start of the nineteenth century, approximately one in five American seamen were African American.[40]

Despite the difficult and dangerous work of seafaring, labor at sea could offer relief from the constraints of land. The constant and familiar presence of sailors on the city streets meant that the profession of mariner was a known option even for those people, enslaved or free, who might otherwise have no direct experience with the sea. Notably, many free Black men chose to become sailors, for the profession often offered more freedom and opportunities than were available to them on land. For example, in 1806 on board the brig *John*, sailing out of Providence, Rhode Island, wages were based on skill rather than color: Black and white experienced seamen earned eighteen dollars per month, while the white cook and white ordinary seamen only received fourteen dollars per month.[41] By the mid-nineteenth century 20 percent of all sailors shipping out of American ports were Black.[42] Life at sea offered freedoms not afforded to African Americans on land.

Furthermore, the regular movement of Black sailors into New York City also gave enslaved African Americans opportunities to escape bondage. Just as Ned had done, some runaway men chose to don sailor jackets, whether they had any experience in the profession or not.[43] Wearing a sailor jacket—usually blue or red in color and made out of sturdy canvas or duck cloth that could stand up to the harsh elements at sea—these men would have fit in with the scores of actual sailors who strolled along the New York waterfront. The distinctive dress of a mariner immediately marked them as professional seamen in port cities. Indeed, the moniker "Jack Tar" referred to the fact that sailors "tarred" their clothes to help make them waterproof. To the eyes of the public, all sailors were similar.

Working as a sailor was not necessary for enslaved men to take advantage of port conditions to escape. In an international, deep-water port such as New York, there were few personal ties between mariners and captains, a circumstance that made it easier for enslaved men to pose as free sailors. A small but steady stream of Black bondsmen dressed as sailors when they enacted their escapes. In May 1799 two enslaved men were noted to have run away, both wearing sailor jackets.[44] The following year, Harry ran away from his master (who called him Orri), dressed in "a blue sailor jacket." The newspaper did not mention whether Harry was from the city or from some other place, but it was "supposed said Negro is lurking about this city," and the ad warned "Masters of vessels" against carrying him off. [45] Similarly, when Charles escaped slavery in Morristown, New Jersey, in April 1805, the master assumed that he had made his way to New York. Charles had taken a sailor's jacket with him and had gone off "in company with a yellow negro man by the name of David Solomons who wears a red sailor's jacket."[46] He also began calling himself Charles Johnson. Wearing the distinctive garb of seamen, Black men were less likely to be marked for their skin color and viewed with suspicion. Black sailors were a common sight in New York City, particularly in the harbor and along the waterfront.

The transient lifestyle expected of African American sailors made it possible for Black escapees, when dressed as sailors, to move through urban spaces with less or little suspicion.[47] Perhaps most famously, Frederick Douglass dressed as a sailor and used borrowed seamen's protection papers to seek and claim his freedom. In his autobiography, Douglass recounted using a protection paper to escape enslavement in 1838. He recalled, "I had one friend—a sailor—who owned a sailor's protection, which answered somewhat the purpose of free papers—describing his person and certifying to the fact that he was a free American sailor."[48] Even though after the War of 1812 American elites no longer viewed protection papers as a means to declare American sovereignty, they still served a vital purpose for enslaved Americans. As members of the floating population who continued to exist on the margins of national ideology, African Americans could draw on the older Atlantic understandings of protection papers to exert some type of agency in their labor and lives.

In addition to dressing in the distinctive garb of sailors, 7 percent of escaped enslaved men arrived in New York via a ship. Desertion was a common practice for Black and white sailors who hoped to secure better employment and sought to combat the exploitation of their labor.[49] Historian Jeffery Bolster notes that New York laws prohibiting the desertion of sailors were similar to those targeting fugitive slaves.[50] As with runaways who relied on local networks within the city to enact their escape, enslaved seamen also relied on networks of knowledge when leaving their ships. For example, upon arriving in New York harbor in 1801, an enslaved sailor named Hercules followed the path of many unfree sailors: he used his ship's stop in the city to make a bid for freedom.[51] When the brig *Rosetta* sailed from New Orleans in the early summer of that year, Hercules worked on the ship as an enslaved sailor.

When the *Rosetta* arrived in New York, Hercules had "gone off and secreted himself in the city." Apparently, he made his decision to escape with "the advice of the crew." Although the crew list for the *Rosetta* no longer remains and its racial makeup of the crew has been lost to time, crew lists for similarly sized vessels that arrived in the port of New York from New Orleans around the same time suggest a mixture of white and Black sailors.[52] For some, this voyage to New York may have been one among many, and their familiarity with the city might have enabled them to direct Hercules and help him make a successful escape. Even if none of the crew members had ever been to the port of New York themselves, they would doubtless have heard tales of the port from other sailors.

Through such a web of personal networks, both Black and white sailors shared knowledge of sympathetic boardinghouse keepers, notary publics willing to forge protection papers, and friendly support and camaraderie in cheap taverns. In port, sailors crowded into neighborhoods along the waterfront, areas described by residents of many port cities as "sailortowns," because of the high concentration of sailors and other maritime workers in these waterfront communities, which were home to maritime trades and many of the city's poor and transient workers.[53] In New York, sailors and other maritime workers congregated in an area known as "topsail alley," which stretched from the shipyards near Corlears Hook down to the tip of Manhattan, where wharves and slips jutted into the East River.[54] Coastal traders and trans-Atlantic voyagers lived alongside each other and socialized with other mariners, laborers, riggers, and dockworkers in waterfront taverns. They would also have shared knowledge of how best to pass unnoticed in the city as an enslaved person seeking to escape from bondage. Runaways such as Hercules took advantage of the chaotic and camouflaging mixture of enslaved and free African Americans who populated New York City.

For many, the escape attempt that earned them a mention in the runaway slave advertisements of the New York City newspapers was not their first escape attempt. For example, as the schooner *Favourite Elsey* from Petersburg, Virginia, sat in New York harbor in June 1796, two enslaved crew members seized the chance to escape.[55] The *Daily Advertiser* reported that Sam and Joshua "ran away . . . about three weeks ago and have not been heard of since." For Sam, at least, who was reported to have "an R on one side of his face" publicly marking him as a runaway, this was not a first attempt to claim freedom. Similarly, a "sailor negro man" named Jack escaped from the schooner *Cato* in the middle of the night in November 1802.[56] Prior to his escape, Jack had been confined on board the ship for four days. Perhaps this incarceration was punishment for an unknown crime and prompted his escape, or perhaps the schooner's master suspected he might try to escape as the ship lay in the harbor.

Regardless of what prompted his flight, for Jack and so many other enslaved African Americans, the ocean did not act as a barrier or a border, but rather as a conduit through which they could slip into a free haven, using both formal and informal methods. Some, such as Ned the hack driver from New Rochelle, had previously lived in New York, while others from Brooklyn, Staten Island, and parts of New Jersey had previously visited the city for market days or other business. Perhaps most significantly, although employment at sea and the ability to masquerade as a sailor were only available to men, women also made use of these maritime escape routes.

Maritime networks to escape slavery expanded well beyond the movement of enslaved people along the Eastern Seaboard of the United States. In addition to the strong trade networks that developed between New York and southern ports in the 1780s, New York had enjoyed robust trade ties with the West Indies since the colonial period.[57] These maritime networks could also sow the seeds of rebellion. Most relevant to Americans in the Early Republic was the Haitian Revolution. White Americans were fearful such violent rebellion would come to the United States and overturn the carefully constructed, guardedly representative government that they had created. Such fears intensified as refugees from Saint Domingue began appearing in American ports. From roughly 1791 to 1810, over 25,000 refugees arrived in the United States from Saint Domingue—about 4,000–5,000 in New York City.[58] Black Saint Domingue refugees did not escape to New York City using water routes, but their flight from slavery was nevertheless shaped by maritime networks.

CONCLUSION

The informal routes to freedom created by enslaved African Americans were a constant challenge to the system of slavery within the United States. Although the period under study in this chapter, spanning from roughly 1790 to the 1810s, was well before the better-known Underground Railroad network helped to ferry enslaved people to freedom, the constant clandestine movement of enslaved people into and out of New York City helped create an atmosphere of resistance within the city. As the nineteenth century progressed, antislavery movements in the city became more public and more organized that were in the period explored in this chapter. For example, the city's Vigilance Committee, an organization comprised of white and Black radical abolitionists, was founded in the 1830s. This organization drew heavily on the ideology of "practical abolitionism," which advocated for civil disobedience, self-defense, and self-emancipation—all practices that runaways within the city had been using for decades.[59] Throughout the early republic, the maritime world of New York's port created a gateway to freedom for enslaved Blacks from the New York hinterland and the southern United States, the Caribbean and West Indies, and even Africa. The constant movement of ships and people in the port created networks through which enslaved people could share vital information about methods of escape and provided community support to resist slavery. In the chaotic atmosphere of the growing port city, enslaved African Americans claimed their freedom.

NOTES

1. *New York Daily Advertiser*, 2 May 1800.
2. Ibid., 24 May 1800.
3. Graham Russell Hodges, *Root and Branch: African Americans in New York and East Jersey, 1613–1863* (Chapel Hill: University of North Carolina Press, 1999), 173–74.
4. Ibid., 32–33; David N. Gellman, *Emancipating New York: The Politics of Slavery and Freedom, 1777–1827* (Baton Rouge: Louisiana State University Press, 2006), 8–9; Leslie M. Harris, *In the Shadow of Slavery: African Americans in New York City, 1626–1863* (Chicago: University of Chicago Press, 2004), 4.
5. Shane White, *Somewhat More Independent: The End of Slavery in New York City, 1770–1810* (Athens, Ga.: University of Georgia Press, 2012), 121–49.
6. For this project, I searched digitized New York newspapers to gather 313 individual advertisements. This number excludes ads that ran multiple times for the same person. For instance, the two advertisements which appeared in newspapers noting Ned's escape in May 1800 are only counted once.
7. Pennsylvania was the first state to enact gradual emancipation in 1780, and Connecticut was the last state to abolish slavery in 1848.
8. Eric Foner offers a comprehensive study of the antislavery movements that existed in New York City in the antebellum period. Eric Foner, *Gateway to Freedom: The Hidden History of the Underground Railroad* (New York: W. W. Norton, 2015).
9. The maritime networks mentioned in runaway advertisements included speculations that runaways were trying to travel to New York from elsewhere in the country, suppositions that runaways were trying to leave the city, warnings that masters of vessels should not hire or carry off runaways, notices that runaways were dressed as sailors or had expressed a desire to go to sea, and reports that runaways employed as sailors had jumped ship.
10. *New-York Packet*, 11 December 1787; *New York Daily Advertiser*, 10 March 1795.

11. New York City Customs Records, 1799–1801, Customs and Shipping Papers (1794–1820), Alexander Hamilton United States Custom House Records, 1794–1893, New-York Historical Society; Billy G. Smith, *The "Lower Sort": Philadelphia's Laboring People, 1750–1800* (Ithaca, N.Y.: Cornell University Press, 1994), 58–62.
12. *New-York Packet*, 21 July 1791.
13. *New York Daily Advertiser*, 23 June 1797.
14. Shane White, "'It Was a Proud Day': African Americans, Festivals, and Parades in the North, 1741–1834," *Journal of American History* 81, no. 1 (1994): 13–50; Hodges, *Root and Branch*, 88.
15. Edwin G. Burrows and Mile Wallace, *Gotham: A History of New York City to 1898* (New York: Oxford University Press, 1998), 398–400; W. Jeffrey Bolster, *Black Jacks: African American Seamen in the Age of Sail* (Boston: Harvard University Press, 2009), 160.
16. Hodges, *Root and Branch*, 15.
17. *New-York Packet*, 10 May 1784.
18. Hodges, *Root and Branch*, 75, 139.
19. Graham Russell Hodges and Alan Edward Brown, *"Pretends to Be Free": Runaway Slave Advertisements from Colonial and Revolutionary New York and New Jersey* (New York: Taylor & Francis, 1994); White, *Somewhat More Independent.*
20. Decennial Censuses, New York County, 1790 and 1800, Social Explorer Dataset, digitally transcribed by Inter-university Consortium for Political and Social Research, ed. Michael Haines, Comp. and ed. Social Explorer, accessed 18 December 2018, http://www.socialexplorer.com.
21. Harris, *In the Shadow of Slavery*, 49; White, *Somewhat More Independent, 85–86.*
22. Harris, *In the Shadow of Slavery*, 73.
23. Decennial Censuses, New York County, 1790, 1800, 1810, and 1820, Social Explorer Dataset, accessed 18 December 2018, http://www.socialexplorer.com.
24. Hodges and Brown, *"Pretends to Be Free,"* xxi.
25. Ibid., 3–5, 43–45.
26. Frances Sargent Locke Osgood, *The Cries of New York* (New York: John Doggett, Jr., 1846); Charles H. Haswell, *Reminiscences of New York by an Octogenarian (1816 to 1860)* (New York: Harper and Brothers Publishers, 1896), 444; Christine Stansell, *City of Women: Sex and Class in New York, 1789–1860* (Urbana: University of Illinois Press, 1987), 13–14.
27. This occupational list is drawn from examinations of New York City directories published from 1790–1806. The directories were accessed digitally through Early American Imprints, Series 1, https://www.readex.com/products/early-american-imprints-series-i-evans-1639-1800.
28. See, for example, *New York Morning Chronicle*, 13 March 1806; *New-York Gazette*, 18 February 1799.
29. English traveler quoted in William T. Lhamon, *Raising Cain: Blackface Performance from Jim Crow to Hip Hop* (Cambridge: Harvard University Press, 1998), 9.

30. Harris, *In the Shadow of Slavery*, 69–70.
31. David S. Cecelski, *The Waterman's Song: Slavery and Freedom in Maritime North Carolina* (Chapel Hill: University of North Carolina Press, 2012), 147–48; Ashli White, *Encountering Revolution: Haiti and the Making of the Early Republic* (Baltimore, Md.: Johns Hopkins University Press, 2010), 21.
32. Harris, *In the Shadow of Slavery*, 73.
33. Julius S. Scott, *The Common Wind: Afro-American Currents in the Age of the Haitian Revolution* (New York: Verso, 2018), 3.
34. Robert Greenhalgh Albion, *The Rise of New York Port, 1815–1860* (Boston: Northeastern University Press, 1939), 95–101.
35. Harris, *In the Shadow of Slavery*, 73.
36. From 1786–1805, over 75 percent of reported runaways were men, the majority between sixteen and twenty-five years old. White, *Somewhat More Independent*, 143; *New-York Gazette*, 9 May 1810; Albion, *The Rise of New York Port*, 107.
37. Peter H. Wood, *Black Majority: Negroes in Colonial South Carolina from 1670 through the Stono Rebellion* (New York: W. W. Norton, 1996); Edmund S. Morgan, *American Slavery, American Freedom* (New York: W. W. Norton, 2003).
38. White, *Somewhat More Independent*, 127. Given that White's figures are drawn from advertisements ranging from 1771–1805, another 12.9 percent of runaways in his survey intended to join the army during Revolution.
39. *New York Commercial Advertiser*, 14 August 1799.
40. Bolster, *Black Jacks*, 2–6.
41. Ibid., 76, 161.
42. White, *Somewhat More Independent*, 159; James Oliver Horton and Lois E. Horton, *In Hope of Liberty: Culture, Community, and Protest among Northern Free Blacks, 1700–1860* (New York: Oxford University Press, 1996), 111–14.
43. Although only eight advertisements specifically mention this practice, it is likely that many escaped slaves who intended to board vessels also dressed in sailor clothes to disguise themselves.
44. *New York Daily Advertiser*, 31 May 1799.
45. Ibid., 26 May 1800.
46. *New York Commercial Advertiser*, 16 April 1805.
47. Cecelski, *The Waterman's Song*, 136–37. For more on the place of Black sailors in the Early Republic, see also Martha Putney, *Black Sailors: Afro-American Merchant Seamen and Whalemen Prior to the Civil War* (New York: Greenwood Press, 1987).
48. Frederick Douglass, *The Life and Times of Frederick Douglas* (Boston: De Wolf and Fiske Co., 1892), 245–46.
49. Marcus Rediker, *Between the Devil and the Deep Blue Sea: Merchant Seamen, Pirates, and the Anglo-American Maritime World, 1700–1750* (New York: Cambridge University Press, 1989), 115, 291–92.
50. Bolster, *Black Jacks*, 73.

51. *New York Daily Advertiser*, 6 June 1801. The ad appeared in subsequent issues of ibid., 16 June 1801 and 30 June 1801). *New York Mercantile Advertiser*, 26 June 1801.
52. New York City Customs Records, 1799–1801, Alexander Hamilton United States Custom House Records, 1794–1893, New-York Historical Society.
53. Scholars who use the term *sailortown* to describe the maritime-oriented communities that emerged along urban waterfronts include Graeme J. Milne, *People, Place and Power on the Nineteenth-Century Waterfront: Sailortown* (New York: Springer, 2016); Isaac Land, "The Humours of Sailortown: Atlantic History Meets Subculture Theory," in *City Limits: Perspectives on the Historical European City*, ed. G. Clark, J. Owens, and G. Smith (Montreal: McGill-Queen's University Press, 2010); Judith Fingard, *Jack in Port: Sailortowns of Eastern Canada* (Toronto: University of Toronto Press, 1982).
54. *New York Daily Advertiser*, 14 October 1791.
55. Ibid., 27 June 1796.
56. *New York Evening Post*, 19 November 1802.
57. Peter Linebaugh and Marcus Rediker, *The Many-Headed Hydra: Sailors, Slaves, Commoners, and the Hidden History of the Revolutionary Atlantic* (Boston: Beacon Press, 2000), 199; Cathy D. Matson, *Merchants and Empire: Trading in Colonial New York* (Baltimore, Md.: Johns Hopkins University Press, 1998), 183–85. Enslaved people also escaped ships that had arrived from Caribbean ports. For example, in 1801 a "negro boy" named Job fled from the schooner *Jack* from Saint Lucia. *New York Daily Advertiser*, 2 September 1801.
58. Burrows and Wallace, *Gotham*, 314.
59. The Black activist David Ruggles, a founding member of the city's Vigilance Committee, played an essential role in the development of the later Underground Railroad network in New York City. See Graham Russell Hodges, *David Ruggles: A Radical Black Abolitionist and the Underground Railroad in New York City* (Chapel Hill: University of North Carolina Press, 2010). The Vigilance Committees that existed throughout the United States were a precursor to later Underground Railroad networks. Jesse Olsavsky, "Women, Vigilance Committees, and the Rise of Militant Abolitionism, 1835–1859," *Slavery & Abolition* 39, no. 2 (2018): 357–82.

7

ABOLITIONISTS AND SEABORNE FUGITIVES IN COASTAL EASTERN CONNECTICUT

Escaping Slavery in New London, Mystic, and Stonington

ELYSA ENGELMAN

A fugitive slave case occurred in New-London, Conn., on Friday. A coasting vessel arrived from North Carolina with a fugitive on board. The Captain, discovering the negro, went ashore at New-London and apprised the Federal officials, who went to the vessel, but the man had taken alarm, jumped overboard and swam ashore. Collector MATHER instituted a search, found "JOE" concealed in a clothing store, and captured him; but Dr. MINER interfered, advised the negro to run, and he did. The Collector got out a handbill offering a reward of $50 for his arrest, but the man escaped, and is supposed to be on his way to Canada.

—*New York Times*, 4 October 1858

Capt. Potter of the schooner Eliza of New London, in whose vessel a slave from Wilmington, N.C. secreted himself, last summer, and was liberated at New London, has paid the owner at Wilmington, the value of the slave, so that he can make his usual trips without hindrance. We presume he has charged the price over to Profit and Loss, as the negro is in Canada.

—*Hartford (Conn.) Daily Courant*, 11 February 1859

These two short newspaper notices, tucked among other local and regional items of interest such as carriage accidents and arrests, detail a single incident both common and curious along the Atlantic Seaboard in the pre–Civil War period. It's a simple enough story. A North Carolina man born into slavery makes his way onto a northbound schooner but is discovered at sea. The captain complies with the federal Fugitive Slave Law, turning him over to the proper authorities. The freedom seeker ultimately escapes, using the coastal Connecticut city of New London as a temporary waypoint on a much larger journey. The case of "Stowaway Joe" (identified in other articles as Benjamin Jones or Benjamin Tebo) is the best-documented case of an antebellum maritime escape in southeastern Connecticut, after the Amistad incident of 1839. The discovery of this fugitive from Wilmington, North Carolina, in 1858 spawned more than half a dozen newspaper articles from Worcester, Massachusetts, to Charleston, South Carolina. A close look at the circumstances of his experience opens up a larger examination of the complicated dynamics and contradictory impulses informing and driving a prominent local shipbuilding family's abolitionist activities.

As with any escape incident on the maritime Underground Railroad, knowing where to begin this story or who belongs at the center is a challenge. In my role as a public historian—director of exhibits at Mystic Seaport Museum—I have experimented with how best to introduce this narrative to a host of audiences, weaving the threads into different patterns to emphasize one aspect over another. I've tried different approaches with different groups: college students being graded on how they used this escape as the central "mystery" in their general education history course; summer museum-studies interns eager to build a project engaging the public at our site; and museum visitors peeking inside the large, green Georgian Revival house perched on the edge of the Mystic River.

Each time we investigate this 1858 escape, the same questions inevitably arise: What else can we discover about this fugitive? What light does his experience shed on other similar maritime escapes, either successful or failed? Ultimately, the largest question in my mind remains, how can my maritime museum responsibly interpret the local conditions and individual actions that contributed to drawing this fugitive to this region? And how can we, as museum professionals, splice together his well-documented story with that of a prominent, shipbuilding, civic-minded, Sabbath-day–keeping, abolitionist, white Mystic family that may (or may not) have sheltered maritime fugitives? The Greenman family's homes and church survive as part of the Mystic Seaport historic village; they stand as potential object lessons about the complex social and political local landscape within the larger U.S. Atlantic maritime world of the 1840s and 1850s. This episode provides an excellent example of how even ardent abolitionists in a New England port town were entangled in the economies of American

FIGURE 13. View of the George Greenman House and Row of Two Adjacent Greenman Family Homes along Greenmanville Avenue in Mystic, Connecticut, ca. 1885. These residences had access to the Mystic River banks and the Greenman shipyard directly behind. Photographic Collections, G. W. Blunt White Library, Mystic Seaport Museum, Connecticut.

slavery. At first glance, these two threads—of Benjamin Jones in New London and the Greenman family in Mystic—have very little in common. Yet, taken together, they point to a larger story, and a complicated one, with layers of complicity and contradiction, making a very human story about money, religion, the close connections between the North and South during the antebellum era, and demonstrating how the maritime world linked it all.

The only surviving sources about "Stowaway Joe" are newspaper notices of varying lengths, pithy sketches printed in disparate places, with often contradictory details. Word of his escape, capture, and release spread quickly in late September and early October 1858, through pro-abolitionist national papers such as William Lloyd Garrison's *The Liberator*, and local papers from Connecticut,

Massachusetts, and New York, down to the border state of Maryland, and as far south as Wilmington, North Carolina, and Charleston, South Carolina. All the papers were located either in coastal port cities or those with strong abolitionist activities, such as Worcester, Massachusetts, presumably reaching populations with vested interests in maritime escapes.

The accounts differ on some basic facts, most noticeably the fugitive's name: some call him "Joe," one identifies him as "Benjamin Tebo," others as "Benjamin Jones."[1] Most likely, he gave a false name to the ship captain and New London customs official, to avoid being identified and returned to Wilmington. Several other maritime fugitives also gave the last name of Smith or Jones when captured, a practice suggesting that creating a name was a common ploy either to assist with escape or to stake a claim for a new identity.[2] Despite the high probability that Jones was not his real name, I will refer to him from here on as Benjamin Jones, since that name appears in the longest and most accurate article, which was published months after he left New London County and had reached safety in another country.

Other details in the early newspaper articles are also incorrect. For example, customs records indicate that the schooner on which Jones hid himself was named *Eliza S. Potter*, not *Eliza*. Also, the vessel's intended destination was not New London on the Thames River but the town of Mystic on the next river east, some ten miles away. Later accounts corrected these mistakes. Other inconsistent details are more minor but illuminate the unreliability of the press at the time. Garrison's *Liberator* reprinted a New London newspaper's claim that Jones had a jug of water and a ham with him when he left Wilmington. A week later, the Worcester *Spy* claimed it was a couple of pounds of crackers and a piece of cheese.[3]

For twenty-first-century readers, the newspaper accounts are problematic primary sources in other ways, peppered as they are with colloquial sayings and thinly veiled but racially charged puns that can be easy to miss. For example, one refers to the African American fugitive deciding to "lie low and keep dark" when hidden onboard the vessel. It also mocks the speed at which he fled New London after his final release, comparing him to a racehorse "going at a 2.40 pace."

Oddly, even the reporting in antislavery newspapers often struck a jovial note, such as that found in the New London article reprinted in *The Liberator*. College students and interns are quick to find and list the range of terms describing the fugitive, unnamed in this account. Jones is referred to variously as "a fugitive slave," "fugacious chattel," "runaway," "colored gentleman," "the darkey," and, finally, again "the fugitive" upon his release from the New London Customs House. However, the students often miss the sly, dehumanizing humor in the mock-elevated description of the customs inspector "and his sable companion sitting very quietly and peaceably together in improving social converse [conversation]," as if they were taking tea and not embroiled in a crisis over Jones's personal liberty.[4] This article provides an opportunity in the classroom to analyze how antebellum abolitionist sentiment often walked hand in hand with the racist attitudes and humor so common in the day.

With so many articles but so few details or consistent elements, many questions remain about Benjamin Jones's maritime escape from Wilmington. It's worth examining what is known to see how his experience resembles and differs from that of other antebellum maritime escapes. In some cases, we can make credible assumptions based on other incidents.

There are conflicting accounts of where Jones started his journey to freedom. According to one paper, he belonged to an African American woman some two hundred miles upriver from Wilmington.[5] More likely, as the Charleston, South Carolina, paper reported, he was from "on the Sound"—presumably Middle Sound, approximately ten miles east of downtown Wilmington, where he boarded the schooner. Wilmington was notorious among southern slaveowners as a popular port for fugitives fleeing north. One called it "an asylum for Runaways," because it attracted so many fugitives to the ships trading with northern ports. They often found help from the large population of free and enslaved African Americans in maritime trades there.[6] Historian David Cecelski has revealed the patterns of maritime escapes out of Wilmington. Like the other maritime fugitives Cecelski traces, Jones probably had help along the way, possibly from sympathetic whites and, more likely from Black stevedores, ferrymen, fishmongers, or sailors. It's hard to conceive that he had no help finding a northbound schooner, getting aboard, then evading detection by the inspectors who fumigated each outbound vessel. Assuming he lived "on the Sound," he came from a maritime environment. Perhaps Jones was a waterman himself or had friends and relatives who were—relationships that increased his chances of leaving Wilmington undetected.

Benjamin Jones's gender and solo passage are consistent with larger patterns of escape. None of the articles mention his age but probably would have noted if he had been a boy or elderly. Clearly, he was limber enough to climb on board, maneuver in tight spaces, survive the week-long voyage, get ashore, and be walking around New London the next day. No accounts mention any physical impairments or difficulties. As historian Deborah Gray White has pointed out, statistics on runaways show that physically able men, traveling alone, were the most common runaways.[7] In a male-dominated maritime environment of wharves and cargo vessels, Jones had a better chance of blending in than a female fugitive or a group.

Newspaper accounts of solo stowaways like Jones are quite common in the 1850s. Of course, it is impossible to know how many seaborne fugitives evaded detection and never prompted public notice in the papers. But the frequent accounts about a captain's discovery of a runaway and decision to hand the him or her over to the federal authorities show the challenges of coastal trade between the North and South in this decade. Captains suspected of assisting fugitives were often levied with expensive fines, barred from trading in southern ports, and threatened with imprisonment or even hanging if they returned. According to the southern newspapers, Captain Potter of the *Eliza S. Potter* was aware of the risk to his reputation and trade when Benjamin Jones escaped from his schooner. He "or some of his friends" visited the New London newspaper offices and "begged that nothing would be said in the papers about it; that if such should happen his business would be ruined." He wanted the publisher to understand "that he had done all in his power to hold the negro until he could be returned to his lawful master; that he had the usual search certificate, etc."[8] The Wilmington newspaper editor wrote: "We are satisfied that the Captain acted honorably in the whole matter—that he did all in his power to return the negro—that he did not know he was on board until several days out. But the moment he found he was onboard, he should have put back and surrendered the negro to his master, or if he could not be found, to the authorities of Wilmington."[9]

Of course, captains—and stowaways—were at the mercy of wind and tide. If Potter discovered Jones six days after leaving Wilmington, as some articles claim, then returning directly to North Carolina would have added considerable hassle, expense, and time to his voyage. Some captains did return to the port of departure, or stopped in another southern port to turn the fugitive over to authorities. Perhaps Potter feared his reception back home in Connecticut if he did so. Six months later in May 1859, Boston-bound Captain John Orlando discovered fugitive Columbus Jones onboard and turned back his brig *Rolerson* several days into his voyage from Pensacola. After unsuccessfully attempting to land Columbus Jones in Key West and Norfolk, he continued on to Hyannis, where he and the brig's owners chartered a vessel for $500 to transport the fugitive to Norfolk. While he protected his ability to continue trading in Pensacola, Captain Orlando was soon arrested in Massachusetts for kidnapping, conspiracy, and violating the state's personal liberty law. The ordeal dragged out for seven months before he and his associates were acquitted.[10]

Captain Josephus Potter anchored the *Eliza S. Potter* off Noank (his hometown) at the mouth of the Mystic River and left the fugitive onboard with the crew. He traveled west across the town of Groton, taking a ferry or small boat across the Thames River to the New London federal customs house to arrange for the arrest of Benjamin Jones.

Jones did not sit patiently on the schooner while the captain fetched an official to arrest him. Was he rowed ashore by a sympathetic crewmember? Or, perhaps, despite the risk to his future trading in Wilmington, Captain Potter may have given Jones a chance to escape, telling him furtively as he left the schooner, "Don't be here when I return. If I see you again, I'll bring you in," or words to that effect. Maybe Jones jumped off the schooner and swam ashore. The water temperature in Noank in late September would be bearable, especially to a man in dire need and accustomed to swimming on the North Carolina shore. As Kevin Dawson has demonstrated, many antebellum southern Blacks were better swimmers than their white counterparts, thanks to the requirements of their work and to West African swimming, diving, and maritime traditions brought by their enslaved ancestors.[11]

Suddenly ashore in a strange land, Jones went in the same direction, if not the exact route, as Captain Potter—west to the city of New London, which had a sizeable Black population and, crucially, a direct train to Norwich, whence he could travel on to Worcester, Massachusetts, a documented Underground Railroad hub. No bridge spanned the Thames River.[12] So he must have taken a ferry or private boat to get from Groton to the city of New London, where Potter spotted him the next day in a clothing store.[13] As Andrew German has pointed out, the landing for the Groton ferry, the train station, and customs house were (and still are) all on the same street, only a few blocks from each other.[14] It's difficult to believe Jones didn't receive local help—help getting there from Noank, finding shelter for the night, and securing money to buy new clothes and a train ticket to push farther north. New London had a sizeable Black community at the time, along with white abolitionists among its prominent citizens, including Augustus Brandegee, a police-court judge who stormed the customs house with others demanding Jones's release. No record has been found regarding who assisted Jones or how.

Where did Benjamin Jones think he was going when he left Wilmington? In other words, where was the schooner delivering its cargo? Despite early reports that the *Eliza S. Potter* was destined for New London, later accounts agree it was headed for the shipyards on the Mystic River. In the six years prior, twenty-two vessels, all brigs or schooners, sailed into Mystic from southern ports. In order of frequency, they left from Wilmington, North Carolina (nine vessels), Darien, Georgia (nine), Jacksonville, Florida (two), and Georgetown, South Carolina (one), all ports that traded in southern pine sawn timber as well as marine supplies like tar, pitch, and turpentine. The busiest season was late spring and summer, with sixteen of the twenty-two vessels arriving between May and July. The year of Benjamin Jones's escape, only two schooners arrived—the *Eliza S. Potter* and the *Red Eagle*, both in October, both from Wilmington, North Carolina.[15] So, turning our attention to Mystic, apparently Jones's intended destination, historians can ask who might have been ready to help him or who may have sent word south disclosing that Mystic was ready to receive fugitives. The answer might lie with a prominent local shipbuilding family, the Greenmans of Mystic.

More than a century after Benjamin Jones's foiled attempt to reach Mystic by sea, another young man, a white teenager in tennis shoes and a t-shirt, mows the lawn for his grandmother's neighbor on Greenmanville Avenue, a few hundred feet from the Mystic River. The homeowner, Mary Greenman Davis, invites him into her kitchen for a glass of milk and a slice of apple pie, then tells him the story of her house's secret history as a stop on the Underground Railroad. She even shows him the secret compartment next to the fireplace where she says her ancestor George Greenman and his family sheltered runaway slaves.

It's an engaging story to today's audiences—whether college students, interns, or museum visitors. The teenaged boy, named William Peterson, is of our era (he currently lives in nearby North Stonington). We can easily imagine his open-eyed, slack-jawed reaction to the venerable Mrs. Davis's stories of escaped slaves sneaking off the lumber schooners berthed in her great-grandfather's shipyard and into the house. Certainly, starting the story there has been easiest for me, since I know and respect Bill Peterson as a colleague. Now curator emeritus of Mystic Seaport Museum, he published the seminal work about Mystic shipbuilding and did much of the primary research about the Greenmans and their religious and social activities. The George Greenman house still stands on the museum campus, complete with the hidden compartment that Mrs. Davis spoke about, nearly six decades ago. So, I also have a physical structure around which to build my museum narrative—an ever-present visual reminder of the story, built into my daily landscape.

When I give tours of the George Greenman house, people are riveted by this Underground Railroad story and how it links our age to the Civil Rights era of the 1960s, to the 1850s build-up to the Civil War, and even to the schooner *Amistad* incident of 1839, the same year the house was built. It's reassuring to think of this structure standing solid even as legal, social, and cultural winds whirled around it. In exploring how to re-interpret this house for visitors, Mystic Seaport museum staff have considered leaving the mid-twentieth-century kitchen intact and unaltered as a stepping-stone to the 1960s story. A glass of ersatz milk and a piece of half-eaten pie could be placed on the built-in breakfast nook table. Visitors could sit down after a day of walking the grounds and hear Mrs. Davis's voice telling her story of a maritime Underground Railroad escape and the role her ancestors played in that very house. This scenario feels honest and authentic. The problem is that it may not be true.

That numerous fugitives from slavery escaped the South by sea and came ashore in Connecticut ports there is no doubt. We have, for example, the story of freedom seeker James Lindsey Smith recounted in his published autobiography. He came to Connecticut in 1838 by steamboat from New York, after using various waterborne means to escape from his master in tidewater Virginia, via the Chesapeake Bay, in the company of an enslaved sailor named Zip.[16] Historian Nancy Finlay observes about his ordeal:

> For Smith, as for many passengers on the Underground Railroad, Connecticut was both a way station and a terminus. Connecticut abolitionists helped Smith to make good his escape; Connecticut was his ultimate destination and became his home. During the 1830s, '40s, and '50s, many other fugitives arrived by ship as he did, landing in Hartford, New Haven, Norwich, and other towns along Long Island Sound and the Connecticut River.[17]

However, as historian David Blight and others have reminded us, the stories white New Englanders have told about their Underground Railroad houses are often more about themselves than about actual fugitives, revealing a desire to claim ancestors who were on the right side of history during the age of abolition.[18] It may not be coincidental that Mrs. Davis boasted about her abolitionist ancestors during the height of the Civil Rights era. It's likely that she believed the story was factual, having heard it as a girl, recounted by her parents or grandparents as family lore. But can this compelling, beguiling tale be confirmed?

The physical evidence in the Greenman house conjures its own puzzles: access to the hidden "fugitives' compartment" is through a cupboard that slides back into the cavity, which is today lined with shelves. No architectural historian yet has been able to date when this cryptic space was built or the clever mechanism controlling the concealed cupboard door's movement. Jones or any other fugitive would have had to crouch to avoid being crushed by the cupboard as it slid back, then somehow squeeze back and around the lower panel as it swung inwards—not a very practical design. More than one person has wondered whether this wasn't more likely a storage cabinet for the family silver or even a Prohibition-era addition—a secret liquor cabinet. After all, each age has its own secrets to hide from the federal government. Perhaps the abolitionist, temperance-minded first generation of the Mystic Greenmans were succeeded by descendants who also bent the rules but this time in their drinking habits.

In addition, there appears to be no documentary evidence of fugitives passing up the Mystic River to freedom, except for Benjamin Jones, who didn't even make it that far. The Greenman family's personal papers do not seem to have survived among its business records and church meeting minutes. Their name is not linked with any fugitive accounts. Yet, a closer look at their business, religious, and abolitionist activities reveals the many contradictory forces that tied them to the system of slavery that Benjamin Jones sought to escape.

It was the broad interconnected maritime culture of coastal port communities that provided the sea links of northern to southern harbors, thus creating the conditions that allowed safe havens for shipping to be conduits for seaborne refugees, as well. Yet, each port had its own distinctive characteristics and conditions, making it more or less likely to receive or even welcome saltwater fugitives. Mystic is an excellent example of that. Southeastern Connecticut was not a place guaranteed to provide a warm welcome to fugitives. Gradual emancipation began in the 1790s, but more than a dozen enslaved people were still residents when the state finally abolished slavery in 1848. The *Amistad* incident of 1839 had increased support for the abolitionist cause in the region. But as late as 1859, the *Mystic Pioneer* noted that an antislavery speech by traveling abolitionist speaker Miss Sallie Holly attracted three hundred people, claiming it a good sign that local residents were "now willing to hear what can be said in favor of a cause which has been so unpopular." Still, the editor doubted that "the majority of people here are ready to adopt and carry into practice" the "unpopular doctrines" she espoused.[19]

The three Greenman brothers—George, Clark, and Thomas—stood out from the local crowd in many ways. Prominent and prolific shipbuilders, they constructed nearly one hundred vessels, ranging from sloops to steam vessels and from barges to brigs, clipper ships, and even a yacht, between 1837 and 1878.[20] They were also devout Seventh Day Baptists, attending services on Saturday and refusing to conduct any business—even take delivery of a schooner-load of needed lumber—on that day. And they were vocal about their beliefs in temperance and the abolition of slavery.

Mystic, Connecticut, might appear geographically removed from the centers of slavery or the corridors of Congress, but the port town was in fact closely linked to them through its multiple maritime endeavors—shipbuilding, shipping, whaling—as well as the new railroad that frequently brought abolitionists and other reformers to local halls and churches for speaking engagements. In 1856, Greenmanville minister S. S. Griswold bragged in *The Liberator* that the town had hosted seven different prominent antislavery speakers (including Lucy Stone and William Wells Brown) in the past five years. "It may be encouraging to know that there is one spot in Connecticut where abolition has a foothold," he wrote to "Friend Garrison."[21]

The Greenmans, Reverend Griswold, and a few neighbors and religious brethren voiced their discontent with slavery explicitly, repeatedly, and loudly. Although younger brothers Clark and Thomas Greenman made several voyages to South America in the 1830s as journeymen shipwrights, there is no evidence they ever witnessed slavery—in the United States or abroad—in person. But fellow Sabbatarian William Ellery Maxson did. In January 1846, having signed on as carpenter for the newly launched, Greenman-built vessel *Niagara*, Maxson went ashore in Norfolk, Virginia, when the ship stopped to repair a major leak. That Sabbath day, he stumbled across a slave auction where a young person was sold for $340, recording his horror in a diary entry: "This scene is the first I ever saw stired [*sic*] up my indignation to a high pitch. I discard the country that boast of light and liberty and the[n] tolerate the system of slavery in all its worst forms. It is a curse to our country."[22] Maxson returned home to Mystic with this memory burned into his consciousness and, no doubt, spoke about it to friends, neighbors, and fellow church members. Four years later, the Greenmans and thirty other families joined together to found the Greenmanville Seventh Day Baptist Church, announcing in the national church newspaper, *The Sabbath Recorder*, "By its constitution it holds no fellowship with slavery, with the traffic in or use of intoxicating drinks, or with Secret Societies."[23]

Maxson and the Greenmans spoke out publicly against the evils of slavery. In 1852, the Greenmanville church held a special Fourth of July meeting. Clark and Thomas Greenman spoke to the assembled crowd, while Maxson served as moderator. The meeting's final resolution condemned the Fugitive Slave Law of

1850 as "violating of the Declaration of Independence, the rights of humanity, and the principles of the gospel" and disavowed support for either Whig or Democratic presidential nominees.[24]

Throughout the 1850s, the Greenman brothers spent both time and maritime-derived profits on abolitionist activities. They hosted abolitionist speakers on tour, donated to antislavery societies, and supported groups that assisted fugitives after their escapes. The family account book includes an 1860 entry of a three-dollar donation to the Canadian Fugitive Mission, presumably one of the several organizations established to assist American-born fugitives beginning new lives across the border. At the end of the Civil War, George Greenman was among the Mystic residents who gave a total of fifty-eight dollars to speaker Reverend J. Root Miller, in support of the American Colonization Society.[25] For men who took their many civic, family, and business responsibilities so seriously, their continued commitment of energy, effort, and funds was noteworthy.

The George Greenman family also hosted abolitionist-feminist Lucy Stone in their home on her whistle-stop tour to Mystic in 1852. Stone probably used Greenman towels to dry off after speaking in one local Baptist church on a warm evening when an unnamed opponent shot her in the face with a water pistol. "Such are the arguments our opponents offer," she calmly declared and continued her speech.[26] Fellow abolitionist Lewis Ford also recorded the water-pistol incident, along with noting in a *Liberator* notice about the 1852 trip: "The meeting was also addressed by the Rev. Charles Milner, Rev. Mr. Griswold, Clarke [*sic*] Greenman, and Ann Watrous, all manifesting a decided opposition to the system of slavery."[27]

Greenman efforts extended to defending abolitionists in trouble. Thomas Greenman was one of three church elders to serve on the Eastern Committee working for the release of Pardon Davis, who was imprisoned in a New Orleans jail for aiding a fugitive slave. Their argument was that his incarceration was an unconstitutional infringement of his right to freely practice his religion because he was not allowed to observe the Sabbath on Saturday.[28]

Yet, as historians and journalists have revealed, Connecticut shipbuilders, mariners, and manufacturers such as the Greenman brothers were, through their extended business interests, economically dependent upon U.S. slavery up to the Civil War—though this fundamental link was often obscured by physical distance and superficially innocuous trade exchanges.[29]

From the colonial era through the antebellum years, Connecticut residents reaped profits from slave-linked trade in the maritime sector, as well as in agriculture and industry. In 1770, Connecticut sent a far greater tonnage of commercial shipping outbound to the slave-dependent West Indies (9,923) than to Great Britain (426) or Southern Europe (180), and almost as much as along and down the entire Atlantic Coast (9,734). Incoming cargoes of mostly slave-produced goods from the West Indies to the Connecticut colony totaled 8,656 tons, again second only to that arriving via the coastal trade. In 1772, those West Indies imports to Connecticut consisted primarily of rum, molasses, sugar, and cocoa.[30] Over the next few decades, Connecticut ships brought Connecticut-raised cattle to the Caribbean for enslaved people's food. When the Continental Army needed provisioners who had expertise with moving large numbers of livestock, they turned to Connecticut shippers.[31]

This economic entanglement with slavery had shifted by the 1850s, yet the Greenman brothers were deeply dependent on maritime trade with southern U.S. ports for slave-harvested raw materials. Their twelve-acre shipyard relied on southern lumber, turpentine, and pitch to build their many vessels. Lumber schooners came directly to their yard on the Mystic River behind their homes. Their reliance on slave-produced goods didn't end when the Greenmans removed their muddy boots at their backdoors, for their households purchased sugar, cotton goods, rice, and molasses for domestic consumption.[32]

Their economic investment went even deeper. During the 1840s and 1850s many of the vessels that the Greenman yard built—some of which also counted the Greenmans as investors—were engaged in the "Southern trade," carrying slave-grown cotton out of the South. As of 1847, these vessels included *Pilgrim, Niagara, Rose Standish,* and the newly launched *Ocilla.*[33] In *Mystic-Built*, his authoritative study of Mystic shipyards and their trade, William Peterson (the same teenage kid who mowed the lawn on the George Greenman house) documents twenty barks, brigs, and schooners built in the Greenman brothers yard that followed the "Southern trade" in the two decades before the Civil War. Many ran between Key West and New York, a common route for Mystic-built vessels. Others were in the coasting trade between New Orleans and Apalachicola, or Mobile, Alabama, and St. Marks, Florida, a few extending that link up to New York or Newport. One vessel, the bark *William Rathbone*, built in 1849, "operated in the cotton trade to Liverpool and New York in the 1850s and early 1860s."[34]

In some cases, the Greenman family continued to profit from the southern trade years after the vessels were built, launched, and carrying cotton, lumber, and other slave-produced materials. Of the Greenmans' $9,087.31 in ship-investment income recorded in 1860, ledgers reveal that $2,281.25 came from five vessels identified as either built for or actively engaged in the southern trade. They were launched as early as 1848 and as late as 1859.[35] These maritime profits paradoxically provided the funds for the Greenman family's abolitionist endeavors.

In at least one case, a Greenman-built vessel even became engaged in the illegal slave trade, albeit after the family was no longer financially invested in it. In 1862, the U.S. consul in Havana reported that the Mystic-based vessel *Ocilla* had just left Cuba on a voyage to bring enslaved Africans to Cuba in violation of U.S. and international laws. Later that year, he reported that *Ocilla* had successfully returned to Cuba—with human cargo. There is no record of the abolitionist Greenman brothers' reaction to the news that a vessel built by them had been used as a slave ship.[36]

Clearly, in the decade following the Fugitive Slave Law, even as the Greenmans and their religious brethren were speaking out publicly against slavery, hosting abolitionist speakers, and donating money to antislavery causes, they continued to make money off the unpaid, forced labor of enslaved African Americans. My intention is not to condemn them as hypocrites or unusually mercenary capitalists but rather to point out just how complex and all-entangling the slave economy was at the time. The maritime world in which the Greenmans were enmeshed before the Civil War makes visible the very real and human forces implicit in nineteenth-century slavery—powerful currents and violent tides that threatened to drown the entire nation. Only a very few people in antebellum America remained untouched by the slave economy. Those few did not include New England shipbuilders.

Still, taken together, the various known threads—economic, familial, geographic, religious, political—that reveal Greenman family sentiments suggest that, if Benjamin Jones (or any other fugitive) had presented himself on their property, the Greenmans would have answered the call of conscience by giving him or her assistance. There is of course a fair chance that Jones was headed to Greenmanville but not to the Greenmans. Just as likely, he expected help from their minister, Reverend S. S. Griswold, who preached, wrote, and acted tirelessly against slavery. And Jones almost certainly would have received his aid, considering Griswold's attitude toward racial equality, so unusual for its day. Boasting about his congregation's welcoming stance, the minister claimed that there was "in Greenmanville no distinction as it respects color" and that "in our families, and in our congregation, the spirit of caste cannot enter." When a fellow Sabbatarian from Virginia asked how Griswold would react if his daughter married a Black man, Griswold replied that "he would sit at the same table with us, sleep in as good a bed, have free access to our parlors, be admitted to all of our social circles, and sit in the same slip at meeting with the minister's family, or with other families."[37]

There is evidence to suggest that Griswold's bombastic statement was grounded in truth. In 1891, George Greenman's obituary stated that he "loved liberty and hated oppression. In his home, and at his board, every man, Black or white, was his equal."[38] There is no record of the Greenmans' employment of any African American workers at their shipyard, farm, or other business. But at home, a different story emerges. Even as Benjamin Jones sat on the schooner *Eliza S. Potter* at anchor in Noank, just a mile or so upriver, a young Black woman named Sarah Mundy from New Jersey was living with the Thomas Greenman family as a domestic worker. She had been a member of the Greenmanville Seventh Day Baptist Church for five years. Her younger sister, Elizabeth, age thirteen, lived next door with the Clark Greenman family and attended the local school. Both sisters were still living with the Greenmans a decade later when the next census-taker came by, suggesting the sisters had become fixtures in the households and community. Perhaps the Mundys were the real Underground Railroad activists, more so than the Greenmans.

Historians Larry Gara and David Blight have pointed out that a focus on white abolitionists ignores the fact that northern Blacks played a major and perhaps the biggest role in physically assisting southern fugitives to freedom.[39] Port cities with sizable free Black communities, such as Philadelphia, New York, Boston, and New Bedford, had well-organized networks through religious, neighborhood, and kinship connections. William Still in Philadelphia recorded the stories of dozens of fugitives he assisted as chairman of the Vigilance Committee of the Pennsylvania Anti-Slavery Society, a group that crossed racial barriers.[40] The Johnsons in New Bedford assisted, housed, and arranged transportation for fugitives wishing to continue onward or found jobs and housing for those who, like Frederick Douglass, wanted to settle there.

Key components for African American northerners' participation in the maritime Underground Railroad—religious and social organizations—were present just across the state border from Mystic. Elizabeth Buffum Chace, a stationmaster on the Underground Railroad in nearby Valley Falls, Rhode Island, wrote in her 1891 memoir how fugitives usually arrived there: "Slaves in Virginia would secure passage, either secretly or with consent of the captains, in small trading vessels at Norfolk or Portsmouth, and thus be brought into some port in New England, where their fate depended on the circumstances into which they happened to fall."[41]By the 1850s, that state had nine Black churches:

five in Providence; two in Narragansett; and one each in Wakefield and Morresfield. There were also several Black improvement societies, including a Female Literary Society and Female Tract Society.[42]

This strong community stood ready to defend its members and to assist strangers on the run. Six days after the passage of the 1850 Fugitive Slave Act, the free Black community in Rhode Island voted to "sacrifice our lives and our all upon the altar of protection to our wives, our children, and our fellow sufferers in commons with us." Black Newport residents created a group to "be on the lookout, both for the panting fugitive and also for the oppressor when he shall make his approach."[43]

A Providence newspaper reported hundreds of fugitive slaves were living in Newport among the free-born Black community there. No doubt many had arrived by sea. For some freedom seekers, Newport was a first stop on a longer northward journey; for others, it was the final destination after working their way from other northern ports. It should be no surprise that several documented stops on the Rhode Island Underground Railroad were houses of Black residents such as Isaac Rice or Black organizations such as the Bethel American Methodist Episcopal Church.[44]

The situation in Mystic was far different. There has never been a Black community in Mystic sizeable enough to support a Black church or social organization. None of the shipyards, the Greenmans' facility included, employed any Black workers. The 1860 census lists Sarah Mundy as the sole Black domestic worker among prominent Mystic families—the others employed Irish or English-born domestics.[45] Still, one wonders whether it was some combination of the two sisters, the reverend, and the shipbuilding brothers who sent word to Wilmington that they were ready to welcome maritime fugitives.

Regardless of whether the residents of Greenmanville ever knew that Benjamin Jones was headed their way, they surely found his story familiar from an article about an earlier, remarkably similar maritime escape in their church newspaper, the *Sabbath Recorder*.

The 1856 account is worth quoting in full, because of the many parallels and because of its straightforward tone, which contrasted to the later newspaper coverage of Benjamin Jones's escape. The author reported:

> Slave case in Boston.—Joseph Williams, a slave in Mobile [Alabama], escaped in the brig *Growler*, which arrived at Boston, July 16. The captain, on entering the harbor, attempted to secure him, for the purpose of taking him back, but Williams jumped overboard and was picked up by a boat, and the Vigilance Committee being immediately notified, a writ of habeas corpus was issued. The slave was

> brought before Judge Metcalf, of the Supreme Court, on the writ of habeas corpus and on one appearing as claimant against him, he was told to go free. An outburst of applause greeted this order, which the officers and Court in vain tried to check. Meantime, the colored man was seized by his friends and hurried out of the Court-room. He was taken to the house of a colored citizen, and hence put on board the first train of cars for Canada.[46]

Here are the common elements of an 1850s maritime escape along the Eastern Seaboard. A single man stows away on a coastal vessel. The fugitive escapes twice—first from the south and then from the captain, who, willingly or not, acts as a slave-catcher. The fugitive reaches land, then successfully disappears from the port city, or, in the case of Benjamin Jones and this Joseph Williams, winds up in a federal court. News spreads quickly as supporters obtain a legal writ, confront the court official, then help the fugitive to finally escape.

Today, only a few pieces of material evidence remain of the Greenmans, Benjamin Jones, and their maritime connection. For the Greenmans, these include a silver-plate coffee pot and sugar bowl that date to the 1850s and belonged to George and Abigail Greenman—and speaks to their domestic consumption of slave-produced foods. A desk and some half-hull ship models represent the Greenman brothers' maritime economic activities. A family Bible lists the names and life dates of several Greenman generations. The headstones for Elizabeth and Sarah Mundy lie inside the Greenman plot in the Elm Cemetery upriver from the houses where they lived, worked, and died. A stained and chipped China chamber pot attests to the types of domestic duties that the Mundy sisters would have performed during their years as domestic servants. The houses of all three Greenman brothers still stand, their backs lining the Mystic River.

The only visible evidence of Benjamin Jones's escape through the area is not in Mystic but New London. Screwed tightly to the front of the former U.S. Customs House, a bronze plaque was installed by the local newspaper in 1991 "to celebrate the blessings of freedom." The headline shouts in all-caps, "DO YOU WANT TO BE SLAVE OR FREE?"—supposedly quoting Customs Collector Mather, the U.S. official who detained "Joe" (Benjamin Jones) briefly before allowing the fugitive to depart. Few passersby notice the New London plaque; even fewer know the story behind it.

Together, the stories of Benjamin Jones and the Greenman family reveal how money, politics, religion, race, and memory swirl through the larger saltwater fugitive story. Their experiences are representative of so many maritime Underground Railroad accounts, where fugitives covered long distances relatively swiftly and secretly, leaving no tracks on the water. Benjamin Jones seemed fated never to meet the Greenmans, yet the circumstances they helped to create in Mystic meant that, had he arrived there as planned, they were ready for him.

NOTES

I am greatly indebted to numerous past and present Mystic Seaport Museum interns, volunteers, and staff, especially William Peterson, Andrew German, and Paul O'Pecko, for their foundational research and thinking about the Greenman family, their shipbuilding and social reform work, and this escape; and to the Connecticut Humanities Council and National Endowment for the Humanities for supporting the Greenmanville project.

1. "News of the Day," *New York Times*, 4 October 1858; "The Wilmington Fugitive," *Charleston (S.C.) Courier*, 11 October 1858; "The End of a Fugitive Slave Case," *New London (Conn.) Daily Chronicle*, 9 February 1859.
2. The most famous example is the case of Orlando Jones described below.
3. "A Fugitive Slave in New London," *Boston Liberator*, 8 October 1858, 163; "Fugitive Slave Case in New London," *Worcester* (Mass.) *Spy*, 13 October 1858.
4. "A Fugitive Slave in New London," *Boston Liberator*, 8 October 1858, 163.
5. Andrew German, "The Wilmington Fugitive: A Perspective on the Underground Railroad" (unpublished report, Mystic Seaport Museum, Connecticut, January 2007).
6. As quoted in John Michael Vlach, "Above Ground on the Underground Railroad: Places of Flight and Refuge," in *Passages to Freedom: The Underground Railroad in History and Memory*, ed. David W. Blight (New York: Harper Collins/Smithsonian Books, 2004), 104.
7. Deborah Gray White, "Simple Truths: Antebellum Slavery in Black and White," in ibid., 60–61.
8. "The Wilmington Fugitive," *Charleston (S.C.) Courier*, 11 October 1858.
9. *Wilmington (N.C.) Herald*, as quoted in ibid.
10. "A Fugitive Slave Returned to Florida," *Charleston (S.C.) Mercury*, 18 May 1859, 1:7; "The Fugitive Slave Case," *Augusta (Ga.) Daily Chronicle & Sentinel*, 22 November 1859, 2; "Hyannis Kidnapping Case," *Boston Liberator*, 16 September 1859, 147.
11. Kevin Dawson, "Enslaved Swimmers and Divers in the Atlantic World," *Journal of American History* 92, no. 4 (March 2006): 1327–55.
12. In 1858, passengers could take a train from Worcester through Norwich to New London, then catch a direct steamboat to New York. See Don Chamberlayne, "Railroads of Worcester: From Court House to Round House" (unpublished manuscript, 2015), 13, accessed 14 August 2020, http://www.worcesterthen.com.
13. "The End of a Fugitive Slave Case," *New London (Conn.) Daily Chronicle*, 9 February 1859.

14. Andrew German, private correspondence with the author, 12 August 2020.
15. Andrew German, "Vessels Arriving in Mystic from Southern Ports in the 1850s," unpublished list, compiled from William Peterson's database of newspaper references to Mystic-related vessels, December 2006. A copy is held in Greenmanville project files, Mystic Seaport Museum, Connecticut.
16. James Lindsay Smith, *Autobiography of James L. Smith, Including, Also, Reminiscences of Slave Life, Recollections of the War, Education of Freedmen, Causes of the Exodus, etc.* (Norwich, Conn.: Press of The Bulletin Company, 1881), 36–53.
17. Nancy Finlay quoted in "James Lindsey Smith Takes the Underground Railroad to Connecticut," Connecticut History.Org,, accessed 14 August 2020, https://connecticuthistory.org/james-lindsey-smith-takes-the-underground-railroad-to-connecticut/. See also Horatio T. Strother, *The Underground Railroad in Connecticut* (Middletown, Connecticut: Wesleyan University Press, 1962), 107–18, 128–36.
18. David W. Blight, "Why the Underground Railroad, and Why Now? A Long View," in *Passages to Freedom,* 3–5, 239.
19. "Miss Holly's Lecture," *Mystic (Conn.) Pioneer*, 23 April 1859.
20. William N. Peterson, *"Mystic Built": Ships and Shipyards of the Mystic River, Connecticut, 1784–1919* (Mystic, Conn.: Mystic Seaport Museum, 1989), 41.
21. Reverend S. S. Griswold, "The Valley of the Mystic," *Boston Liberator*, 11 April 1856.
22. William Ellery Maxson, 31 January 1846, Journal diary kept on ship Niagara, Log 863, William Ellery Maxson Diaries, Manuscripts Collection, G. W. Blunt White Library, Mystic Seaport Museum, Connecticut.
23. *New York Sabbath Recorder*, 17 April 1851, 174.
24. Ibid., 29 July 1852.
25. "Receipts of the American Colonization Society," *African Repository* 41, no. 8 (August 1865): 255.
26. George H. Greenman, unpublished reminiscence, dated 1921, VFM 857, Manuscripts Collection, G.W. Blunt White Library, Mystic Seaport Museum, Connecticut.
27. Lewis Ford, "Labors in Connecticut," *Boston Liberator*, 26 March 1852.
28. "Minutes of the Eastern Association," *New York Sabbath Recorder*, 31 May 1855, 202, cited in Don A. Sanford, "Pardon Davis: A Prisoner in Louisiana," Underground Railroad of Wisconsin Network to Freedom, accessed 19 May 2011, www.wlhn.org/wnf/stories/pardondavis.htm (site discontinued). Copy of article in possession of the author.
29. Anne Farrow, Joel Lang, and Jennifer Frank, *Complicity: How the North Promoted, Prolonged, and Profited from Slavery* (New York: Ballantine Books, 2006), xviii.
30. Robert G. Albion, William A. Baker, and Benjamin W. Labaree, *New England and the Sea,* rev. ed. (Mystic, Conn.: Mystic Seaport Museum, 1994), 38.
31. Brenda Milkofsky, "Connecticut and the West Indies: Sugar Spurs Trans-Atlantic

Trade," 7 January 2016, Connecticut History.Org, accessed 14 August 2020, https://connecticuthistory.org/connecticut-and-the-west-indies-trade.

32. Greenmanville General Store, George Greenman & Co., Records, 1836–1904, Misc. Vols. 236–276, Manuscripts Collection, G. W. Blunt White Library, Mystic Seaport Museum, Connecticut.
33. *New London (Conn.) Morning News*, 20 September 1847.
34. Peterson, "*Mystic Built*," 244.
35. Financial ledger for 1860, George Greenman & Co., misc. vol. 239, Blunt White Library; Peterson, "*Mystic Built*," 168, 206, 227, 233, 244.
36. Farrow, Lang, and Frank, *Complicity*, 132.
37. "Slavery-Again," *New York Sabbath Recorder*, 21 October 1856, 66.
38. Obituary of George Greenman, *New York Sabbath Recorder*, 22 October 1891.
39. Larry Gara, *The Liberty Line: The Legend of the Underground Railroad* (Lexington: University of Kentucky Press, 1967), 18; David Blight, "Why the Underground Railroad, and Why Now?" 243.
40. Vlach, "Above Ground on the Underground Railroad," 103.
41. Elizabeth Buffum Chace, *Anti-Slavery Reminiscences* (Central Falls, R.I.: E. L. Freeman & Son, State Printers, 1891), 27.
42. Christy Clark-Pujara, *Dark Work: The Business of Slavery in Rhode Island* (New York: New York University Press, 2016), 130.
43. Quoted in Ibid., 137.
44. Ibid.; Clark-Pujara, *Dark Work*, 197.
45. Sandra Oliver, "The Greenmans of Greenmanville" (unpublished paper, prepared for a course at Clark University, 1977), 52. Copy in Mystic Seaport Museum files, Connecticut.
46. "Slave Case in Boston," *New York Sabbath Recorder*, 24 July 1856, 27.

8

SEABORNE FUGITIVES FROM SLAVERY AND THE PORTS OF EASTERN MASSACHUSETTS

KATHRYN GROVER

> Let us be bold, if any man flies from slavery, and comes among us. When he's reached us, we'll say, he's gone far enough. If any man comes here to New Bedford, and they try to take him away, you telegraph to us in Boston, and we'll come down three hundred strong, and stay with you; and we won't go until he's safe. If he goes back to the South, we'll go with him. And if any man runs away, and comes to Boston, we'll send to you, if necessary, and you may come up to us three hundred strong, if you can—come men, and women, too.
>
> —Robert Morris, reported in *The Liberator*, 13 August 1858

In late November 1874, the veteran African American abolitionist William P. Powell stood up before the people assembled at San Francisco's Zion African Methodist Church to eulogize Lewis Berry (1805–1874), whom he had known for more than forty years. Powell, who began his career as a blacksmith but by the early 1830s was running a mariners' "temperance" boarding house in New Bedford, had known him since 1832, during Berry's early years on Nantucket. Berry had come to the island with his brother, Wesley, from New Jersey, where a provision in the state's 1804 gradual manumission law made it possible to hold formerly enslaved people in long-term indentures. In 1830, more than two-thirds of the 3,568 African Americans still enslaved in the North were living in New Jersey, and in 1865 a census found eighteen people of color were "apprentices for life" in that state. Neither Lewis Berry nor his brother ever claimed any place other than New Jersey as their place of birth, and whether they were enslaved, apprenticed, or free when they left New Jersey "to engage in whaling" at Nantucket is so far unknown.[1]

In his eulogy, William Powell was interested in recounting not Berry's origins but his work in fugitive assistance:

> He was one of the pioneers in the great anti slavery war under the leadership of that consistent, uncompromising advocate, Wm. Lloyd Garrison. He was associated with such stern, patriotic men as Capt. Absalom Boston, Capt. Edward J. Pompey, Messrs Godfrey, Harris, Young and Borden of Nantucket; and Capt. Richard Johnson, Nathan Johnson, Norris Anderson, Cuffee Lawton, and John Briggs of New Bedford. Men, who were inspired with the spirit that "right is of no sect, truth is of no color, God is the father of us all, and we are all brethren." New Bedford, Nantucket, Boston; near the State of Maine were the eastern termini of that celebrated mysterious underground railroad. Brother Berry and the above-named men, together with myself, and a host of the good and true were stockholders, Managers and Conductors who controlled the road running from the extreme south, and delivered the fugitive passengers with safety, security and dispatch to the land of freedom.[2]

Powell's statement linking New Bedford, Nantucket, and Boston in a general system of fugitive assistance is unusual; no other assertion of cooperation between the ports in fugitive assistance is known to exist. All the men Powell mentioned, including himself, became active before organized fugitive assistance in the form of "vigilance committees" arose in the 1830s and 1840s, and most of them continued to operate largely outside its sphere. Far-flung and diverse connections existed throughout the Atlantic coastal states, and though these individuals and organizations fell far short of forming a centralized "Underground Railroad" operation, they may be understood as an extensive series of largely unconnected networks covering regions of varying extents and linked internally by sociopolitical sentiments, kinship, friendship, and religious affiliation. However, the Underground Railroad did not operate entirely, or perhaps even mostly, in this way. Given the vast number of escapes that either happened outside their purview or are largely or wholly undocumented, it is possible that most occurred outside the knowledge and grasp of these networks, however formally or informally organized.[3]

The existence of commercial maritime connections initially unrelated to the movement of fugitives from slavery helps explain why Boston and New Bedford became Underground Railroad entrepots and other Massachusetts ports did not. To a great extent, fugitive traffic to Massachusetts paralleled the main

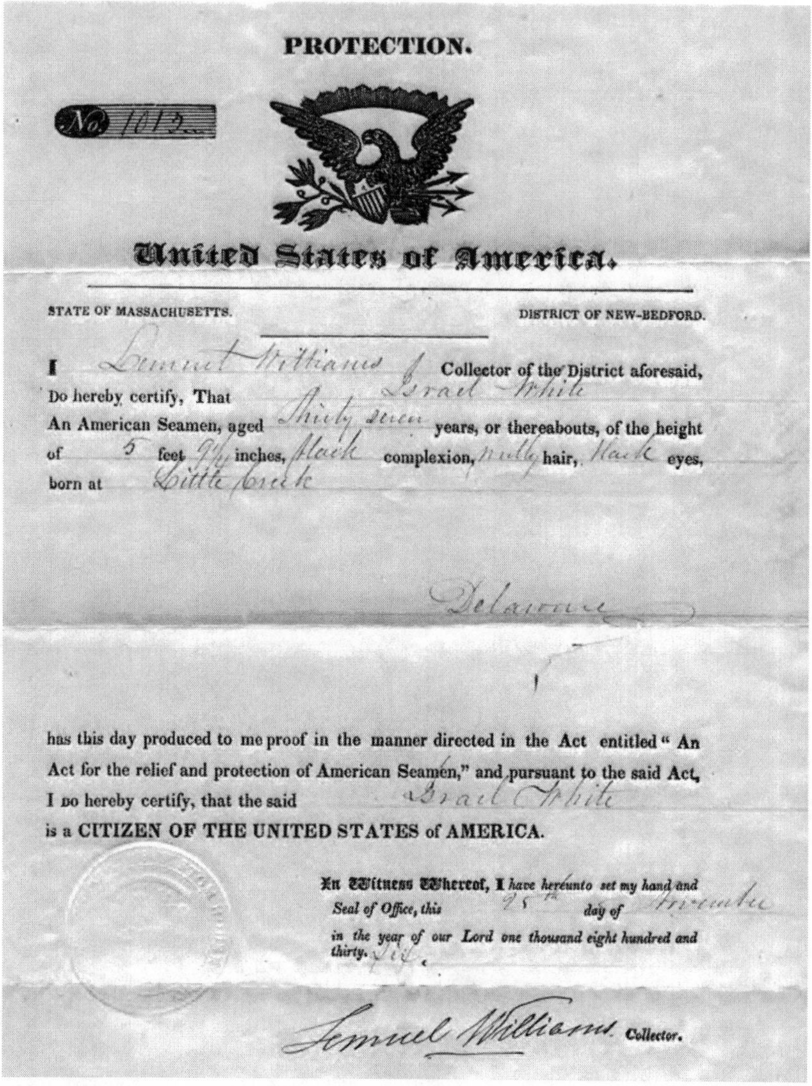

PROTECTION.

No. 1012

United States of America.

STATE OF MASSACHUSETTS. DISTRICT OF NEW-BEDFORD.

I Lemuel Williams Collector of the District aforesaid, Do hereby certify, That Israel White An American Seamen, aged Thirty seven years, or thereabouts, of the height of 5 feet 9¼ inches, black complexion, woolly hair, black eyes, born at Little Creek

Delaware

has this day produced to me proof in the manner directed in the Act entitled "An Act for the relief and protection of American Seamen," and pursuant to the said Act, I do hereby certify, that the said Israel White is a CITIZEN OF THE UNITED STATES of AMERICA.

In Witness Whereof, I have hereunto set my hand and Seal of Office, this 25th *day of* November *in the year of our Lord one thousand eight hundred and thirty.* Six.

Lemuel Williams. Collector.

FIGURE 14. Seaman's Protection Paper for Israel White, an African American mariner, stating his birthplace as Little Creek, Delaware, ca. 1799. The document was issued at New Bedford, Massachusetts, Port District, by Collector Lemuel Williams, District Customs House, on 25 November 1836. Document, KWM Loose Manuscripts, New Bedford Whaling Museum, Massachusetts.

patterns of maritime commerce, but it focused more narrowly on those ports that offered relatively large African American populations, an interracial group of abolitionists, and opportunity for work. Both Boston and New Bedford carried on substantial business through southern ports. More than a thousand packets ran on a regular schedule between Boston and New York, Albany, Philadelphia, Baltimore, Norfolk, Charleston, Savannah, Mobile, and New Orleans between 1820 and 1860. New Bedford vessels had been carrying candles, whale oils, and manufactured goods to southern ports virtually since the town was settled in the 1760s, and by 1834 it ranked behind only New York, Boston, and Philadelphia in the total tonnage of vessels registered and licensed in its district. In 1845 it was still the fourth-largest tonnage district in the country behind New York, Boston, and New Orleans. New Bedford's total tonnage increased from 64,049 in 1834 to 233,262 in 1845, a spectacular rate of growth that principally reflects the robust growth of the whaling industry but also concomitant growth in the trade carrying whale and other products across the ocean and along the Eastern Seaboard.[4]

When slavery existed in the North and South, both enslaved and free people of color were drawn to maritime work on deck and on shore because it was among the few spheres of the economy that was relatively open to employing them. As historian Jeffrey Bolster has put it, people "ran *to* the relatively anonymous wharves and ships of the eighteenth-century Atlantic world" to escape enslavement. Throughout much of the eighteenth century, northern newspapers routinely warned vessel masters not to take fugitives on board, yet the practice nonetheless continued.[5] Of eighteenth-century maritime fugitives, Crispus Attucks is the best known. Born about 1723 and enslaved by William Brown of Framingham, Massachusetts, Attucks ran away in 1750. Documents record him serving in the crew of a Nantucket whaling vessel then in port at Boston when he became the first casualty of the Boston Massacre on 5 March 1770.[6] Venture Smith, born about 1729 in Africa and brought to Rhode Island aboard a slaving vessel when he was six years old, made at least one whaling voyage during his enslavement to Oliver Smith of Stonington, Connecticut.[7]

African American populations in Massachusetts rose and fell on the strength of maritime trade. Salem, for example, carried on immense waterborne commerce, particularly with the East Indies between the late 1700s and the War of 1812. In 1765 it was second only to Boston in the proportion of its population that was of African descent—173 of 4,254 persons or 4.1 percent. By 1790, because many of the town's merchants and much of its commerce had moved to Boston, that proportion fell to 3.2 percent. Salem is scarcely mentioned in letters or narratives of fugitives and their assistants, and only 8.4 percent of Salem's Black population claimed a slave-state birthplace in 1855.[8] In New Bedford, by contrast, African Americans were 7.5 percent of the total population in 1855; their numbers had grown from 38 in 1790 to 1,527 in 1855. In 1850, 29.9 percent of the African American population in New Bedford claimed to have been born in the South. By 1840, Nantucket's early primacy in the whaling industry had given way to New Bedford's, and its population of color dropped from 579 in 1840 to 128 in 1860, while New Bedford's more than doubled over those twenty years.[9] Men of African descent were a principal pool of the low-wage(though they in fact received no wage at all but instead a small share of a vessel's profit) labor on which whaling depended as voyages grew longer and more onerous, and they also were often crew on trading vessels. The suspicion that Black crewmen enticed enslaved African Americans onto or hid fugitives on their vessels inspired the southern states' Negro Seamen's Acts. Beginning in 1822, these legislative acts endeavored to keep Black sailors from influencing enslaved southerners by confining them to their vessels while in any southern port. The penalty for violating the law was imprisonment and even sale.[10]

Vessels running in to Boston and New Bedford from the South before about 1830 carried flour, corn, tobacco, lumber, and ship stores such as tar and turpentine. They also carried fugitives from slavery either knowingly or unwittingly. African American cleric William H. Robinson, born in 1858, recalled how his father Peter, an enslaved vessel pilot, worked with Quakers Samuel Fuller and "Mr. Elliott" to guide their oyster sloops along the Cape Fear River to and from Wilmington, North Carolina. "Father was with Messrs. Fuller and Elliott every day towing them in and out from the oyster bay," Robinson wrote in 1904. "This gave them an opportunity to lay and devise plans for getting many into Canada (the only safe refuge for the negro this side the Atlantic,) and my father was an important factor in this line." The three devised a system for carrying fugitives, often wagons with "double linings, with corn and wheat visible, while the cavity was filled with women and children."[11] In 1830 Joseph H. Smith stowed away on a vessel carrying lumber from North Carolina to New Bedford.[12]

Increasingly after 1830, the explosive growth of cotton culture as it moved from the played-out soils of the Atlantic coastal states to the South's interior and Gulf states accelerated sales of enslaved people to work these vast new plantations, and those sales in turn heightened the perceived necessity among enslaved people to escape to the North.[13] Cotton moved North after 1830 to feed New England's burgeoning textile industry, and the frequency of traffic between the regions is attested by a trope common to many fugitive narratives—that of seeing in a northern place one's former enslaver or some other person from a fugitive's homeplace in the South. In 1854, the "Marine Intelligence" columns of the *New Bedford Evening Standard* listed 168 vessels entering from Philadelphia and fourteen different southern ports.

Where fugitives had earlier concealed themselves amid lumber cargoes on northbound vessels, they now concealed themselves amid bales of cotton—another trope of the fugitive narrative. Boston cotton broker C. F. Atkinson, whose father Edward was a member of the Boston Vigilance Committee yet also a cotton broker, told Underground Railroad historian Wilbur Siebert in 1898: "Although my Father was active in the cause, and I lived in an atmosphere of Anti-Slavery Effort, I have only a boy's remembrance of it myself. 'The White Pigeon' and rescue of slaves from cotton ships off the harbor was the branch of the 'Underground' Father had most to do with—and the news of the slave came, if I remember rightly, from an old gentleman in New Bedford."[14] The vessel Atkinson recalled was the *Wild Pigeon*, the second of two "yachts" built by master mariner Austin Bearse on behalf of the Boston Vigilance Committee "with the purpose to rescue fugitive slaves, who were coming all the while to Boston."[15] Unitarian cleric Thomas Wentworth Higginson was clearly speaking of the Boston Vigilance Committee when he told Siebert that one of the "secret societies in Boston aimed to impede the capture of fugitive slaves . . . [and] owned a boat, in which men used to go down in the harbor to meet Southern vessels. The practice was, to take along a colored woman with fresh fruit, pies, &c. She easily got on board & when there, usually found out if there was any fugitive on board; then he was sometimes taken away by night." Bearse noted, "People used to write to Mr. [Wendell] Phillips from the South, out in those places just before slaves were about to start. Mr. Phillips got the letters, and so was on the lookout when the vessels got into Boston harbor. He would know the name of the vessel, and who was on board, and be all ready to help them."[16]

Fugitives came to Boston and New Bedford not only because maritime commerce was most active there but also because both had relatively large populations of people of color—1,999 in Boston and 1,027 in New Bedford in 1850, according to the federal census. And as seaports, both were populated or visited by a large number of nonresidents, many of whom manned the vessels of those ports. Just as people of color found relative anonymity and freedom aboard ships in the eighteenth and nineteenth centuries, fugitives could become relatively invisible among a large population of resident and transient African Americans.

Though New Bedford's whaling industry far overshadowed Nantucket's by 1850, that island had a long-standing and stable African American population and enough maritime and service work to sustain it. In 1850 its population of free people of color was 394; though far smaller than the number living in Boston and New Bedford, Nantucket's Black community was still the third-largest in the commonwealth.[17] By that same year Nantucket's lack of a deep water port and difficulty of access made it an outlier both in terms of economic activity and fugitive traffic. Like Nantucket, the ports on Martha's Vineyard and Cape Cod were too shallow and small for large vessels, and they otherwise offered little employment to people of color. Even though some of the most daring of Massachusetts's Underground Railroad activists—Jonathan Walker, Austin Bearse, and the African American journalist and activist Charles B. Ray—were from the Cape, the census recorded only 123 free people of color out of a total population of 35,153 in the thirteen Cape Cod towns. Some slight presence of fugitives from slavery on the Vineyard and the Cape is documented, but they too were outliers.[18]

Virtually from the time slavery was declared "inconsistent" with the Massachusetts Constitution and therefore banned in 1783,[19] fugitives from the South and from places in the North where slavery still existed made their way to the commonwealth. In 1787 William Rotch Sr., then Nantucket's preeminent whaling merchant, attempted to secure the freedom of Cato, who had escaped to Nantucket from his Newport, Rhode Island, enslaver John Slocum in 1783 and had been working for Rotch's son-in-law, Samuel Rodman, "near two years."[20] Another early fugitive was Robert Voorhis, the so-called Hermit of Massachusetts, who was born about 1770 in New Jersey and had been "sold South." He attempted to escape by vessel from Charleston several times before he succeeded in reaching Boston in the late 1790s. He then sailed as crew from both Salem and Boston for nearly a decade before moving to Providence about 1807 and ultimately living the rest of his life in a cave in Seekonk, now part of Massachusetts.[21]

New Bedford's first documented fugitive incident had its roots in 1791, when master mariner Peleg Smith Jr. brought the fugitive Jack Cotton to New Bedford; the next year Cotton returned South on a New Bedford sloop to bring his enslaved wife and children North.[22] At least three other fugitives were brought into the town on coastwise vessels between 1794 and 1799. Master mariners Noah Stoddard and William Taber claimed to be unaware of their presence on board—certainly to try to shield themselves from fines, imprisonment, or worse.[23] Both declared that once they discovered the fugitive on board, it seemed "inconsistent for me to return, the wind being ahead."[24] The third, however, was quite evidently an intentional transport to the North. Thomas Wainer, the Afro-Indian master of the schooner *Ranger*, "carried off" a man and wife, enslaved by separate people, from Snow Hill, Maryland, in late March 1799. Wainer was the nephew of Afro-Indian master mariner Paul Cuffe (1759–1817), who owned the *Ranger* with his brother-in-law and business partner, Michael Wainer, Thomas's father. Cuffe and Wainer (Michael) had been trading in southern ports such as Norfolk, Savannah, and Baltimore at least since the late 1790s. Samuel Sloane's runaway notice for Harry and his pregnant wife, Lucy, noted that Thomas Wainer had come to Snow Hill to take on "a load of corn and staves, and cleared for Norfolk, Virginia." Instead, Wainer probably sailed the *Ranger* to Philadelphia, where he may have left the fugitive couple.[25]

These early fugitive cases occurred well before the formal organization of antislavery reform and of vigilance committees. The first vigilance committee in the Northeast was probably the New York Committee of Vigilance, organized on 20 November 1835 and managed principally by its secretary, African American mariner, bookseller, and grocer David Ruggles. In 1841 Ruggles stated that he had helped six hundred persons in "their flight from bonds" over the past three years. He had sent the fugitive Frederick Douglass and others to New Bedford in the 1830s, and the records and letters of Sydney Howard Gay, active in fugitive assistance by 1846, document his frequent work with vigilance committees in both Massachusetts ports.[26]

Boston's first vigilance committee was formed in early June 1841 after the captain and mate of the Boston schooner *Wellington* returned a stowaway fugitive named John Torrance to New Bern, North Carolina. The *Wellington*'s mate, James S. Higgins, wrote that Torrance "convayed him self on board of Capt [Benjamin] Higgins vessel Probably by the aid of sum of the Crue which I discovered 5 days after wards" and stated too that the crew refused to allow him to put the fugitive on shore at Norfolk. Torrance attempted to escape from the vessel as it lay in Boston harbor by jumping overboard, but he was caught, put in irons, and kept on the vessel while first mate James S. Higgins tried in vain to raise money among Boston abolitionists to buy Torrance's freedom. Boston abolitionists were outraged. As Charles Turner Torrey stated in a New Bedford newspaper, Torrance's enslaved status was never proved, Higgins had no claim as his enslaver or an agent of his enslaver, and no "title" to ownership had ever been presented; Torrance was simply brought back to New Bern. Torrey charged, "No candid person can for a moment doubt, that the real reason of such a perversion of law and evidence, is to be found in the fear that the profitable trade of Boston with the slave States will be embarrassed."[27]

In December 1846, another instance of "attempted kidnapping" involving a fugitive in Boston Harbor triggered the formation of the second, interracial Boston Vigilance Committee. In early August of that year, an enslaved man identified only as George hid himself on the brig *Ottoman* at New Orleans and was discovered on board a week later. James W. Hannum (1823–1888), the *Ottoman's* captain, and its crew knew George, for he had earlier sold milk for his enslaver aboard the vessel during its time in New Orleans. Hannum knew that he could suffer penalties in both Louisiana and Massachusetts on account of George's presence on—or removal from—his vessel, but he judged the punishment he would face in the South to be worse. Thus, as the *Ottoman* approached Boston Harbor, he placed George in a small boat and took him first to Lighthouse Island and then to Spectacle Island. George escaped in the boat to South Boston, where Hannum and his men overtook him, and when the *Niagara*—owned by the firm John H. Pearson and Company, which also owned the *Ottoman* and, more infamously, the *Acorn* (the vessel that later returned the fugitive Thomas Sims to slavery from Boston in 1851)—was leaving the harbor for New Orleans, they placed George on board. Hannum later testified that a steamer with "darkeys of every hue" had pursued the *Ottoman* with cries to fire upon or ram it until they realized that George was aboard the *Niagara*, which the steamer could not overtake.

Hannum was arrested and placed in jail in Boston. At a meeting at Faneuil Hall about the *Ottoman* case, Stephen C. Phillips alleged that "there was not another merchant in Boston who would have advised or countenanced" sending a fugitive back, but Pearson retorted that for every one master who would not have done so five certainly would have. "There is no philanthropy held out towards our shipmasters who may be innocently caught with a secreted slave," Pearson wrote to Phillips, "but it is very philanthropic to *steal* the property of our southern neighbors, and have our white citizens imprisoned in exchange."[28]

The second Boston Vigilance Committee kept a record of the nineteen fugitives who sought its aid between 30 November 1846 and 24 April 1847. Its last record related the story of John Armstrong, or John Hill, whose enslaver had hired him out to work in Baltimore in order to purchase his freedom but had reneged on the agreement. "Left Baltimore about 6 weeks ago in a packet to Brandywine, & came through Philadelphia, & New York to N. Bedford," committee secretary John White Browne quoted Armstrong to have stated. Armstrong reported, "Mr. Ray, a white man, in N. Bedford to whom I went, advised me to go to Boston." The committee sent Armstrong to Pembroke, Massachusetts.[29]

Records other than those of vigilance committees document fugitives who came to Boston and New Bedford and traveled between the two. In 1839 New Bedford tax collector Henry Howland Crapo noted that William Henry, "a runaway slave," had shipped out on the whaling ship *Hope*; the July 1839 crew list for the vessel, which did not record race, lists Henry as a twenty-three-year-old man from Petersburg, Virginia. The *Hope* returned to New Bedford in May 1841, but whether Henry returned with it is not known.[30] Probate records also sometimes revealed former enslavement. Henry Steward shipped aboard New Bedford whalers twice in the 1840s and was listed as a mariner living in New Bedford's African American West End neighborhood in 1849. He told census takers that he was born in Pennsylvania, but his death record and grave indicate that he was born in Maryland, either in Queen Anne's or Talbot County. His will, signed with a mark three days before he died in late December 1869, left a dollar each to his children, "really named Elizabeth and Cordelia Steward but have sometime been named or styled Brooks—These two daughters are the only children I have & were born in Slavery and have been so long separated from me that the above identification is made."[31]

The passage of the Fugitive Slave Act in September 1850 triggered the creation of a third Boston Vigilance Committee. From its formation on 21 October 1850 to February 1859, the Boston Vigilance Committee aided more than four hundred fugitives, and its records indicate that it assisted at least forty-six more between February 1859 and its last record in April 1861.[32] This third committee was involved in one of the most open and spectacular fugitive "rescues" of the 1850s, that of Jane Johnson and her sons, Isaiah and Daniel, enslaved by John Hill Wheeler of North Carolina, then the U.S minister to Nicaragua. Philadelphia abolitionist Passamore Williamson took them from a docked steamboat in broad daylight; Williamson was jailed for refusing to state where Johnson and her sons were taken. Philadelphia Vigilance Committee secretary William Still wrote that Johnson "very naturally and wisely concluded to go to Canada, fearing if she remained in this city . . . that she might again find herself in the clutches of the tyrant from whom she had fled." Yet she and her sons were in fact sent to Boston. "The woman—Jane Johnson for whom Passamore Williamson had been imprisoned—I had the pleasure of escorting from the depot in Boston recently on her destination," William C. Nell wrote to Rochester, New York, abolitionist Amy Kirby Post on 13 August 1855. "She is a woman who can take care of herself."[33] The fugitive Henry Lewey, whom Still described as "one of the most dexterous managers in the Underground Rail Road agency in Norfolk," also came to Boston shortly before his wife, Rebecca, and fourteen other fugitives escaped by schooner from Norfolk to Philadelphia in early July 1856. Still sent part of that party to Boston and the rest to New Bedford and stated that Lewey had sent his wife "on in advance as he had decided to follow her soon in a similar manner." "Before many months had passed," Still added,

Lewey had gone to Canada. Oddly, though, Still's book includes a letter from a fugitive in Hamilton, Ontario, dated 26 June 1856—before Rebecca Lewey and her fellow fugitives left Norfolk—telling Still that Henry Lewey "had left this city for Boston about 2 weeks ago, we have not herd from him yet." Lewey died in Boston in 1906.[34]

The existence of a vigilance committee in New Bedford in 1851 is known only through newspaper accounts of a rumored "raid" originating in Boston to undertake "the seizure of and carrying away of fugitive slaves from New Bedford." Upon hearing of it, the Boston Vigilance Committee telegraphed its counterpart in New Bedford with the news that a vessel and "marines" were on their way to the city, but for some unstated reason the wire failed, and the committee ultimately sent two men by train and steamboat to the city to warn of the visit. The vessel never arrived, which left the New Bedford *Republican Standard* to speculate that "the requisite papers from the South" that would authorize any seizure had not arrived.[35] This 1851 vigilance committee may not have been the same as the Vigilant Aid Society, which appears to have been formed by African Americans in New Bedford at least by 1855. Of the six known members of the Vigilant Aid Society, two were born free, two were documented fugitives, and two were probably fugitives.[36] Connections between New Bedford and Boston fugitives and abolitionists of both races are amply documented in vigilance committee and other records, and the African American attorney Robert Morris of Boston made those ties explicit in his address to a Massachusetts convention of "colored citizens" in 1858.[37]

Documenting the movement of fugitives between Boston, New Bedford, and the islands, and the interactions between abolitionists in these places, are far more difficult tasks. And it is not possible to know whether that difficulty reflects the rarity of their presence or simply that formal sources did not acknowledge it. A wide kinship network existed among often-intermarried people of African and native American descent on the islands, on Cape Cod, and in New Bedford. Such families as the Capeys, Sharpers, Peterses, Cuffes, Harrises, Webquishes, Walmsleys, Mingos, Haskinses, and Johnsons had members in all these places.[38] The largest community of Afro-Indians and Indians on Martha's Vineyard existed at Gay Head (Aquinnah), and it figured centrally in the most celebrated fugitive case known to have taken place in part on that island.

Newspapers mention other events—the presence of an enslaved man on a schooner in January 1837 whose enslaver presented him at a Vineyard antislavery meeting as contented with his lot and unwilling to deal with New England's cold weather; the landing of several fugitives on the Vineyard who were sent on to New Bedford in May 1855[39]—but the Edinbur Randall/John Mason case was widely discussed in the press and the abolitionist community when it occurred in 1854. In September that year, the enslaved Edinbur Randall stowed away on the Portland, Maine, bark *Franklin*, then loading with pine lumber at Jacksonville, Florida, and bound for Bath, Maine. Randall was discovered while the vessel was at sea, and its captain put in at Holmes Hole (now Vineyard Haven) on Martha's Vineyard. There he remained for a week while he sought a federal officer to warrant the fugitive's return to Jacksonville. For some reason, the Boston Vigilance Committee believed the *Franklin* had left the Vineyard for Bath and dispatched one of its members, S. P. Hanscom, "to Bath Me. to rescue John Mason," the name Randall had by then taken, "from Bark Franklin," Francis Jackson's accounts note in September 1854.[40] When the bark arrived at Bath, however, it was without its captain and without Mason, who had in fact escaped in one of the *Franklin's* boats and rowed it to West Chop on the island.

One account states that Mason then hid in a swamp at Gay Head for several days until two women, whom Francis Jackson later identified as "Gay Head Indians," entered the swamp, fed the frightened Mason, and convinced him to put on the women's clothes they had assembled in Holmes Hole when they hired a carriage. Neither Jackson, the newspapers, nor Theodore Parker, who described the case in his Thanksgiving sermon that year, identified these women; Parker declared that "he had the names of the two Indians that most befriended the fugitive, but he dare not tell them, for do we not know that there is a Fugitive Slave law?"[41] However, Jackson's vigilance committee accounts make clear that they were Beulah Vanderhoop and Mary Ann Cooley. Cooley's identity remains obscure, but Vanderhoop was a Gay Head Wampanoag (her father was probably of African descent) who had married William Adrian Vanderhoop of Surinam in New Bedford in 1837 and lived in New Bedford at least through the early 1840s.[42]

Vanderhoop and Cooley carried Mason, dressed in women's clothing, in a wagon to Menemsha Bight, north of Chilmark on the northeast coast of the island, and Gay Head Indian Samuel Peters took Mason and the women in a boat to New Bedford. In 1921 Netta Vanderhoop told the *Vineyard Gazette* that her grandmother, Beulah, had said to her that "the people of Gay Head knew that if he once reached there [New Bedford] he would be perfectly safe. On the shore," presumably at Menemsha, "there gathered a large number of men, armed with guns, pitchforks, clubs, and almost anything that would do to fight with" in case the deputy sheriff of Chilmark, who had a warrant to arrest Mason for stealing the *Franklin's* boat, should attempt to arrest his flight. The boat carrying Mason reached New Bedford at seven o'clock the next morning, and the women took the fugitive "to the residence of an abolitionist, and arrangements were made by him, which resulted in the forwarding of the slave to Canada." Yet Netta Vanderhoop stated that Mason took the name Edgar Jones, "remained for some time, working about the wharves" in New Bedford, and sometimes visited Vanderhoop on the Vineyard.[43]

A similar case in December 1858 played out in part at Holmes Hole, when the fugitive Philip Smith stowed away on the Boston brig *William Purrington* at Wilmington, North Carolina. Captain James L. Bryant discovered him after three days at sea and confined him in the hold amid a nauseating cargo of turpentine and rosin, but high winds at sea prevented the vessel from returning to Wilmington or docking at Norfolk. The *William Purrington* finally reached Holmes Hole, where the captain confined Smith on the ship. When the weather improved, he set off for Boston. At the Narrows in Boston's outer harbor Captain Bryant ran the vessel aground, and as Smith helped the crew try to free the brig, he jumped overboard and swam to Lovell's Island. From there he hailed a small sailboat, which took him to Boston's Commercial Wharf. William Lloyd Garrison recorded Smith's story and presented it as "from the fugitive's own lips" at a Boston meeting in March 1859. Smith is supposed to have been sent to Canada, but nothing more is known of him, and Boston Vigilance Committee records do not state or intimate any involvement in the case.[44]

Nantucket was tied more closely to New Bedford than the Vineyard, for its whaling industry and whaling merchants had moved to the mainland port after 1820. Some research has indicated that few African American mariners made the move, perhaps because they were an increasingly small presence on whaling crews as the century went on.[45] As in Martha's Vineyard, family ties—particularly those of the Boston-Borden-Cook-Cuffe family–strengthened the connection between Nantucket's and New Bedford's African American communities. Yet, despite Powell's declaration, neither kinship nor business relations appear to have affected the presence and movement of fugitives on Nantucket. Aside from the well-documented case of Arthur and Mary Cooper in 1822 and the newspaper notice of fugitive John Williams in 1826 that he wished to be known thereafter by "his real name," Joseph Mason, fugitives were either few or simply unnoted on Nantucket.[46] Historians are left to speculate about others who might have been fugitives, among them Lewis Berry. He was on Nantucket by 1830, the year he married Eliza Boston (1808–1883).[47] On Nantucket, Lewis worked as a whitewasher, and his brother, Wesley, kept a boardinghouse for mariners for some time, as William P. Powell did in New Bedford and New York City. Like Powell, Wesley Berry was "one of the most zealous workers in the anti-slavery cause, and his voice was often heard in public, in behalf of his race," his obituary stated.[48] Yet, so far, only Powell's eulogy attests to Lewis Berry's work in "the great anti slavery war" and on behalf of fugitives. Berry, as so many others, remains underground in that history.

NOTES

1. On slavery in New Jersey, see the Slavery in the North website, http://slavenorth.com/newjersey.htm. Wesley Berry obituary, 25 April 1883, Edouard Stackpole Papers, Nantucket Historical Association, Massachusetts (hereafter NHA). Powell's address is reprinted in part in "Reverend Chairman," *San Francisco Elevator*, 21 November 1874, 2.
2. "Reverend Chairman," *San Francisco Elevator*, 21 November 1874, 2.
3. Samuel J. May, *Some Recollections of Our Antislavery Conflict* (Boston: Fields, Osgood & Co, 1869), 144, 296–97.
4. Robert G. Albion, William A. Baker, and Benjamin W. Labaree, *New England and the Sea* (Middleton, Conn.: Published for the Marine Historical Association, Mystic Seaport, by Wesleyan University Press, 1972), 40, 127–28; table exhibiting the registered tonnage of each shipping district in the United States as of December 1831, in "Hospital Money," *Sailor's Magazine and Naval Journal*, July 1834, 334–36. For 1845 see Zephaniah W. Pease, *History of New Bedford* (New York: Lewis Historical Publishing Company, 1918), 1: 37.
5. Lorenzo Johnston Greene, *The Negro in Colonial New England* (1942; reprint, New York: Atheneum, 1971), 145–48; Robert J. Cottrol, *The Afro-Yankees: Providence's Black Community in the Antebellum Era* (Westport, Conn.: Greenwood Press, 1982), 26–27; W. Jeffrey Bolster, *Black Jacks: African American Seamen in the Age of Sail* (Cambridge, Mass.: Harvard University Press, 1997), 28.
6. *Boston Gazette*, 2 October 1750; also folder 51, Stackpole Papers, NHA.
7. Venture Smith, *A Narrative of the Life and Adventures of Venture, a Native of Africa, but Resident above Sixty Years in the United States of America. Related by Himself* (New London, Conn.: C. Holt, 1798), 27, online at Documenting the American South, https://docsouth.unc.edu/neh/venture/venture.html.
8. Samuel Eliot Morison, *The Maritime History of Massachusetts, 1783–1860* (1961; reprint, with a foreword by Benjamin Woods Labaree, Boston: Northeastern University Press, 1979), 79–95, 213–24; Kathryn Grover, "The Underground Railroad in Salem: Draft Case Study" (unpublished report, National Park Service and Massachusetts Historical Commission, 30 November 2003). See also United States, Census Bureau, Sixth Census, 1840, *Compendium of the Enumeration of the Inhabitants and Statistics of the United States . . .* (Washington, [D.C.]: T. Allen, 1841),

https://www2.census.gov/library/publications/decennial/1840/1840v3/1840c-02.pdf#.

9. Frances Ruley Karttunen, *The Other Islanders: People Who Pulled Nantucket's Oars* (New Bedford, Mass.: Spinner Publications, 2005), 83, 90.

10. Philip M. Hamer, "Great Britain, the United States, and the Negro Seamen Acts, 1822–1848," *Journal of Southern History* 1 (February 1935): 3–28; Peter P. Hinks, *To Awaken My Afflicted Brethren: David Walker and the Problem of Antebellum Slave Resistance* (University Park: Pennsylvania State University Press, 1996), 239; Kathryn Grover, *The Fugitive's Gibraltar: Escaping Slaves and Abolitionism in New Bedford, Massachusetts* (Amherst: University of Massachusetts Press, 2001), 229–30.

11. William H. Robinson, *From Log Cabin to Pulpit: or, Fifteen Years in Slavery*, 3d ed. (Eau Claire, Wisc.: James H. Tifft, 1913), 13.

12. Unidentified New Bedford, Massachusetts, newspaper, 1911, cited in Robert C. Hayden, *African-Americans & Cape Verdean-Americans in New Bedford* (Boston: Select Publications, 1993), 29. See also R. C. Smedley, *History of the Underground Railroad in Chester and the Neighboring Counties of Pennsylvania* (1883; reprint, Mechanicsburg, Penn.: Stackpole Books, 2005), 355–61.

13. Daniel M. Johnson and Rex R. Campbell, *Black Migration in America: A Social Demographic History* (Durham, N.C.: Duke University Press, 1981), 25, 33; Albion, Baker, and Labaree, *New England and the Sea*, 128.

14. C. F. Atkinson to Wilbur Siebert, 2 May 1898, Boston, vol. 2 (unpaginated), Notebooks Concerning the Underground Railroad Collected by Professor Wilbur H. Siebert, Ohio State University, Houghton Library, Harvard University, Cambridge, Massachusetts (hereafter Siebert Notebooks).

15. Austin Bearse, *Reminiscences of Fugitive-Slave Law Days in Boston* (Boston: Warren Richardson, 1880), 34; Sidney Kaplan, "The *Moby Dick* in the Service of the Underground Railroad," *Phylon* 12, no. 2 (1951): 173–76.

16. Thomas Wentworth Higginson to Wilbur H. Siebert, 24 July 1896, Dublin, New Hampshire, vol. 2, Siebert Notebooks; Bearse, *Reminiscences of Fugitive-Slave Law Days in Boston*, 33.

17. Barney placed the total number of people of color on Nantucket at 342, which is 52 persons fewer than the federal census offered.

18. In 1850 federal census enumerators counted more than 150 people of color in only ten towns and cities in Massachusetts—Boston (1,999), New Bedford (1,027), Nantucket (394), Salem (324), Pittsfield (285), Springfield (271), Charlestown (206), Worcester (192), Sheffield (182), and Northampton (158).

19. Massachusetts Chief Justice William Cushing ruled that "there can be no such thing as perpetual servitude of a rational creature." See *Commonwealth v. Jennison* (unreported, Mass.,1783).

20. William Rotch Sr., to Moses Brown, Providence R.I., 8 November 1787, Nantucket, Moses Brown Papers, Special Collections and University Archives, University of Massachusetts, Amherst; Wilbur H. Siebert, "The Underground Railroad in

Massachusetts," *Proceedings of the American Antiquarian Society* 45, pt. 1 (April 1935): 27.

21. *Life and Adventures of Robert, the Hermit of Massachusetts, Who Has Lived 14 Years in a Cave, Secluded from Human Society* (Providence, R.I.: for H. Trumbull, 1829).
22. On this case see Kathryn Grover, *"Testimony against the Sin of Our Nation": The Abolitionism of William Rotch Jr.* (New Bedford, Mass.: Rotch-Jones-Duff House and Garden Museum, 2018), 20–30.
23. David S. Cecelski, *The Waterman's Song: Slavery and Freedom in Maritime North Carolina* (Chapel Hill: University of North Carolina Press, 2001), 126. See also Gerald W. Mullin, *Flight and Rebellion: Slave Resistance in Eighteenth-Century Virginia* (New York: Oxford University Press, 1972), 127–28.
24. Stoddard and Taber published a "Public Notice!" in the *New-Bedford (Mass.) Medley* respectively on 26 August 1794 and 28 April 1797.
25. *New Bedford (Mass.) Medley*, 26 April 1799. On Cuffe, see in particular Lamont D. Thomas, *Paul Cuffe: Black Entrepreneur and Pan-Africanist* (Urbana: University of Illinois Press, 1986); Rosalind Cobb Wiggins, ed., *Captain Paul Cuffe's Logs and Letters, 1808–1817: A Black Quaker's "Voice from within the Veil"* (Washington, D.C.: Howard University Press, 1996).
26. *The First Annual Report of the New York Committee of Vigilance, for the Year 1837* (New York: Piercy and Reed, 1837), 3–5, 13–14, 84; "Soiree in Honor of David Ruggles," *Liberator* (Boston), 20 August 1841, 3; "British and Foreign Anti-Slavery Convention," *Liberator* (Boston), 7 July 1843, 2; Graham Russell Gao Hodges, *David Ruggles: A Radical Black Abolitionist and the Underground Railroad in New York City* (Chapel Hill: University of North Carolina Press, 2010), 10, 132–35; Dorothy B. Porter, "Family Records, a Major Resource for Documenting the Black Experience in New England," *Old-Time New England* 53, no. 3 (Winter 1973):71; Amelia Hickling Nye to Thomas Hickling Jr., 7 January 1855, New Bedford, 1855, box 1, Hickling-Nye Papers 1769, Ms. N-65, Massachusetts Historical Society, Boston.
27. "A Letter" from Charles T. Torrey, 10 June 1841, Boston, in *New Bedford (Mass.) Register*, 23 June 1841, 4; "From the Boston Daily Mail: Extraordinary Case of Kidnapping!" *Liberator* (Boston), 11 June 1841, 94. For a far different account of the event, see *Newbern (N.C.) Spectator*, 26 June 1841, 2–3.
28. See *Address of the Committee Appointed by a Public Meeting, Held at Faneuil Hall, September 24, 1846, for the Purpose of Considering the Recent Case of Kidnapping from Our Soil, and of Taking Measures to Prevent the Recurrence of Similar Outrages* (Boston: White & Potter, 1846), https://archive.org/details/addresscommoowhitrich/page/n59. Parker quoted in "Speeches of Wendell Phillips and Theodore Parker," *Liberator* (Boston), 4 December 1846, 2.
29. Irving H. Bartlett, "Abolitionists, Fugitives, and Imposters in Boston, 1846–1847," *New England Historical Quarterly* 55, no. 1 (March 1982): 107–8. "Mr. Ray" was Isaiah C. Ray (1802–82), a native Nantucketer and abolitionist who worked in New Bedford.

30. Henry Howland Crapo, "Memorandum of Tax Delinquents," 1837–41, Special Collections, New Bedford Free Public Library, Massachusetts.
31. Protection papers for Henry Steward, 25 March 1842, 1 October 1842, 28 July 1846; crew list bark *Favorite*, 1 August 1846; Bristol County Register of Probate #9307, will of Henry Steward, 20 December 1869, Briston County Probate and Family Court, Taunton, Massachusetts.
32. "Aid to Fugitive Slaves," *Liberator* (Boston), 18 February 1859, 3. The February 1859 to April 1861 figures are derived from [Jackson], "Boston Vigilance Committee Appointed at the Public Meeting in Faneuil [*sic*] Hall October 21st 1850 to Assist Fugitive Slaves," facsimile by the Bostonian Society, n.d.
33. William Still, *The Underground Rail Road: A Record of Facts, Authentic Narratives, Letters, &c., Narrating the Hardships, Hair-breadth Escapes and Death Struggles of the Slaves in Their Efforts for Freedom, as Related by Themsleves and Others, or Witnessed by the Author* (1871; reprint, Chicago: Johnson Publishing Co., 1970), 86–97; Henry Louis Gates Jr., ed., introduction to *The Bondwoman's Narrative*, by Hannah Crafts (New York: Warner Books, 2002), xliv–xlix; Dorothy Porter Wesley and Constance Porter Uzelac, eds., *William Cooper Nell: Selected Writings, 1832–1874* (Baltimore, Md.: Black Classic Press, 2002), 419; Katherine E. Flynn, "Jane Johnson, Found! But Is She 'Hannah Crafts'? The Search for the Author of the *Bondswoman's Narrative*," *National Genealogical Society Quarterly* 90, no. 3 (September 2002). The Flynn article was reprinted in *The Search for Hannah Crafts: Essays on the "Bondswoman's Narrative,"* ed. Henry Louis Gates Jr. and Hollis Robbins (New York: Basic Civitas, 2004).
34. Still, *Underground Railroad*, 293, 559–65; "Rescuer of Slaves: Wm. H. Lewey, Famed in Underground Period of Civil War, Buried from West End Church," *Boston Globe*, 29 June 1906, 4.
35. Grover, *Fugitive's Gibraltar*, 223–24. See also "Fugitive Slave Excitement in New Bedford," *New Bedford (Mass.) Republican Standard*, 20 March 1851, 3, and "Extradition Extraordinary," *New Bedford (Mass.) Mercury*, 21 April 1851.
36. "Public Meetings," *Liberator* (Boston), 14 March 1856; *New Bedford (Mass.) Republican Standard*, 6 December 1855; Still, *Underground Railroad*, 254–59; Grover, *Fugitive's Gibraltar*, 255–56; *New Bedford (Mass.) Evening Standard*, 19 December 1896; Ray Patenaude collection, New Bedford.
37. See the passage quoted in the epigraph to this chapter. "Anniversary of British West India Emancipation: Convention of Colored Citizens of Massachusetts," *Liberator* (Boston), 13 August 1858, 4.
38. John Milton Earle, *Report to the Governor and Council, Concerning the Indians of the Commonwealth, Under the Act of April 6, 1859* (Boston: William White, 1861), 34, quoted in Carter G. Woodson, "The Relations of Negroes and Indians in Massachusetts," *Journal of Negro History* 5, no. 1 (January 1920): 48.
39. N. S., "An Agent's Adventures," *Liberator* (Boston), 21 January 1837, 2; article from

Vineyard (Mass.) Gazette (Edgartown), in *New Bedford (Mass.) Republican Standard*, 17 May 1855, 1.

40. Note entered in September 1854 by Francis Jackson, "Boston Vigilance Committee," 30.
41. "Rev. Theodore Parker's Thanksgiving Sermon," *Liberator* (Boston), 8 December 1854, 2; Francis Jackson's comments, in "Rhode Island State Antislavery Convention," ibid., 19 January 1855, 2.
42. *New Bedford (Mass.) Standard*, 29–30 September 1854; Francis Jackson, "Fugitive Slaves," *The Liberty Bell* (Boston: American Anti-Slavery Society, 1858), 29–43, reprinted in *Slave Testimony: Two Centuries of Letters, Speeches, Interviews, and Autobiographies*, ed. John W. Blassingame (Baton Rouge: Louisiana State University Press, 1977), 320–25; "A Fugitive Slave Case—A Villanous Captain," *Liberator* (Boston), 22 September 1854, 3; "The Bath Slave Case," *Liberator* (Boston), 6 October 1854, 3 (from the *Martha's Vineyard [Mass.] Gazette*); and Netta Vanderhoop, "The True Story of a Fugitive Slave: Or the Story a Gay Head Grandmother Told," *Martha's Vineyard [Mass.] Gazette*, 3 February 1921. See also [Jackson], "Boston Vigilance Committee," 30 (September 1854), 32 (1 December 1854), and 50 (18 July 1856), and [Jackson], "Fugitive Slaves Aided by the Vigilance Committee."
43. *New Bedford (Mass.) Standard*, 29 and 30 September 1854. Article from the *Liberty Bell* (Boston), 29–43, reprinted in *Slave Testimony: Two Centuries of Letters, Speeches, Interviews and Autobiographies, ed.* John W. Blassingame (Baton Rouge: Louisiana State University Press, 1977), 320–25; "A Fugitive Slave Case—A Villanous Captain," *Boston Liberator*, 22 September 1854, 3; "The Bath Slave Case," reprinted from the *Vineyard (Mass.) Gazette* (Edgartown), in *Liberator* (Boston), 6 October 1854, 3; and Netta Vanderhoop, "The True Story of a Fugitive Slave: Or the Story a Gay Head Grandmother Told," *Vineyard (Mass.) Gazette* (Edgartown), 3 February 1921. See also [Jackson], "Boston Vigilance Committee," 30 (September 1854), 32 (1 December 1854), and 50 (18 July 1856), and [Jackson], "Fugitive Slaves Aided by the Vigilance Committee."
44. "Escape of a Fugitive Slave from a Vessel in Boston Harbor," *Liberator* (Boston), 31 December 1858, 2; "No Slave-Hunting in Massachusetts—Another Hearing,"ibid., 4 March 1859, 2.
45. Martha S. Putney, *Black Sailors: Afro-American Merchant Seamen and Whalemen Prior to the Civil War* (Westport, Conn.: Greenwood Press, 1987), 2; Edward Byers, *The "Nation of Nantucket": Society and Politics in an Early American Commercial Center, 1660–1820* (Boston: Northeastern University Press, 1987), 255. See also Kathryn Grover, "Whaling and Kinship: African American Migration between Nantucket and New Bedford, 1790–1860" (James Bradford Ames Fellowship Lecture, Nantucket Historical Association, 5 May 2005), and Nathaniel Philbrick, *Away Off Shore: Nantucket Island and Its People, 1602–1890* (Nantucket, Mass.: Mill Hill Press, 1994), 182.

46. See Grover, *Fugitive's Gibraltar*, 94–98; *Nantucket (Mass.) Inquirer*, 29 October 1822, 2; Robert Johnson Jr., introduction to *Nantucket's People of Color: Essays on History, Politics, and Community*, ed. Robert Johnson Jr. (Lanham, Md.: University Press of America, 2006), 4–6; Francis Ruley Kartunnen, *Other Islanders: People Who Pulled Nantucket's Oars* (New Bedford, Mass.: Spinner Publications 2005), 76; *New Bedford (Mass.) Republican Standard*, 14 March 1878; "Looking Backward: 111 Years Ago—1826," *Nantucket (Mass.) Inquirer*, undated clipping in folder 51, Stackpole Papers, NHA, cited in Kartunnen, *Other Islanders*, 69 n. 3.
47. Leesburg (Va.) *Genius of Liberty*, 13 June 1826, featured a runaway ad for a Lewis Berry, 23 or 24 years old, who was enslaved by John B. Hunter of Fairfax County but had hired out to George Henry in Loudoun County for the past year. The advertisement stated that he had "a free mulatto wife" near Waterford, Virginia, and was expected to go there or "to some free state." The given age of the fugitive roughly matches that of Lewis Berry of Nantucket.
48. Unidentified newspaper clipping, dated 25 April 1883, folder 51, Stackpole Papers, NHA. Lewis Berry was killed by his son Isaac, who in 1875 was declared insane and sent to the state asylum. See "Memorial Meeting," *San Francisco Elevator*, 21 November 1874, 2; "Parricide," ibid., 31 October 1874; "The Parricide," ibid., 14 November 1874; "The Parricide," ibid., 8 November 1875, 3.

9

MAKING A LIVING IN THE "FUGITIVE'S GIBRALTAR"

People of Color in New Bedford, 1838–1845

LEN TRAVERS

> The colored population of New Bedford is very large, numbering not less than 1,000. Very many of them are fugitives from "Southern *service*."
>
> —*The Liberator*, 3 February 1854

On a late summer afternoon in 1838, Frederick Augustus Washington Bailey, a fugitive from justice, took a stroll from a house near the corner of Seventh and Spring Streets in New Bedford, Massachusetts, where he had taken refuge. He was not particularly worried about running afoul of the law, for his "crime," as he would later express it, had been to "steal himself" from slavery in Maryland, and his new hideout was renowned for its hostility to slave-catchers seeking their human prey.

But he was concerned with how he would now make his living as a free man. In Baltimore he had learned the trade of caulking—sealing a ship's hull to make it watertight—and it seemed only natural that America's premier whaling port would have need of his services. Recalling the experience of his first walk about the busy town years later, Bailey (who changed his surname to Douglass) wrote, with tongue firmly in cheek:

> I was quite disappointed at the general appearance of things in New Bedford. . . . I had very strangely supposed, while in slavery, that few of the comforts, and scarcely any of the luxuries, of life were enjoyed at the north, compared with what

> were enjoyed by the slaveholders of the south. I probably came to this conclusion from the fact that northern people owned no slaves. . . . I had somehow imbibed the opinion that, in the absence of slaves, there could be no wealth, and very little refinement.

But to the contrary, he found himself "surrounded with the strongest proofs of wealth. Lying at the wharves, and riding in the stream, I saw many ships of the finest model, in the best order, and of the largest size. Upon the right and left, I was walled in by granite warehouses of the widest dimensions, stowed to their utmost capacity." "Added to this," he continued, "almost every body seemed to be at work, but noiselessly so, compared with what I had been accustomed to in Baltimore. . . . I heard no deep oaths or horrid curses on the laborer. I saw no whipping of men; but all seemed to go smoothly on. Every man appeared to understand his work, and went at it with a sober, yet cheerful earnestness. . . . To me this looked exceedingly strange."[1]

His amazement increased, he wrote, as he left the wharves and moved back up the slope on which New Bedford rested, "gazing with wonder and admiration at the splendid churches, beautiful dwellings, and finely-cultivated gardens; evincing an amount of wealth, comfort, taste, and refinement, such as I had never seen in any part of slaveholding Maryland." To the eye of this newly liberated man, "Every thing looked clean, new, and beautiful. I saw few or no dilapidated houses, with poverty-stricken inmates; no half-naked children and bare-footed women, such as I had been accustomed to see in . . . Baltimore. The people looked more able, stronger, healthier, and happier, than those of Maryland. I was for once made glad by a view of extreme wealth, without being saddened by seeing extreme poverty."[2]

In his classic *Narrative of the Life of Frederick Douglass*, the now-famous abolitionist gave us an evocative, impressionistic portrait of New Bedford in 1838 that rivals the opening chapter of Herman Melville's *Moby Dick*, published thirteen years later. New Bedford was well-known to his contemporaries as a terminal on the "underground railroad," a place where runaway slaves could find work, assume new identities (as did Douglass), and live in comparative safety. From the observant passages sampled above, one would expect that Frederick Douglass' autobiography, first published seven years later, would provide a treasure-trove of detail concerning his fellow escapees and how they got on.

And yet, apart from vague or general references, Douglass tells us almost nothing about the people of color who had assembled in New Bedford, by then the second-largest African American community in the state—indeed the largest of any Northern city if reckoned as a percentage of the population. He found "astonishing" the "condition of the colored people. . . . I found many, who had not been seven years out of their chains, living in finer houses, and evidently enjoying more of the comforts of life, than the average of slaveholders in Maryland." His host in town, Nathan Johnson, was the only man he named; he "lived in a neater house; dined at a better table; took, paid for, and read, more newspapers; better understood the moral, religious, and political character of the nation, than nine tenths of the slaveholders in Talbot county Maryland." To demonstrate to his audience the superiority of free labor, Douglass hastened to add: "Mr. Johnson was a working man. His hands were hardened by toil, and not his alone, but those also of Mrs. [Polly] Johnson." But Douglass never tells the reader what the Johnsons actually *did* for a living, nor even that his hosts were people of color like himself. Douglass wrote that he found the "colored people" "much more spirited than I had supposed they would be. I found among them a determination to protect each other from the blood-thirsty kidnapper [bounty hunters who returned fugitives to slavery], at all hazards," and offered an anecdote (all names withheld) illustrating the point. But that is nearly all he has to say about the Black community in New Bedford.[3]

As it happens, Douglass had good reason to be reticent. Just as he did not want to furnish slaveholders with details of his flight, in case another fugitive tried to escape similarly, neither did he wish to supply any clues regarding other Black men and women at risk of arrest and return to slavery. But that reticence still leaves the reader with questions: how large was the community of color in New Bedford; how many of its members were fugitives like Douglass; how did they get there; and what did they do to support themselves; what were their living arrangements? To become the "fugitive's Gibraltar," New Bedford had to offer runaways sufficient employment and adequate housing, as well as security from slave hunters. On the surface at least, it would seem strange if New Bedford, virtually a one-industry town dependent on a specialized "fishery," did not offer and encourage maritime work for its refugee inhabitants. And certainly, the opportunity for escapees like Douglass to change their names, board a whaling vessel that might be at sea for several years, and thus remain out of reach of slave-catchers while in active employment would seem an appealing proposition.

But Douglass's recorded experience does little to suggest any such smooth or natural fit. On his third day in town, he got a job "in stowing a sloop with a load of oil, which he found "new, dirty, and hard work," and of course nothing like permanent employment—he had a wife and would soon have a family to support. He had learned the caulker's trade while enslaved in Baltimore and quite reasonably expected his skills to be in demand in New Bedford. Caulking involved driving long, tar-infused strands of "oakum"—untwisted fibers of old rope—into the spaces between the planks of a ship's hull with specialized mallets and caulking irons. The seams were then sealed with hot pitch to prevent the oakum coming loose. It was vital to ship maintenance and a highly valued trade. But when Douglass tried to ply his specialized skills, he discovered that "such was the strength of prejudice against color, among the white caulkers, that they refused to work with me, and of course I could get no employment." In his *Narrative*, published in 1845, he was happy to report, "I am told that colored persons can now get employment at caulking in New Bedford—a result of anti-slavery effort." But forced in 1838 to give up on that line of work, Douglass became a common laborer, claiming that "there was no work too hard—none too dirty. I was ready to saw wood, shovel coal, carry wood, sweep the chimney, or roll oil casks,—all of which I did."[4]

But what of the rest? Of the questions proffered above, the number and significance of New Bedford's "colored" residents can be given with fair precision. New Bedford in 1838 held the densest population of color in all of New England: its nearly 1,000 residents of color made up more than 8 percent of a general population of about 12,000. Only Boston, with a population in 1840 seven and a half times greater than that of New Bedford, had more resident African Americans (2,427), but they represented only 2.6 percent of the state capital's population. Nearby Providence, Rhode Island, with twice the population of New Bedford, was home to 1,302 Blacks, 5.6 percent of the total, that same year.[5]

The nucleus of New Bedford's population of color seems to have grown primarily from freemen drawn from southeastern New England as the town's maritime activities expanded in the first four decades of the century. Free Black seamen, laborers, and artisans from outside the area joined them over time, as did fugitive slaves escaping from southern ports. The number and proportion of residents born outside New England increased sharply by midcentury: only about half of New Bedford's total population of color claimed northern origins in the 1850 census, and nearly 30 percent admitted to a birthplace in the South—almost necessarily making a large number of southern Blacks runaways from enslavement or their children.[6]

One example was Joseph M. Smith. Born in 1811, Smith stowed away on a ship bound from North Carolina to New Bedford with a hold full of lumber about 1830. He may have been one of a gang of men assigned to stow the cargo, his absence going unnoticed until the ship had departed. It seems likely he also escaped with the connivance of some of the crew, for the trip would have lasted several days at least. At any rate, once the vessel came to the wharf at the foot of Union Street, Smith made his move. As he recalled some eighty years later, he "waited until the captain went down below to dress for going ashore, and then I made a dash for liberty." Leaping onto the wharf, Smith made a run for it but found the wharf crowded with people, who shouted "a fugitive, a fugitive!" But to Smith's relief and astonishment, instead of closing in to stop the runaway, "they stood aside and let me pass." With the help of William Bush, an African American resident, he soon enough "gained work."[7]

Historians would give a great deal to know the exact nature of that work and the jobs of those fellow fugitives who ended up in or passed through New Bedford. But just as there are no records clearly indicating the proportion of formerly enslaved people who resided there, information concerning their employment is piecemeal and anecdotal. Richmond-born William Henry Johnson, for example, escaped his owner and got to New Bedford sometime in the early 1830s. He may have become a seaman (two men of color named William Johnson are so designated in 1838), but he never claimed in his writings to have gone to sea. No less ambiguous is the career path of William Piper, who settled in New Bedford between 1825 and 1830. He had been born in Alexandria, Virginia, but whether he had been free or enslaved at the time of his arrival is not known. He worked as a laborer in 1836 and 1838 but had become a hostler—a stable keeper and groomsman—at the granite mansion of William R. Rodman, three years later. One who definitely found escape in maritime work was John S. Jacobs. Fleeing slavery the same year as Frederick Douglass, Jacobs arrived in New Bedford in 1839 and soon shipped out on the whaler *Frances Henrietta*—far from the reach of slave-catchers for the ensuing three-and-a-half-year voyage.[8] Another possible fugitive, James W. Harris, who later claimed to come from Philadelphia, took to the sea immediately upon his arrival in New Bedford.[9]

The impression one gets from the scanty anecdotal evidence is that work at sea offered entry-level employment for Black fugitives and that a place on a whale ship's crew may even have been the job of choice for men wishing to "disappear" for a few years. They would certainly have blended in, for men of color could be seen crewing vessels and working the dock areas in every major seaport in the United States. Historian Jeffrey Bolster calculates that Black men made up about 18 percent of American seafaring jobs overall, or one out of six berths, but the proportions were higher in northern ports. By 1838, men of color furnished about 30 percent of the maritime workforce in Providence, Rhode Island, and Kathryn Grover reckons that a similar proportion of New Bedford's African Americans were engaged as sailors about the same time.[10] Five months before Douglass's arrival in the whaling town, a resident estimated that three thousand seamen passed through the town annually.[11] He was not more specific, but if Bolster's and Grover's estimates are correct, hundreds of these Ishmaels must have been people of color—and a sizable proportion of them fugitives from enslavement.

One especially useful source for suppling some of the answers that Douglass did not or could not give in his account is a series of booklets, entitled *The New Bedford Directory*, for the years 1838, 1841, and 1845. The 1838 edition was only the second such guide published in the town and provides far more nuanced data for the year of Douglass's arrival. Directories for American cities first appeared at the end of the eighteenth century; they served as guides to community residents and businesses and aimed at promoting commerce. Boston could boast the first such directory in 1789.[12] The New Bedford directories, published half a century later, attempted to include, alphabetically by surname, "the place of residence, occupation, profession, &c., of every individual in Town . . . as nearly as possible, and in every case where it was practicable, by a personal application to the individuals themselves." And while the compiler, Collector of Taxes Henry H. Crapo, admitted inevitable errors in collecting the data, he insisted it was "my constant aim to render the work as accurate as possible."[13] Given the objects of the directories, children were absented from its pages, as were the great majority of women, unless they too possessed a public occupation or profession or were otherwise independent householders, such as widows. Thus, directories did not constitute a census, but for tracing individual or group occupational histories they are far more useful, especially as they became more regular, even annual, publications.

Finding people of color in the early directories is sometimes problematic, however. Not until 1813 did the Boston guide include them and even then placed them at the end of the directory under the separate heading "Africans"—whether they technically were African or not. But the New Bedford directories, the first one printed in 1836 by a committee of town businessmen and civil officials, shunned this practice and integrated the data for Blacks and whites. Nevertheless—and fortunately for the historian—the early New Bedford directories included a more subtle but still discriminatory code. The name of a "person of color" was followed by a lowercase *c*, presumably so that anyone for whom that information was significant would know in advance of contact.[14]

BLACK EMPLOYMENT IN NEW BEDFORD

As noted above, the lack of any comprehensive register of fugitives who made their way to New Bedford makes it difficult to say with confidence just how and in what capacity the runaways found work. Some of the biographical sketches offered above, such as the one for Joseph Smith, indicate that the town's abolitionist networks, both Black and white, helped by providing immediate shelter and advice, much in the way Frederick Douglass experienced. Douglass, as we have seen, became a laborer, despite his maritime specialty. On the other hand, William Temple, formerly of Richmond, Virginia, was able to ply the blacksmithing trade he had learned there, eventually designing the efficient, toggle-headed whaling harpoon that revolutionized the industry and today bears his name.[15]

The town directories give us a good idea of the categories and varieties of employment available to people of color in New Bedford and reveal the limited range of work fugitives might initially expect. The *Directory* for 1838 includes a total of 3,233 entries for individuals, of which, using the code as a guide, 253 are for people of color (Table 1).

Three general categories of employment stand out. The first, and most numerous, involves maritime workers, indicating that the town's African American population was indeed heavily invested in New Bedford's primary calling. The largest group, "in [vessel]," unites all those listed as "in ship Phenix," "in bark Rajah," "in brig Sarah Louisa," and so forth (ship, bark, and brig being distinct vessel types). Without exception, the vessels named were whaling craft then at sea, indicating that these men were on board as crewmen in some capacity: novice "green hand"; able (experienced) seaman; cook; or related occupation. The 10 men "at sea" suggests that they too were seamen of some sort but that the vessel they had sailed in was unknown to the compilers. The designation "mariner," for which there are 37 entries for men of color, may simply have been a synonym for "seaman" in the minds of the compilers but may also suggest something more than a common sailor. The title is often reserved for a seaman of considerable experience and knowledge of his craft: a pilot, perhaps, or even the master of a sloop or schooner, the workhorses of coastal navigation and commerce.

These three maritime subsets—"in vessel," "at sea," and "mariner"—total 140 men of color, more than half (55 percent) of the total. These are clearly seafaring occupations, but the number of maritime-related livelihoods available for African Americans may not be limited to these categories. The second-largest

TABLE 1. Occupational Breakdown of "Colored" Entries, New Bedford Directory, 1838, with Data Regarding Lodging Status

Occupation	#	boarding house	house	not given
"in [vessel]"	93	72	16	5
laborer	53	2	48	3
mariner	37	18	19	
widow	13	1	12	
"at sea"	10	8	2	
blacksmith	2	2		
boarding house	2		2	
butcher	2	1	1	
clothes-dresser	2		2	
cooper	2		2	
cordwainer	2		2	
trader	2		2	
chimneysweep	1		1	
confectionary	1		1	
dressmaker	1		1	
fruit [retailer]	1		1	
hairdresser	1		1	
oyster [retailer]	1		1	
restaurateur	1		1	
minister	1		1	
shop [keeper]	1	1		
tailor	1		1	
washerwoman	1		1	
not given	21	6	15	
253 total	253	110	135	8

Data from: Henry H. Crapo, *The New Bedford Directory, Containing the Names of the Inhabitants, Their Occupations, Places of Business and Dwelling Houses . . .* (New Bedford, Mass.: J. C. Parmenter Printers, 1838).

occupational group was "laborer," a category that could encompass anything from digging ditches to helping house builders and working in the port's boat shops and candle factories. But in a place like New Bedford, dockworkers were in high demand, and they did not need to put to sea to have work that was just as dependent on maritime pursuits. Douglass's first job, it will be recalled, was stowing oil casks in a sloop, a job requiring brawn, handling block and tackle, and working on shipboard. Each vessel coming into the port needed to be loaded or unloaded; longshoremen and teamsters were naturally ever-present. Laboring men might be doing dockwork one day, digging a ditch the next, and working on the docks a day later. A few of the other occupations in the table may have been "maritime" in nature too, as may have been those of some of the twenty-one persons for whom no occupation was given.[16] The two blacksmiths, as well as the two coopers (barrel makers), likely contributed at least occasionally to the vital process of fitting out the scores of vessels engaged in the whaling and coasting trades. All these employments were likely familiar to men escaping slavery in the South, coming as many did by vessels from southern ports or who, like Lewis Temple and Frederick Douglass, had learned maritime-related trades while enslaved. It seems likely then, if we are willing to stretch the category of "maritime" to include cases where the ship meets the shore, the percentage of Black maritime workers in the New Bedford Directory may have been considerably higher than the raw figure given above. And the *Directory's* data does not include the assumed scores of Black men who passed only briefly through the town before boarding the whale ships, transients who would not have been considered residents in any case.

The third category of employment, numbering twenty-five individuals, had specific occupations or trades ashore. These included skilled trades such as blacksmiths, coopers, cordwainers (shoemakers), clothes-dressers (men who shave the nap from woolen cloth to make it finer), and butchers, as well as a hairdresser and tailor—but no caulkers, as Frederick Douglass observed. Others owned or ran small business establishments, such as the traders, retailers, a shopkeeper, and a restaurateur. Nathan and Polly Johnson, Douglass's hosts, were in fact well-known confectioners and bakers. There were three boarding-house keepers, including William P. Powell, who ran the Seamen's Temperance Boarding House on North Water Street—a "dry" (alcohol-free) establishment, reflecting Powell's commitment to the moral-reform movement.[17] The men who resided in boarding houses were predominantly sailors, as we shall see, and keepers such as Powell acted as recruiters for whaleship crews, connecting green hands (and presumably some fugitives) with captains eager to fill their ships' muster rolls. The inclusion of "widows" (thirteen) in a directory stressing occupation is something of a puzzle, but a clue may reside in the fact that twelve of these women lived in houses: they may have let rooms to some of those men of color who were waiting to ship out and who preferred a quiet room to a crowded boarding house. For example, Avis Williams kept a house at

150 Purchase Street at which seaman Charles Broocher maintained an address while he was at sea, and there are similar arrangements suggested by the *Directory*. On the whole, it would appear from the 1838 *Directory* that maritime labor indeed dominated Black male employment in New Bedford and that such a class of worker, especially the assumedly more-professional "mariners," formed the nucleus of an African American community there.

Is this sample of occupations for New Bedford's population of color in 1838 sufficiently representative of the whole? The 253 named persons in the *Directory*, all but fourteen of whom were men, falls far short of the 1,000 or so "colored" people in New Bedford that year: the 253 represent only 25 percent of the whole (note that the total of 3,233 individual entries in the *Directory* is, similarly, about 27 percent of the whole population of New Bedford). But that total of a thousand includes about 700 "male" and 330 "female" residents of color, with no distinction by age. Only fourteen female residents of color are listed in the *Directory*, not only reflecting the prevailing bias in directories generally but also suggesting that paid work beyond domestic help and occasional, casual employment was particularly problematic for women of color.

Focusing, then, on the better represented male workers of color, the remaining 239 represent 36 percent of the total male population listed in the *Directory* for 1838. Compared with aggregate projections in studies with far less data, this Black cohort is already an impressive sample size, but historians can assume that the sample is even greater. An indeterminate number of the African American males and females were children. If even one-fifth (170) of all males were boys (under sixteen years of age, traditionally), then the 239 men of color in the *Directory* constitute 43 percent of the estimated remainder of grown males. The proportion could well be higher. Subject to countervailing evidence, then, this discussion accepts the employment patterns evidenced in the 1838 *Directory* as representative.

CHANGING PATTERNS OF EMPLOYMENT

But the number and proportion of town-based, Black maritime workers did not remain at such levels. Subsequent directories indicate that the number and proportion of African American seamen who called New Bedford home declined sharply over the next seven years. Indeed, the maritime workers of 1838 were largely gone a mere three years later. Of those 140 men "at sea," "in ship," etc., ninety-four had been dropped from the directory in 1841, although virtually all the ships absent in 1838 (61) had returned to port in the meantime.

A few of these men may have died or deserted, but it rather appears that the vast majority had returned to New Bedford, been paid off, and had moved on.[18] And while 47 new Black crewmen were listed in the 1841 directory, this number did not come close to making up the deficit, totaling only ninety-one—a 35 percent reduction in the category. Such a fluctuation is consistent with what historians know about maritime labor in general, but it is also reflective of New Bedford's restless population. Henry Crapo, who compiled the data for all three years of the *Directory*, claimed in 1841 that 733 names had been removed since 1839, and 1,367 new ones added, "exclusive of removals [within town], which have been very numerous."[19] The downward trend in maritime employment for Blacks continued apace, according to the 1845 directory: in that year only 69 Black men (30 percent) out of 231 in the directory worked at sea.[20] Nor had the persistence of maritime employment for individuals improved: in the seven years since the 1838 peak of 140 resident Black maritime workers, only 23 men of the 1838 cadre, or 16 percent, were still so employed. Almost all the others had apparently left town.

On the face of it, this drop in Black maritime participation, coming just as New Bedford was entering its "golden age" of whaling before the Civil War, seems puzzling. In 1844 Congressman Joseph Grinnell tallied 219 vessels sailing from his home port, manned by 5,888 seamen. Fourteen years later the number of vessels from New Bedford alone had climbed to 320, with about 8,320 crewmen.[21] If anything, shipowners and captains should have been happy to get as much cheap, available labor as possible, regardless of color, but by the period under scrutiny here, the choice may no longer have rested entirely with them. Jeffrey Bolster has discovered that, between 1820 and 1845, the maritime labor market had undergone a significant shift with regard to recruitment. Before that time, ship captains and owners had customarily found their own crews through personal connections and by enlisting the aid and cooperation of boarding house keepers. As the volume of shipping increased and selecting crewmen from the turnover-prone maritime population became more onerous and time-consuming, owners and captains turned over to middlemen the task of finding crews. These "crimps," as they were called, became responsible for filling a ship's complement of men and getting them on board the vessel, in return for fees for each man thus delivered. By employing crimps, ship captains sacrificed a degree of control over their crews' makeup but were spared the hassle of filling the berths themselves. White men dominated the crimping business and tended to hire crews in their own image and according to prevailing prejudices. By midcentury, Blacks were clearly losing ground in maritime employment, being relegated to positions of cooks and stewards—"service" positions little different from counterparts ashore. The trend was certainly noticed in New Bedford, where in 1863 a white selectman remarked that "the proportion of colored men in the whaling business is not as great now as formerly" and that this trend was due expressly to "the prejudice of the whites."[22]

The ups and downs of the national economy also seem to have had something to do with the diminishing proportion of berths for Black men. When sharp economic downturns occurred, as in 1809 and 1819, the smaller number of places aboard ship went disproportionately to white sailors. The worst financial panic before the Civil War came in 1837, the year before Frederick Douglass escaped to New Bedford. The effects of the recession were long-lasting, and with crimps handling more and more of crew recruitment, preference was given to white seamen.[23] Black sailors looking for work, or returning sailors hoping for another voyage, were forced to look elsewhere.

On the other hand, those African Americans explicitly engaged in shore-bound work had far greater staying power over those seven years. In addition, their numbers quickly outstripped those for resident maritime workers. For example, of the 53 Black laborers listed in 1838, 38 (72 percent) were still at their jobs in 1841, and 30 of the original 53 (57 percent) in 1845. Meanwhile, the overall number of Black laborers had climbed to 71 in 1841, then to 83 in 1845. The proportion of Black residents engaged in maritime pursuits was nearly halved, to 30 percent of the men, while those designated "laborers" rose to 36 percent. Some in the latter category had moved into more-distinct occupations. One 1838 laborer became a shop owner within a few years; another a lamplighter, another a trader, plus a hostler, a gardener, two stewards—and one became a mariner. All these occupations were likely considered a step up from the irregular work of ordinary laborers. And the variety of occupations, including skilled trades, increased considerably over time. By 1845, New Bedford African Americans contributed such trades to the directory as housewright (two), barber (four), cabinet maker, sailmaker, saddle-and-harness maker, and a cabman—but still no caulkers, contrary to Douglass's informant. This category of employment, trades, displayed the most persistence over time: of the 1838 cadre, nearly all were still in town in 1845, though some had taken up different occupations. None had opted or been forced to become laborers instead. While much has been written about African American prospects for promotion afloat—and these were real enough, earlier in the century—there were simply more opportunities ashore in New Bedford for a wider variety of work, for advancement, for career change, and, of course, for family life by the time when Douglass and Melville walked its streets.

HOW THEY LIVED

As for the manner in which they lived, the directories offer insights there also. Douglass anecdotally related that there were "many" former slaves like himself, who "[lived] in finer houses" and "enjoyed more of the comforts of life, than the average of slaveholders in Maryland," and there is some support for his claim in the *Directory*. But Douglass's pronouncement did not apply to most of the men whom historians can identify as seafaring. As Table 9.1 indicates, fully 78 percent of those "in vessel" or "at sea" in 1838 were boarders, most giving their addresses at established boarding houses near the waterfront. These men generally had no families in town and had come to New Bedford seeking work. The housing status of "mariners" was nearly evenly split, suggesting the higher status of the more established, experienced, and resident seamen. For shore-based workers, however, the trend was decidedly the opposite: only 30 boarded, while 135 (82 percent) dwelt in houses—like Douglass and his wife. Most of these domiciles were surely rented rather than owned by the Black occupants, but a correspondent to *The Quarterly Anti-slavery Magazine* in 1837 reckoned there were in New Bedford "about twelve hundred colored inhabitants [about 200 over the mark], of which number are fifty owning real estate, valued at seventy thousand dollars," or fourteen hundred dollars each, on average.[24] In any case, the point is more about standards of living than of home ownership. Overall, more than half (53 percent) of New Bedford's working people of color, as indicated by the 1838 *Directory*, lived in households, but only 30 percent of seamen did so and half of these were the mariners.[25]

New Bedford's people of color were not "ghettoized" strictly into poor, Black-only neighborhoods. The directories permit the user to plot the address of each entry, creating a graphic impression of where in town they made their homes. The example here (fig. 9.1) is for 1838. To be sure, there were older, established, or more exclusive parts of town to which wealthy and middle-class whites had laid claim: to County Street at the crest of the hill above town, for example.[26] There is also evident clustering of Blacks about First and South Second Street and on two unfinished streets west of County Street. This latter area became the nucleus of an African American neighborhood that persists to this day. But the first of these clusters, near the waterfront, is interspersed with white residents and white-owned businesses. North of Middle Street, Blacks seem fairly evenly dispersed within the area. Prejudice and preference were probably at work, but it may also be fair to say that Blacks, three-quarters of whom were identified in the *Directory* either as maritime or shore-based laborers, lived where they could afford to, as did the far larger number of laboring whites.

Nor should we take Douglass's impressions of Black prosperity, contentment, and morality at face value. In contrast to his report of "few or no dilapidated houses," another observer, the year before Douglass's arrival, thought that, near the town's waterfront, "Very many of the houses are ordinary, not a few quite mean in their appearance." An editorial in the town's newspaper that same year referred to "the deplorable deficiency here of ample and commodious accommodations."[27] In 1841 at least three Black men and one Black woman rented the basements of houses, as did many white workers. These subterranean accommodations were likely to be damp, poorly lit, and airless spaces, breeding grounds, many believed, for dangerous diseases.

That there were indeed poor—and some desperately poor—people in town, white and Black, is evident from newspaper accounts and from a memorandum book of tax delinquents for the years 1838 to 1840. For example, Black seaman Joseph Durfee, impoverished by the shipwreck he had recently survived, had to pawn his coat to pay his rent and was "helped by town this winter."[28] Douglass's sanguine first impressions of New Bedford, recorded in his *Narrative* and quoted above, were based on his perambulations during the daylight hours. But New Bedford's night life, away from its more genteel quarters, revolved around drink, gaming, prostitution, and occasional violence, especially in "Hard Dig," a waterfront area that the town constabulary "seldom entered." It was likely there that a tavern brawl erupted between a white and a Black patron the same year Douglass arrived. The Black combatant ultimately pitched his opponent into the street and continued to pummel him with a "heavy hand," until the vanquished white man limped away, badly beaten up.[29] Another rough neighborhood, near which some Black townsfolk resided, was "Dog Corner," at the intersection of County, Allen, and Wing Streets. It became notorious on summer evenings for "constant exhibitions of drunkenness, brawling and profanity," as one observer complained in 1841. He elaborated:

> And at dusk such is the concourse assembled there that it is not only disgusting and indecent, but such is the character of the assemblage, that it is dangerous for civil persons to pass in the vicinity. . . . [The corner area] has been a moral stain and a public curse upon our community [exhibiting] atrocious scenes

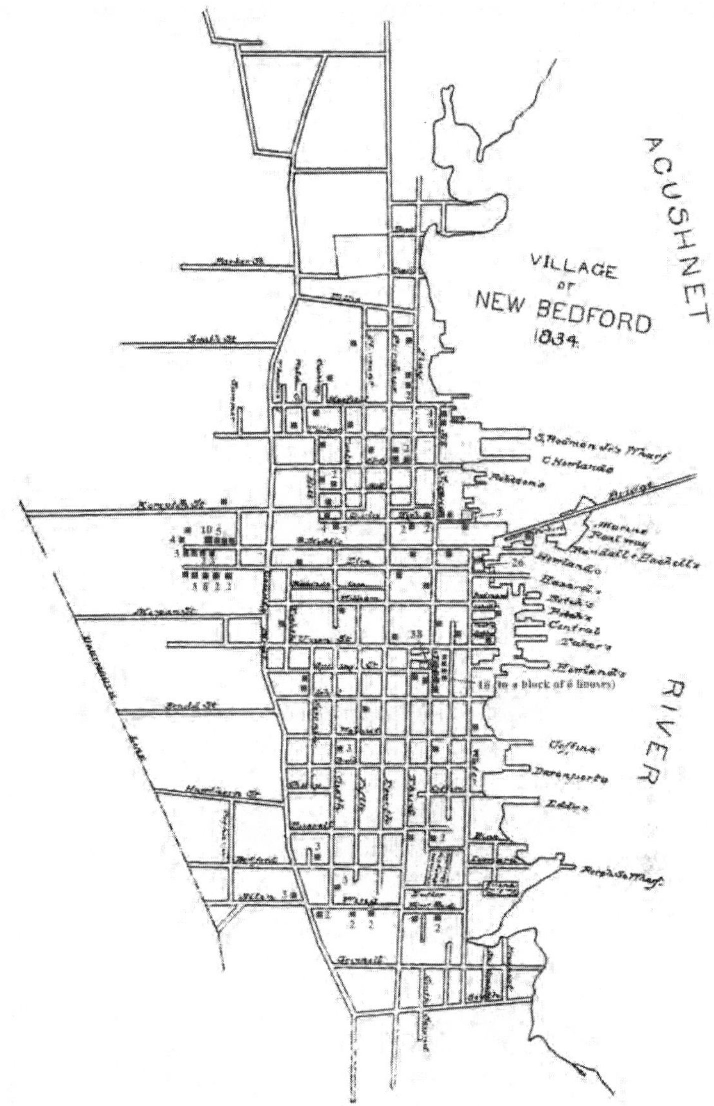

FIGURE 15. Dwellings of New Bedford's "Colored" Population, 1838, Based on the *New Bedford Directory*. Most of the dwellings indicated in this map housed multiple occupants of color. The large hollow squares identify licensed boarding houses used predominantly by African American maritime workers. Map by Len Travers, with special thanks to Daniel Everton. Street plan from George Bolles Ellis, *A History of New Bedford and Its Vicinity, 1602–1892* (Syracuse, N.Y.: D. Mason and Company, 1892), 269.

> of paganism. . . . The houses are occupied by many tenants—some men, some women, some married and some unmarried, some in cellars and some in garrets, each having an apartment that at dark is thronged with visitors—and at that hour the fiddle strikes up and the place swarms. And here also may be seen children by dozens who are becoming initiated into the vilest habits, which cannot fail to lead them to the public prisons.[30]

Douglass could hardly have escaped reading or hearing of such incidents, and of many more, in the years he lived there. But Hard Dig and Dog Corner were not "black neighborhoods"; rather, they were poor ones peopled by those who, for whatever reason, could not share in New Bedford's prosperity.

IMPRESSIONS AND CONCLUSIONS

Fugitives such as Douglass, Smith, Jacobs, and many others found in New Bedford a community of color ready to help them on their journey to freedom and many whites holding sincere sympathy for their plight. Opportunities for employment and improvement, even for modest wealth, beckoned both free and fugitive African Americans to the area's boomtown economy. Although the labor of Black men and women was welcome in New Bedford, that general sentiment did not translate to anything like equality with whites in work or status. Persistent racial prejudice operated to keep skilled men such as Frederick Douglass and Ezra Johnson (a free man trained as a sailmaker but turned away in New Bedford) out of the more prestigious maritime trades.[31] Seamen especially were notoriously overworked and underpaid in this period. Low wages were a grim and grinding reality for most whalemen. Nearly a quarter of the town's total population worked on board vessels in some capacity, while among Blacks the proportion, as we have seen, was at least twice that—at first. Hundreds of whites worked at a dazzling variety of professions—merchants, physicians, printers, block makers, clock makers, dentists, apothecaries, and others—while Blacks, excluding maritime workers and laborers, occupied only a relative handful of skilled positions in New Bedford.[32] Even the waterfront's boarding houses were segregated, at least some of them. The two largest boarding houses in town sheltered Black sailors almost exclusively, while others apparently held none but whites. One whaling brig, the *Rising States,* was notable for its all-Black crew, including its captain, William Cuffe, and officers, but this was an exception occasioned by the ship's having Black partners and investors. The rule is suggested by an observer who noted that, in 1837, there were "now in this vicinity, two [Black] captains, laid up in ordinary for want of employ, owing to the prejudice which exists against people of color. . . . There are two men now at sea, who are fully qualified for masters of vessels, and first rate whale men, but are obliged to serve as common sailors because of their color only."[33]

Maritime employment clearly attracted men of color and escaping slaves, offering relative freedom at sea and a sense of manly pride for those who had not known it before. During the first third of the nineteenth century, it had certainly contributed to the making of an African American community in New Bedford. But by midcentury, white prejudice in the labor market was squeezing Black men out of all but the most menial jobs on board. The way to long-term residence for the town's African Americans, and to the community that such protracted habitation facilitated, no longer lay primarily with "black jacks," but with their less peripatetic and adventurous but more rooted brothers and sisters living and working ashore.

So Douglass the fugitive's rosy first impressions of New Bedford in 1838 must be tempered by other reliable primary sources. In contrast to the white population at large, who enjoyed far greater diversity of employments, the population of color constituted a poorer subdivision of the labor force. Tax Collector Crapo's *Directories* for 1838–1845 reveal a Black workforce heavily invested in the whaling town's maritime pursuits initially, but one lacking permanent residence for the most part and ultimately unlikely to stay long. As opportunities for maritime work deteriorated for men of color, the ever-increasing proportion of the shore-bound remainder labored in menial jobs, worked in service trades, and occasionally found skilled employment, doing well enough to put roofs over their heads, food on the table, and roots of community in New Bedford.

NOTES

1. Frederick Douglass, *Narrative of the Life of Frederick Douglass, an American Slave* (Boston: Printed at the Anti-slavery Office, 1849), 112–13.
2. Douglass, *Narrative*, 114.
3. Ibid., 114–15. Douglass expanded on his activities and experiences at this time in two subsequent autobiographical works, *My Bondage and My Freedom* (1855) and *The Life and Times of Frederick Douglass* (1881), but included little in the way of helpful data concerning New Bedford's Black community.
4. Douglass, *Narrative*, 115–16.
5. See Henry H. Crapo, *The New Bedford Directory, Containing the Names of the Inhabitants, Their Occupations, Places of Business and Dwelling Houses . . .* (New Bedford, Mass.: J. C. Parmenter Printers, 1838), 24–25, for population figures taken in 1836. My estimates for the 1838 population of color are based on data

from 1836 and 1839 found in Henry H. Crapo, *The New Bedford Directory, Containing the Names of the Inhabitants, Their Occupations, Places of Business and Dwelling Houses . . .* (New Bedford, Mass.: Benjamin Lindsey, 1841), 28. For historical population statistics for American cities, see Campbell Gibson and Kay Jung, "Historical Census Statistics on Population Totals by Race, 1790 to 1990, and by Hispanic Origin, 1970 to 1990, for Large Cities and Other Urban Places in the United States by Population," Division Working Paper No. 76 (U.S. Census Bureau, Washington, D.C., February 2005), accessed 13 March 2019, https://www.census.gov/population/www/documentation/twps0076/twps0076.html. The 1840 census statistics for both New Bedford's populations are considerably lower than Crapo's figures. The town's assessors had tallied 12,585 residents in 1840; the U.S. census counted only 12,087, because, as Crapo explained, "in the latter census no persons are included excepting those having actual residence here, either as heads or members of families at the time when taken. This must necessarily be short of the actual population, as there is at all times a large number of persons '*at sea*,' who, nevertheless, to all intents and purposes, are inhabitants of this place." He felt the town's population by 1841 "exceeds 13,000." Crapo, *The New Bedford Directory* (1841), 28–29.

6. Kathryn Grover, *The Fugitive's Gibraltar: Escaping Slaves and Abolitionism in New Bedford, Massachusetts* (Amherst: University of Massachusetts Press, 2001), 56–57.
7. Robert C. Hayden, *African-Americans and Cape-Verdean-Americans in New Bedford: A History of Community and Achievement* (Boston: Select Publications, 1993), 29.
8. Grover, *The Fugitive's Gibraltar*, 118–120, 153–154; Crapo, *New Bedford Directory* for 1836, 1838, and 1841.
9. Grover, *The Fugitive's Gibraltar*, 59, 136.
10. W. Jeffrey Bolster, *Black Jacks: African American Seamen in the Age of Sail* (Cambridge, Mass.: Harvard University Press, 1997), 6, 220, 225; Grover, *The Fugitive's Gibraltar*, 268.
11. *New Bedford (Mass.) Weekly Mercury*, 20 April 1838.
12. *The Boston Directory, Containing, a List of the Merchants, Mechanic, Traders, and Others, of the Town of Boston; in Order to Enable Strangers to Find the Residence of Any Person* (Boston: John Norman, 1789).
13. Crapo, *The New Bedford Directory* (1841), iii–iv.
14. The "code" is in a list of abbreviations used in the 1838 *Directory*, 4.
15. "Lewis Temple's Real Innovation," New Bedford Whaling Museum, accessed 27 May 2019, https://www.whalingmuseum.org/learn/lewis-temple,.
16. Considering that New Bedford's economy enjoyed virtually full employment and that the purpose of the *Directory* was to identify actively working people, entries lacking a specific occupation cannot be dismissed as simply "unemployed." Incomplete data collection, printer's errors, or the status of being "between jobs" offer more-plausible explanations.

17. Powell was also a blacksmith. To avoid counting him twice, I so characterized his occupation for the table of occupations.
18. If these men had stayed in town or shipped on another vessel, they presumably would still have been listed in the *Directory*, as they had been in 1838.
19. Crapo, *The New Bedford Directory*, 1841, *iii*. My thanks to University of Massachusetts student Courtney Beauregard for her help with the 1841 data.
20. In separate studies and using different methods, both Kathryn Grover and Martha Putney identify this downward trend. See Grover, *The Fugitive's Gibraltar*, 311 n. 81, and Martha S. Putney, *Black Sailors: Afro-American Merchant Seaman and Whalemen Prior to the Civil War* (New York: Greenwood Press, 1987), 33–48, 125.
21. Elmo P. Hohman, *The American Whaleman: A Study of Life and Labor in the Whaling Industry* (1928; reprint, Clifton, N.J.: Augustus M. Kelley Publishers, 1972), 323, 314.
22. Bolster, *Black Jacks*, 226–28.
23. Ibid., 175–76.
24. "Fourth Annual Report of the American Anti-Slavery Society," *Quarterly Anti-Slavery Magazine* 2, no. 4 (July 1837): 427.
25. The dwelling houses were small by modern standards—a handful of such houses remain in New Bedford's historic center—but they were in good enough trim to favorably impress Douglass.
26. Nathan and Polly Johnson, Douglass's hosts, were one exception to the rule. They lived at 21 Seventh Street, a distinctly middle-class neighborhood. They were successful confectioners and bakers.
27. *New Bedford (Mass.) Weekly Mercury*, 18 August 1837. Douglass may have been influenced by his former condition as a slave and by a desire to extol the virtues of free labor. My thanks to Jeffrey S. Heyer for his work in finding references to living conditions in the town's newspapers.
28. Henry H. Crapo, Memorandum Book of Tax Delinquents, 1838–1840, Special Collections, New Bedford Free Public Library, Massachusetts.
29. Grover, *The Fugitive's Gibraltar*, 115; *New Bedford (Mass.) Weekly Mercury*, 30 March 1838.
30. Firsthand observation of Dog Corner quoted in "Local New Bedford Ma[ssachusetts] History, 1840–1849," *Whaling City.net*, accessed 20 January 2019, http://www.whalingcity.net/new_bedford_local_history_1840%20-%201849.html.
31. Grover, *The Fugitive's Gibraltar*, 136.
32. Douglass was right about the caulkers: all twenty-five of them in 1838 were white, and this situation had not improved by 1845.
33. "Fourth Annual Report of the American Anti-Slavery Society," 427.

10

FREEDOM ON THE MOVE BY SEA

Evidence of Maritime Escape Strategies in American Runaway Slave Advertisements

MEGAN JEFFREYS

> RUN away from the Subscriber, on Saturday Night last, a likely Negro Man named Prime, about 25 Years of Age, and about Five Feet Four Inches high; he took with him when he went away, two striped linsey Woolsey Jackets, a red Cloth one, and a blue Camblet one: He was seen coming out of the Mouth of the Kills in a Canoe on Sunday Morning last, with an Intention of coming to New-York, in Order to get on Board some Vessel: Whoever takes up and secures said Negro, so that his Master may have him again, shall have a reward of Five Dollars and all reasonable Charges paid by JOHN MERCEREAU. N.B. All Masters of Vessels and others, are forbid to carry him off or harbour him at their Peril.—It is very likely he is gone to Mr. David Provost's Farm, about Six Miles from New-York, as he formerly lived there. Staten-Island, August 11, 1767.
>
> —*New-York Gazette: or, The Weekly Post Boy*, 13 August 1767

Before technology enabled news, advertisements, sales, and trends to be accessed instantly via the internet, regional newspapers were the central hubs of information in eighteenth- and nineteenth-century America. They relayed knowledge regarding local policies, state laws, national political developments, and international reports. They announced marriages, business partnerships, and deaths and advertised the arrival of new goods and information essential to the smooth functioning of the contemporary economy.[1] Prominently featured among these advertisements, slave-owners, hoping to recover their property, placed notices that advised the public to be on the lookout for individuals who had fled bondage, choosing fugitivity over enslavement. These notices provided physical descriptions, lists of mannerisms and characteristics, suspected means of escape, and, whenever feasible, potential routes or destinations to help with the location and capture of the runaway. Usually headed by an attractive reward offer, these advertisements villainized their subjects and promised a bounty for their capture and re-enslavement. Now, more than 150 years after the end of legal slavery in the United States, those advertisements sit in archives, libraries, and basements, holding valuable information about slavery, master-slave relations, the frequency of escape, and the ways in which enslaved individuals sought pathways to freedom.

For decades, historians looked at slave narratives as primary sources elaborating stories of life in slavery, successful escapes, and contemporary ideas regarding abolition. The diverse approach of each narrative articulated new circumstances, experiences, and methods of escape. From the numerous attempts to escape by Frederick Douglass, to the rescue of Solomon Northup by prominent white northerners he knew prior to his capture and twelve-year enslavement, these stories convey circumstances of oppression, resistance, and survival while highlighting the firsthand experiences of the enslaved.[2] However, using runaway slave advertisements as a source, historians can discover other factors that help paint a more complete, albeit fraught, escape experience. In every slaveholding state and almost every county and town therein, slave-owners advertised for the loss of runaway, escaped, stolen, or missing individuals of whom they claimed ownership. In recent years, though, historians have turned increasingly to runaway slave advertisements to understand the impact of fugitive slave laws, the value of the enslaved as determined by slave-owners, and the anticipated destinations of fugitives.

Recent targeted research analyzing these newspaper advertisements reveals that, to an extent heretofore unappreciated, enslaved people frequently utilized the sea as a viable route to escape bondage, especially from the coastal regions and ports of the Deep South. From the moment of colonization in North America through the beginning of the twentieth century, the use of waterways to establish and maintain commerce increased exponentially. With the rise of maritime commerce, ports expanded to accommodate growing demand. The increased frequency of imported and exported goods and services directly correlates with the rise of runaway slave advertisements that allude to the use of vessels or maritime routes in the suspected escape of fugitives. As fleeing individuals turned towards waterways to escape the bonds of slavery, slaveowners increasingly reflected their fears of fugitive egress by sea in their advertisements, warning the public to be vigilant in ports.

However, limited access to these rich sources, dispersed in antebellum newspapers in many state and local depositories, complicates the production of more complete, encompassing, and illuminating scholarly studies.[3] In an effort to eliminate this barrier, many state libraries and archives have created their own digital databases that house runaway slave advertisements from regional newspapers.[4] Yet, the disparate and disconnected nature of such regional databases continues to hinder comprehensive studies of fugitivity and escape.

To ease these obstructions and expand possibilities for research, data collection, and education, Professor Edward Baptist, with the help of fellow historians and the staff of the Cornell Institute for Social and Economic Research (CISER), has established a digital database that will house runaway slave advertisements from across the United States and beyond. Entitled "Freedom on the Move" (hereafter FOTM), this online project database will store a comprehensive collection of North American runaway slave advertisements.[5] Featuring a rigorous crowdsourcing application to ensure accurate cataloging of transcriptions, the FOTM database is an ongoing effort that will incorporate new runaway-advertisement information for future research and educational purposes.[6] Since the creation of the first data model in 2013, the project continues to gain momentum, attracting new contributors, team members, and ideas. With a team of five core historians, the creative, productive crew at CISER, support from the staff of numerous universities, and funding from the National Endowment for the Humanities, National Historical Publications and Records Commission (NHPRC), the Mellon Foundation, and Cornell University, the project is now a reality. Moreover, FOTM is an ongoing project, designed to grow by the input of newfound primary-source materials and augmented through contributions from existing digitized collections.[7] As of August 2019, the database held more than 22,000 individual runaway slave advertisements from thirteen states, the distribution of which is illustrated in figure 10.1. Of these items, many are identical advertisements that were republished multiple times on successive dates by the same newspaper or were picked up and republished by different newspapers.[8] According to the Library of Congress, an estimated 200,000 fugitive slave notices appeared in U.S. newspapers between 1730 and 1865, though even more may exist.[9] Thus, currently the FOTM website holds about 10 percent of these notices. With 4,312 advertisements transcribed, as of the summer of 2019, the FOTM database provides undeniable insight into the lives and experiences of self-liberating individuals—especially those who escaped enslavement by water. As support and momentum increase, the FOTM database will expand to incorporate new contributions from universities, libraries, individuals, and archives from around the nation.

With an increasingly user-friendly interface, FOTM is compiled using two equally helpful applications. The first is a crowdsourcing application that allows the users to be a part of the archival procedure by assisting in the transcription process. Once registered, the user not only transcribes the advertisement but also answers questions about the advertisement, advertiser, event, runaway, and reward. With step-by-step instructions, this application is accessible to seasoned researchers and amateur historians alike. The second application allows the user to search through the advertisements by specific criteria including date, location, name, age, description, among other data or to browse more casually. Designed to be accessible to scholars, students, and citizen historians, the FOTM database provides an in-depth, interactive experience that brings the lives of the self-liberated into any classroom, laptop, or public history installation. As described on the FOTM website, runaway slave advertisements were

> created to control the movement of enslaved people, [but] ultimately preserved the details of individual lives—their personality, appearance, and life story. Taken collectively, the ads constitute a detailed, concise, and rare source of information about the experiences of enslaved people. . . . We are compiling thousands of stories of resistance that have never been accessible in one place.[10]

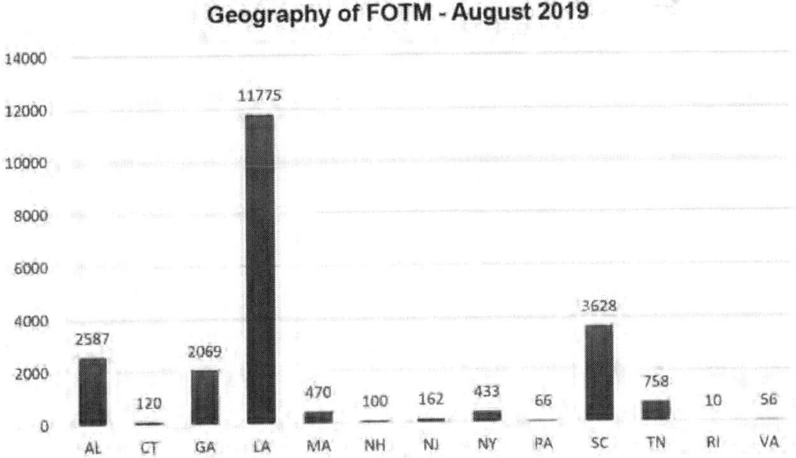

FIGURE 16. The Geography of the Freedom on the Move Project's Runaway Slave Advertisements by State. Graph prepared by author.

With plans to continue developing the project as an educators' tool, researchers' hub, and centralized source of runaway advertisements, FOTM confirms the profound insights that runaway slave advertisements provide about the development of slavery legislation, culture, and resistance in the United States.

What follows, then, is not limited to a discussion of the value of runaway slave advertisements and the necessity of a centralized database, though they do speak to the larger inquiry at hand in this maritime Underground Railroad volume. Instead, this chapter emphasizes the ways that runaway slave advertisements inform discussions about North American slavery while focusing specifically on the prominence of maritime and other waterborne escapes. By deconstructing the advertisements and considering their basic elements, historians and future scholars can better understand the ways in which these advertisements illuminate aspects of slavery that intersect with theories of economics, culture, law, politics, race, and gender.

To best address this complicated study, the present chapter is divided into two complementary discussions. The first section focuses on the use of the FOTM database to identify trends in escape attempts, rewards, departure points, and suspected destinations along the Atlantic Seaboard over time. By looking at larger sets of data, these trends define research parameters more clearly and articulate specific circumstances in which numerous runaways attempted to escape. The second section looks at an individual runaway slave advertisement as a nexus of historical inquiry. This section identifies modes of analysis, ways to connect documentation and sourcing through information found in the advertisements, and methods for using runaway slave advertisements to find more complete stories of escape and resistance. Ultimately, this chapter focuses on waterborne escape as a prominent form of resistance in the context of U.S. slavery by illuminating the frequency and impact of advertisement trends and emphasizing the possible contributions that a single advertisement might provide when it is broken down to its most basic elements.[11]

IDENTIFYING TRENDS OF MARITIME ESCAPE IN EIGHTEENTH- AND NINETEENTH-CENTURY AMERICA

For an institution whose origins ultimately relied entirely on ocean travel, trans-Atlantic slavery scholarship divulges little about the use of vessels as a method of escape.[12] Yet, despite the limited scholarship, water facilitated the escape of innumerable individuals from slavery. Out of the more than one hundred slave narratives written between the height of the slave trade and the end of the Civil

War in 1865, more than 70 percent of them discuss the use of waterways and vessels as means used in the course of their escape.[13] Similarly, in runaway slave advertisements, the subscribers—the individuals who placed notices seeking the return of their human property—refer to the threat of maritime escape consistently and with great frequency. Though more prominent along the Atlantic Seaboard, these trends extend into the interior of the United States, where major river corridors and lakes on state or national borders provided means for escape. Ultimately, the use of water as a viable means of flight occurred in every slaveholding state in America.

Though preliminary in nature, this section examines the prominence of maritime escape—escape as it connects to ocean-linked waterways—as seen through runaway slave advertisements, in which slave-owners published newspaper notices that articulated the escape of individuals enslaved on board vessels, predicted the use of vessels in escapes, and warned captains and shipowners against harboring fugitives.[14] In total, research undertaken for this publication turned up 617 such advertisements published in North American newspapers between 1716 and 1860 (fig. 10.2).[15] Within these chronological parameters, however, the majority (476) of the advertisements appear in the latter half of the time frame, or after 1793, following the introduction of fugitive slave legislation and coinciding with an increase in runaway slave advertisements overall. Utilizing the FOTM search function, these advertisements were identified by searching for terms typically included in contemporary discussions of maritime culture.[16] Though this process produced only 617 advertisements, it should be noted that many port-city advertisements (90 percent of extant examples) have yet to be introduced to the growing database.[17]

In addition, for the purposes of this chapter, FOTM analysis was not undertaken solely using the search criteria for enslaved persons who escaped via the maritime Underground Railroad to freedom in the northern U.S. states or Canada. Instead, to demonstrate the broad utility of the FOTM project, this chapter employs search parameters for all cases in the FOTM database prior to the U.S. Civil War in which runaways fled their enslavement using waterborne means, even if their flight was not always toward a territory or jurisdiction where they would be legally free or where slavery had been outlawed at the time. The data presented here include cases that occurred along the entire North American coast from New Orleans to New Hampshire between 1716 and 1860. It is important to remember, however, that slavery was legal in New England and New York prior to the late eighteenth century and in Canada until 1834. Thus, the enslaved fugitives discussed below may not have been escaping to freedom, necessarily, but they were attempting to escape from their circumstances of enslavement. As runaways, they could have attempted to live secretly amid free Black communities, for example, but it is important to note that waterborne flight occurred in many contexts, and prior to full legal abolition even escapes to northern states did not imply an escape to freedom.

Runaway slave advertisements that discuss the escape of individuals from coastal and seagoing vessels appear throughout the FOTM database. Of the 617 advertisements uncovered to date, 147 describe escapes initiated from a ship, on which the enslaved person was often traveling with the knowledge and permission of the slave-owner. Typically in these cases, the vessel was either under the subscriber's control or was operating in U.S. or British government service, depending on the historical era in which it was published. In many of these cases, the escapee had worked aboard the vessel either as a cook, crewmember, or drummer, illuminating important aspects of American slave life at sea in the eighteenth and nineteenth centuries. Of the 147 advertisements discussing escape from vessels, 108 pertained to escapes taking place in or around New York Harbor. Published in newspapers such as the *Royal Gazette* and *New-York Gazette*, these advertisements highlight the popularity of the New York port and the feasibility of escape in this particular area. Of the 433 total runaway slave advertisements in New York newspapers available in the FOTM database, these 108 advertisements describing flight from vessels represent 24.9 percent. The remaining 39 advertisements discussing escape from vessels also occurred

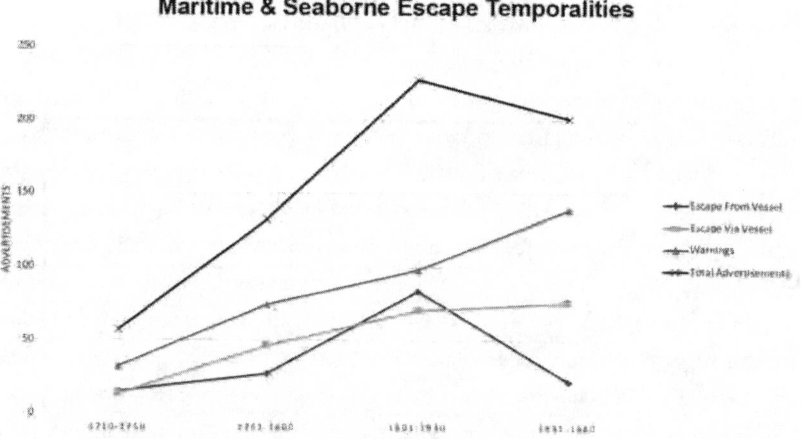

FIGURE 17. Maritime and Seaborne Escape Temporalities of the Freedom on the Move Project's Runaway Slave Advertisements. Graph prepared by the author.

in important port cities, such as Charleston, Newark, and New Orleans, with very few emanating from smaller coastal towns. Advertisements concerning escape from vessels also cover a broad timespan, with the first advertisement published in 1747 and the last in 1844 (fig. 10.2). Enslaved individuals appear to have escaped from vessels throughout slavery's long duration in North America.

Finally, in addition to location and era, this trend also illuminates advertisement consistencies regarding gender, age, and occupation. This sampling contains only males, who ranged in age from fourteen to fifty-four. Given the era and the history of maritime occupations, the predominance of male subjects is justified and not surprising.[18] Had these records indicated a woman, extended research would be required to understand the woman's role on the ship and why she had been employed when most captains favored employing or enslaving men. When the occupation is mentioned, most of the advertisements describe the escaped individuals as experienced sailors, drummers, and cooks. In 43 advertisements reporting escape from vessels, the subscriber describes the incident as desertion, and 38 of those same advertisements mention that the vessel from which the fugitive escaped was either a "ship of war" or "his majesty's ship."[19] This phenomenon, of course, speaks to the frequency with which enslaved individuals served on vessels belonging to or associated with the U.S. military and the Royal Navy prior to the nineteenth century. Thereafter, escape from seagoing vessels is limited to merchant or privately owned vessels dealing in the import or export of goods and materials. Nevertheless, the appearance of advertisements discussing maritime escape are not solely bound to escapes from seafaring vessels.

While 147 of the 617 maritime escape advertisements feature escape from a vessel, 205 advertisements describe escape situations in which the subscribers who placed the notice suspected that the escaped individuals attempted to flee through the use of ships or vessels. Representing just over 33 percent of the maritime escape advertisements from the current FOTM database, these advertisements typically articulated suspicions that the persons named in the notice had attempted to pass as free or gain employment on a vessel bound for a free state. While the location of the first trend—where individuals attempted to escape from a vessel—is highly representative of New York, advertisements in which the named fugitive escapes with the use of a vessel are more spatially diverse. These advertisements appear in New York, Charleston, Newark, Mobile, New Orleans, Boston, and Philadelphia in almost equal numbers. This underscores the significant use of port cities along the U.S. Atlantic Coast by fugitives as an accessible and immanently viable means for escape. During the eighteenth and nineteenth centuries, waterborne transportation provided the easiest, cheapest, safest, and fastest means for transporting goods and materials. With a continuous movement of ships coming in and going out of port, enslaved individuals seeking to run away could potentially find a vessel that would employ or hide them on the next voyage.

Not only was there an abundance of ships moving in and out of all U.S. ports on a regular basis, but there were also questions regarding the issue of slavery in what is now regarded as "international waters."[20] Prior to the global dominance of the U.S. and European naval powers in the twentieth century, maritime law recognized the open ocean as an international trade zone free to all nations but belonging to none.[21] The questionable jurisdiction and dominion of the Atlantic provided some protection for escaped individuals and the ships that harbored or employed them. With increased accessibility to vessels and greater possibilities of finding a path for freedom, escape via the sea became a persistent trend in runaway slave advertisements.

When compared, the two trends illuminate differences in frequency and representation of maritime escapes. Similar to the advertisements about escapes initiated from vessels, notices suspecting escape via vessels appeared in newspapers throughout the eighteenth and nineteenth centuries. From the first published advertisements in 1716 to the last occurrence in 1846, advertisements that suspected the use of vessels in escape appeared in almost every decade (see fig. 10.2). This category of advertisement clearly increases as the nineteenth century wore on because of the increase in published newspapers and the frequency with which newspapers reprinted identical advertisements in successive issues, but the consistency remains, demonstrating the continuing prevalence of maritime escape. Finally, though escape-from-vessel advertisements included only male subjects, notices suspecting escape via vessel include a mixture of men and women, with an increase in the latter after 1825. This trend illuminates a couple of key components of maritime escape. First, maritime escape attempts cross gendered boundaries. Though ship captains preferred to employ men, it appears that, in some cases, they allowed fugitive women to gain passage on their vessels. Consequently, in most runaway advertisements in which the subject is a female, the subscriber does not suspect she will search for employment on board a vessel. Instead, the subscriber proposes that she will likely gain passage on a ship. On the other hand, in most of the advertisements where the subjects are men, the subscribers warn that the fugitive will most likely look for employment aboard a vessel. Of course, there are exceptions to this rule. In one advertisement, published in New Orleans in 1837, the subscriber explains that Caroline, the enslaved subject of the advertisement, was last "seen on the Levee in man's clothes."[22] Her owner expected that, through the use of this disguise, she would attempt to board a ship as a man, perhaps gaining employment as a mariner. Regardless of the exceptions, however, it is clear that numerous fugitives viewed escape via vessel as conceivable, a belief that explains its abundant appearance in runaway slave advertisements.

Even in cases of advertisements wherein an escapee is not directly expected to use or escape from a vessel, subscribers and slave-owners clearly understood the risk of maritime escape and actively took measures to prevent it. The last major trend that appeared in these advertisements is the inclusion of warnings to ship captains and vessel owners. Appearing in 343 advertisements—more than half of the sample—vessel warnings were often included in advertisements that followed one of the previous trends.[23] Such warnings typically appeared at the end of a runaway slave advertisement and stated, essentially, that "all persons are hereby warned not to harbor or receive [an enslaved person] on board any vessel under the penalties of the law."[24] Much like the advertisements that predict escape via vessel, these warnings appeared in numerous states along the Atlantic Seaboard, but this trend also extends into the interior of the United States, particularly along major rivers. The expansive geography covered in this advertisement trend illuminates the scope of maritime and other waterborne escapes throughout the eighteenth and nineteenth centuries. The fear that enslaved individuals would escape by water extended beyond bustling port cities to include small towns and cities along most large waterways across America. Though much more prevalent in the intensive maritime communities of the U.S. East Coast, long-distance waterborne escape was not only a possibility but a reality in all the slaveholding states.

Advertisements that included warnings to ship captains and owners also constituted the largest chronological breadth of advertisement publications and subjects across all three trends. Spanning the early eighteenth century through the 1860s—as demonstrated in figure 10.2—these advertisements demonstrate the abundance of maritime escape in the United States. They also include the largest presence of escapes achieved by multiple fugitives acting together. While all of the advertisements about subjects who escaped from vessels and most of the advertisements that predicted the subject would escape via vessel focused on a single individual, these warnings accompanied numerous advertisements that announced the escape of entire groups of fugitives. From what may be assumed to be a family—a group including a man, a woman, and a young boy—to a small group of men, these advertisements articulate the importance of family and comradery among enslaved individuals while they attempted a seaborne escape from bondage.[25] They also include a fairly balanced mix of men and women, as well as many younger individuals, some even including infants. The inclusion of numerous subjects, despite age and gender differences, is telling in its own right. Maritime escape was not only a reality but one that was potentially present in escapes from any region with nearby long-distance water routes.

Among the many benefits of this comprehensive runaway slave database is its utility as a tool to understand the frequency with which certain historical trends appear. This cability will undoubtedly facilitate research to track Underground Railroad activities across space and through time. Though the numbers and trends examined and explained here are preliminary in nature due to the ongoing development of FOTM, they articulate the numerous ways that a centralized, integrated database for advertisements aids in the development of innovative scholarship. Maritime escapes of one type or another appear in almost every state represented in the FOTM database. As FOTM expands, encompassing additional print advertisements from different locations and eras, new trends may appear to offer fresh insight into maritime or waterborne escape as a feature of slavery experienced in North America. In the meantime, however, one should not discount the research possibilities available through examining a single runaway slave advertisement.

BASIC ELEMENTS OF RUNAWAY SLAVE ADVERTISEMENTS

In any given runaway slave advertisement, there are certain elements that must exist: the subject (the fugitive or fugitives), a physical description of the runaway(s), the subscriber (typically the slave-owner), a location, and a reward. Within each of these elements is the possibility to connect these advertisements with other documents and sources. A single runaway slave advertisement may serve as a nexus of historical inquiry; it is the beginning, center, and core of a broader research effort. As researchers analyze the elements of a runaway slave advertisement, the information gleaned becomes threads that connect different types of sources to the nexus. Through the use of single advertisement analysis, or the use of a small, controlled sample set, historians and researchers can analyze the various aspects of a runaway slave advertisement in order to identify new information about the era in which the incident it describes took place and the people discussed in the advertisement, as well as the role of newspapers in the escape and possible apprehension of the enslaved individual(s).[26]

On 20 June 1836, slave-owner James Deery published a runaway slave advertisement in the *Charleston Mercury*. In hopes of finding his lost human property, Deery included pertinent information that could aid in the fugitive's recapture. The advertisement reads:

> TEN DOLLARS REWARD Will be paid for the apprehension of my Negro Fellow NED, he is about 35 years old, dark complexion, stout made, about 5 feet 8 inches high, walks lame, good countenance when spoken to, and speaks good English. He has a wife on Edisto Island, and is supposed to be on Col. Ashe's plantation, as he left in his Sloop from South Bay, about three weeks ago. If it can be proved that he is harbored by any white, or free colored person, the law shall be most rigidly enforced. The above reward will be paid by delivering him to the work House.
>
> June 20 JAMES DEERY[27]

Within the advertisement, Deery incorporated all five elements of a typical runaway slave advertisement. In the eighteenth and nineteenth centuries, these elements conveyed crucial information that aided in the recapture of escaped individuals. In the present era, however, they provide a starting point for new historical inquiries into the characteristics of American slavery.

The first and perhaps most important element of a runaway slave advertisement is the subject, the enslaved individual. The entire advertisement revolves around this individual, since recovering human property is its entire objective and purpose. As such, the subject is the perfect place to begin examining a

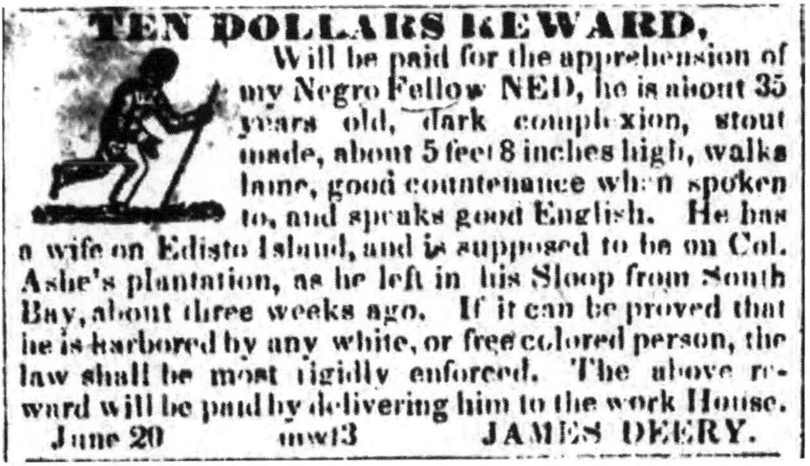

TEN DOLLARS REWARD,
Will be paid for the apprehension of my Negro Fellow NED, he is about 35 years old, dark complexion, stout made, about 5 feet 8 inches high, walks lame, good countenance when spoken to, and speaks good English. He has a wife on Edisto Island, and is supposed to be on Col. Ashe's plantation, as he left in his Sloop from South Bay, about three weeks ago. If it can be proved that he is harbored by any white, or free colored person, the law shall be most rigidly enforced. The above reward will be paid by delivering him to the work House.
June 20 mwf3 JAMES DEERY.

FIGURE 18. Runaway Slave Advertisement for "Ned" Placed by His Proclaimed Owner, James Deery, in the *Charleston (S.C.) Mercury*, 20 June 1836.

runaway slave advertisement. By knowing the enslaved individual's name, researchers can search through historical documents—such as slave narratives, Federal Writer's Project interviews, ship manifests, plantation records, marriage licenses, death certificates, among others—to understand more about the subject's unique experience.

Take, for instance, the above advertisement. As a thirty-five-year-old man in 1836, Ned would not have been alive during the 1930s interviews by the Federal Writer's Project (FWP). That fact eliminates a possible avenue of research. A quick search through slave narratives also reveals that, though some do mention enslaved individuals by the name of Ned, none aligns with his age and the date of the advertisement. Nevertheless, there are other clues to investigate. The advertisement mentions that Ned had a wife who lived on Edisto Island. While many enslaved individuals were married in "unofficial" ways, a substantial number sought federally recognized licenses during and after their enslavement.[28] After a thorough search through marriage records in and around Charleston, there is one possible connection. In a license obtained in 1867, a Ned Freeman—a popular last name adopted by previously enslaved individuals after emancipation—married Nelle Ashe.[29] With the same last name as the colonel mentioned in the advertisement, it is possible that Nelle Ashe was an enslaved woman on Colonel Ashe's plantation on Edisto Island, as enslaved individuals often used or were assigned their owner's last name. Given the possible escape as well as the impact of emancipation and the Civil War, however, it is also possible that Ned may not have remained in the Charleston area.[30] Further research would be necessary to confirm this possible connection, but it is a viable vein of research that could impart an additional piece of Ned and Nelle's full story.

Knowing the subject's name, while helpful in beginning a search, only provides minimal insight into the possible background of an enslaved individual. Equally important is the description of the subject that typically follows the name. This description often provides details about scarring, physical deformities, personas, skin color, clothing, and skills, all of which open up new opportunities for continued research. From the description of the enslaved, researchers can identify possible origins of the cloth or garments they were wearing, learn more about how they obtained their scars, illuminate their working conditions, identify more about their access to medicine—if they survived a disease such as small pox which left scarring—and uncover details about how they escaped. From Deery's description, Ned's height (five feet, eight inches) is fairly average for the era and region. His dark complexion speaks to his heritage, making it less likely that his father or earlier ancestors were of European descent. The fact that he "walks lame" could reflect the grueling environment in which he worked, or his limping gait could have been caused by a punishment, an injury, a birth defect, or an illness. Yet, despite his walking disability, Ned was described as having "good countenance when spoken to" while also speaking "good English." These traits, again, reflect more about his upbringing than his ancestry, but they could provide useful information to distinguish between Ned and another person of similar description. These combined factors work together to create a more nuanced picture of Ned and the circumstances of his escape. These conclusions tend to be more circumstantial in nature, but when combined with primary documentation about other aspects of Ned's life, they paint a more complete picture of his story.

To make more progress in tying Ned to historical documentation, the best route is to search by the subscriber's name. The subscriber of a runaway slave advertisement is typically the legal owner of the subject, unless stated otherwise. Because slave-owners usually left behind more documentation—state, federal, and personal records about themselves and their plantations—than the enslaved, following the subscriber's paper trail into the historical record provides a more nuanced understanding of the life of the people they enslaved, in this case Ned. The subscriber's name opens doors to documentation in the form of slave auction records, property records, tax documents, letters, journals, court documents, census data, and plantation or business records. Within each of these lines of inquiry, researchers have the possibility of finding records that illuminate daily life and the practical operation of slavery in the American South.

The subscriber of the above advertisement was a man named James Deery. That the advertisement asks for Ned to be returned to the "work House" conveys the possibility that Deery may have been connected to a business that housed, rented, and sold enslaved individuals who were not bound to one specific plantation.[31] A quick look through federal documentation provides numerous results for multiple persons named James Deery.[32] Narrowing down the search results to persons in the South Carolina area, however, brings to light an extensive family of Deerys who operated in and around Charleston from about 1790 through the mid-nineteenth century. In particular, a James D. Deery appears in numerous city directories beginning in 1822. This James Deery, a clerk for a local shipping company, could provide valuable insight regarding the mention of the sloop in the advertisement and possibly help illuminate whether it was used in Ned's escape or whether his use of the sloop was by permission, perhaps in an official capacity in connection to the workhouse. Considering that many shipping companies utilized workhouses to obtain inexpensive and reliable labor, this information helps link these disparate aspects of the advertisement in a way that makes Ned's story clearer and more comprehensible.

While the context and circumstances of the subscriber, the fugitive subject, and his or her description are critical to analyzing a runaway slave advertisement, the inclusion of a location is essential to maximizing the possibilities for additional connected research. In the initial search through documents connected to Ned and James Deery, numerous possibilities emerged from across the United States. Knowing that the initial escape began in South Bay near Charleston, South Carolina allowed the search to be narrowed and provided possible further connections pertaining to the subject and subscriber. Knowing the location of the escape incident, combined with other clues from the advertisement, allows for investigative extrapolation. For example, Deery mentions the location of Ned's wife, who resided on Edisto Island, a coastal enclave approximately twenty-five miles southwest of Charleston. In many runaway slave advertisements, the subscriber refers to nearby family residences in hopes of possibly recapturing the lost individual while they attempt to reconnect with their kin. Since Ned was last seen in the Charleston area and had left aboard a sloop, he easily could have sailed to where his wife lived. This scenario is Deery's hypothesis; the clear feasibility of such a plan provided would-be bounty hunters with a direction to pursue Ned. Finally, the location of the advertisement and the subject's community provides critical background that facilitates the construction and understanding of the subject's past. In this case, Ned's proximity to the sea accounts for his access to the sloop used in his flight. As an enslaved individual in a workhouse that happens to be in a large port city, Ned likely worked as a skilled laborer as opposed to a plantation or field hand. This detail, if true, changes the type and circumstances of his enslavement from the archetypal rural slavery of the southern United States to the urban slavery typical in port cities of the American seaboard.

These factors—the subject, description, subscriber, and the location—contribute to the impact and understanding of the final element: the reward. Why did Deery offer a mere ten-dollar reward for Ned, and how is that significant? Examining the monetary value Deery placed on recovering Ned at this specific time and place provides a telling indicator of the value of the fugitive to his proclaimed owner. When compared with those in other advertisements in Charleston from the same decade, rewards for escaped adult male runaways tended to range from twenty to one hundred dollars, depending on age, skills, countenance, and ability. We know that Ned, while in a prime age with a "good countenance," was hindered in performing his labor duties by his walking disability, a physical challenge that may have reduced his value.[33] Though Ned seems to be undervalued by James Deery in Charleston, most escaped men between the ages of thirty and fifty were assigned a similar reward value in New Orleans during the same decade.[34] With further research, the reward offered can also illuminate the subject's value in a given location—by searching through runaway advertisements by the same subscriber and comparing the rewards offered—while also shedding light on regional economic situations during a specific era.

Possibilities for archival corroboration grow exponentially when analysis of the above-mentioned elements yield additional data. Knowing the subject, his or her description, the subscriber, any locations mentioned within the advertisement, and the reward enables the researcher to connect the data points to draw new conclusions regarding specific enslaved individuals and runaway events. Not only do these analyses shed light on individual situations, they also illuminate the importance the fugitive placed on familial connections as compared to the prospect of permanent freedom. While Ned escaped, no doubt in the hope of achieving freedom, James Deery anticipated that he would venture south to find his wife instead of north towards a free state. Each specific runaway advertisement presents opportunities for examining slavery, escape, and resistance in a new light; the investigative potential is exceptional. This study presents only a fraction of possible research avenues available to future scholars in the FOTM database of runaway slave advertisements.

CONCLUSION

Archives, libraries, and other document repositories across the United States hold more than one hundred years of crucial historical documentation about North American slavery in the form of newspaper advertisements for runaway slaves. The abundance of runaway advertisements pertaining to aspects of maritime escape confirm that waterways represented an opportunity for enslaved individuals and simultaneously a threat of losing property for slave-owners. In the many port cities along the Atlantic Seaboard and the Gulf coast and even on major interior waterways across the United States, enslaved individuals demonstrated that increased access to vessels expanded the likelihood that they, or those helping them, would utilize water transport as a feasible means of escape. A significant cache of newly-digitized documentation—runaway advertisements in the FOTM database—provides fresh insight into this under-studied historical trend, and its value will increase as the database continues to grow. Indeed, the close analysis of a single advertisement offers rich information about specific individuals, regions, and eras, contributing to an enhanced understanding of how slavery functioned in the United States.

Newspaper runaway slave advertisements provide a window into an era when escape from enslavement by seaborne means was common and frequent. With the ongoing development and expansion of the Freedom on the Move project, more scholars will utilize this immense resource as a way of uncovering new aspects of this fascinating but hitherto under-researched topic. One thing is clear: the future historiography of the Underground Railroad will undoubtedly include a greater appreciation for maritime means of escape, as well as for the numerous ways that runaway advertisements can bring clarity to such fraught yet common circumstances.

NOTES

The author would like to thank Edward Baptist for his insight on the developing stages of this chapter. Also, a special thank you to the FOTM staff for their assistance and to Bree'ya Brown and Mark Jeffreys for their invaluable feedback. For those people who are unnamed in this acknowledgment, know that it is space, not appreciation, that runs low.

1. On print culture in the United States during the eighteenth and nineteenth centuries, see Isabelle Lehuu, *Carnival on the Page: Popular Print Media in Antebellum America* (Chapel Hill: University of North Carolina Press, 2000); Jonathan Senchyne, *The Intimacy of Paper in Early and Nineteenth-Century American Literature* (Amherst: University of Massachusetts Press, 2019).
2. Frederick Douglass, *Narrative of the Life of Frederick Douglass, an American Slave* (Boston: Anti-Slavery Office, 1846); and Solomon Northup, *Twelve Years a Slave: Narrative of Solomon Northup, a Citizen of New-York, Kidnapped in Washington City in 1841, and Rescued in 1853, from a Cotton Plantation near the Red River, in Louisiana* (Auburn, N.Y.: Derby and Miller, 1853).
3. Numerous monographs and articles have been published regarding this topic, including John Hope Franklin and Loren Schweninger, *Runaway Slaves: Rebels on the Plantation* (New York: Oxford University Press, 1999); Sally Hadden, *Slave Patrols: Law and Violence in Virginia and the Carolinas* (Cambridge, Mass.: Harvard University Press, 2003); and Martha Cutler, "'As White as Most White

Women': Racial Passing in Advertisements for Runaway Slaves and the Origins of a Multivalent Term," *American Studies* 54, no. 4 (2016): 73–97, 185.

4. State or region-based databases include but are not limited to the following: The Geography of Slavery in Virginia, *University of Virginia Library*, http://www2.vcdh.virginia.edu/gos/index.html; North Carolina Runaway Slave Advertisements, 1750–1865, *State Library of North Carolina*, http://libcdm1.uncg.edu/cdm/landingpage/collection/RAS; Julie DeMatties and Louis S. Diggs Sr., "Runaway Slave Ads: Baltimore County, Maryland, 1842–1863," *AfriGeneas*, http://www.afrigeneas.com/library/runaway_ads/balt-intro.html; Documenting Runaway Slaves, *University of Southern Mississippi*, http://runawayslaves.usm.edu/index.html.
5. "Freedom on the Move: Rediscovering the Stories of Self-Liberating People," Freedom on the Move, Cornell University, http://www.freedomonthemove.org.
6. According to Baptist, the creation of the database stems from two separate origins: his idea that began at Cornell University while he was writing *The Half Has Never Been Told* (New York: Basic Books, 2014); and the collaboration of Joshua Rothman and Mary Niall Mitchell of the University of Alabama and the University of New Orleans, respectively. While the database began as multiple separate projects, each with different goals in mind, their creators soon realized the benefits of working together to create one comprehensive database.
7. As of August 2019, the project had ten people on its "interdisciplinary" team. Historians working on the project are Edward Baptist, Vanessa Holden, Hasan Jeffries, Mary Niall Mitchell, and Joshua Rothman, all of whom work closely with the CISER team, which includes William Block, Elena Goloborodko, Janet Heslop, Brandon Kowalski, and Chris Perez. Baptist has also expressed his sincere gratitude for the Cornell Library staff, in particular Michelle Paolillo and Madeleine Casad, without whom this project would never have come into being. For a current list of team members, please visit https://freedomonthemove.org/#team.
8. At this point in the development of FOTM, it is not possible to assess precisely how many advertisements are duplicates; however, this will be a feature available in the future. The states represented in the FOTM database as of August 2019 are as follows: Alabama, Connecticut, Georgia, Louisiana, Massachusetts, New Hampshire, New Jersey, New York, Pennsylvania, South Carolina, Tennessee, Rhode Island, and Virginia.
9. Library of Congress, Research Guides, "Topics in Chronicling America," "Fugitive Slave Ads," accessed 5 October 2019, https://guides.loc.gov/chronicling-america-fugitive-slave-ads.
10. "About the Project," FOTM, accessed August 2019, https://freedomonthemove.org/#about.
11. This study utilizes only the advertisements available in the FOTM database. Consequently, the conclusions discussed here are preliminary and only represent a fraction of advertisements available across the United States. Nevertheless, these discussions and conclusions provide a glimpse into the use of runaway slave

advertisements and the representation of maritime escape on a grander scale. It is hoped that current and future scholars will move forward with these ideas, adding, expanding, and amending the conclusions drawn in this chapter.

12. While this is true for the study as a whole, some scholarship does examine escapes using steamboats along rivers in the interior. These include Thomas C. Buchanan, *Black Life on the Mississippi: Slaves, Free Blacks, and the Western Steamboat World* (Chapel Hill: University of North Carolina Press, 2004); Robert Gudmestad, *Steamboats and the Rise of the Cotton Kingdom* (Baton Rouge: Louisiana State University Press, 2011); Walter Johnson, *River of Dark Dreams: Slavery and Empire in the Cotton Kingdom* (Cambridge, Mass.: The Belknap Press of Harvard University Press, 2017).
13. The role of waterways and vessels in these narratives varies from case to case. Yet from William Wells Brown's escape across Lake Erie into Canada to Ellen and William Craft's use of steamboats, U.S. interior waterways appear in numerous narratives as a viable means of escape.
14. Important to note is that, despite the variety of decades present in this search, none of the individuals who escaped from a vessel were identified as part of a slave cargo. Most likely, missing or escaped unsold slaves would not have been sought through runaway slave advertisements. See "Trans-Atlantic Slave Trade—Estimates," *Slave Voyages*, accessed August 2019, https://www.slavevoyages.org/assessment/estimates; Sowande' Mustakeem, *Slavery at Sea: Terror, Sex, and Sickness in the Middle Passage* (Urbana: University of Illinois Press, 2016); Stephanie Smallwood, *Saltwater Slavery: A Middle Passage from Africa to American Diaspora* (Cambridge, Mass.: Harvard University Press, 2007).
15. The database search done to identify these 617 advertisements derived information only from the 4,312 advertisements transcribed in the FOTM database as of August 2019. As more advertisements are transcribed and added to the database, this number will undoubtedly grow. Nevertheless, the fact that maritime escape is present in approximately 14 percent of the transcribed advertisements demonstrates the prevalence of maritime methods as a viable means of escape.
16. These terms include boat names (schooner, sloop, vessel), occupations (sailor, cook), types of waterways or bodies of water (ocean, river, sea), and other terms that may be associated with water (row, wade, swim).
17. These numbers are based on a thorough search conducted by the author through the FOTM database in August and September 2019. As such, they are preliminary in nature and are sure to expand and change as new advertisements are added.
18. Recent scholarship focused on sailing, seafaring work, and gender includes Margaret S. Creighton and Lisa Norling, eds., *Iron Men, Wooden Women: Gender and Seafaring in the Atlantic World* (Baltimore, Md.: John Hopkins University Press, 1996).
19. While there were numerous advertisements that discussed these types of ships, these exact quotations reference the following advertisements: "ABSCONDED,"

Rivington's New York Gazetteer and Universal Advertiser, 24 December 1783, accessed August 2019, https://app.freedomonthemove.org/advertisements; and Wm. Furnivall, "Deserted," *New York Royal Gazette*, 18 July 1778, accessed August 2019, https://app.freedomonthemove.org/advertisements.

20. See Marcus Rediker, *Outlaws of the Atlantic: Sailors, Pirates, and Motley Crews in the Age of Sail* (Boston, Mass.: Beacon Press, 2014), 120–75.
21. See Edward Gordon, "Grotius and the Freedom of the Seas in the Seventeenth Century," *Williamette Journal of International Law and Dispute Resolution* 16, no. 2 (2008): 252–69.
22. Advertisement subscribed by Jas. Taylor, *New Orleans Daily Picayune,* 13 June 1837, accessed August 2019, https://app.freedomonthemove.org/advertisements.
23. Out of the 617 maritime escape advertisements in the FOTM database, 343 contained warnings to ship captains and owners. Of these, 265 appeared with warnings but followed no other major trends; 32 articulated an escape from a vessel; and 46 noted the possibility of the subject attempting to escape via vessel.
24. Advertisement subscribed by M. D. Eslava, *Mobile (Ala.) Commercial Register,* 14 December 1826, accessed August 2019, https://app.freedomonthemove.org/advertisements. When these advertisements discuss the "penalties of law," most refer to the punishments stipulated in the federal Fugitive Slave Acts of 1793 and 1850. Under these laws, and more aggressively in the latter, the federal government directed that fugitive slaves were to be returned to their owners. Failure to do so could result in a $1,000 fine (approximately $30,000 in 2019) or six months in jail.
25. While groups were present in many advertisements, particularly ones that included warnings, these specific examples stem from the following advertisements: C. Hall Blakely, "Ran Away or Stolen," *Mobile (Ala.) Commercial Register,* 25 November 1825, accessed August 2019, https://app.freedomonthemove.org/advertisements; "RUN-AWAY," *Rivington's New York Gazetteer and Universal Advertiser,* 6 December 1783, accessed August 2019, https://app.freedomonthemove.org/advertisements.
26. It is important to note that the following analysis focuses on uncovering information concerning the enslaved individuals or subjects and their condition. The advertisement itself, however, was written by the slave-owner. I do this in an attempt to demonstrate how scholars can read these advertisements "along the bias grain" to uncover more knowledge about the silent voices in the archive of slavery. For more information on this technique, please see Marisa Fuentes, *Dispossessed Lives: Enslaved Women, Violence, and the Archive* (Philadelphia: University of Pennsylvania Press, 2016), 78, and James C. Scott, *Domination and the Arts of Resistance: Hidden Transcripts* (New Haven, Conn.: Yale University Press, 1992), 3–5, 58, 183–201.
27. Advertisement subscribed by James Deery, *Charleston (S.C.) Mercury,* 20 June 1836, accessed August 2019, https://app.freedomonthemove.org/advertisements.
28. On enslaved marriage and rituals, and gaining licenses after emancipation, see Tera Hunter, *Bound in Wedlock: Slave and Free Black Marriages in the Nineteenth*

Century (Cambridge, Mass.: The Belknap Press of Harvard University Press, 2017), 23, 204–15.

29. Ned Freeman and Nelle Ashe, Marriage Certificate, 12 August 1867, South Carolina Department of Archives and History, digital image available at https://scdah.sc.gov/.
30. Ultimately, there are numerous factors at play. If Ned's escape was successful, he most likely would not have returned or stayed in the Charleston area to acquire the marriage certificate thirty years later. However, given the location of his wife and the short appearance of the advertisement (two weeks), it is likely that he would have been apprehended or stayed close to be with his wife. All possibilities must be considered and researched to identify which situation would be most feasible. Without corroboration, it is all speculation.
31. In the 1800s, the term *workhouse* (sometimes *work house* or *work-house*) typically referred to an establishment, prominent in many European countries and in the United States, designed to employ poor, dissolute, or underprivileged workers. See Martin Ravallion, *The Economics of Poverty: History, Measurement, and Poverty* (New York: Oxford University Press, 2016), 31–54.
32. This discussion of searching for state and federal records that include the subscriber is based on a search through the South Carolina Department of Archives and History at https://scdah.sc.gov/, as well as through the National Archives at https://www.archives.gov/.
33. James Deery, "Ten Dollars Reward," *Charleston (S.C.) Mercury*, 20 June 1836, accessed August 2019), https://app.freedomonthemove.org/advertisements.
34. Based on research from the FOTM database. The author searched for specific physical criteria throughout the database and identified this trend in New Orleans. FOTM offers users the capability to search by specific information in and about the advertisements including details pertaining to its publication, describing the runaway, regarding the runaway event, or identifying the enslaver or subscriber. See https://app.freedomonthemove.org/search.

CONTRIBUTORS

Dr. David S. Cecelski is an independent scholar who has written extensively about history, culture, and politics on the North Carolina coast. Among his books is *The Waterman's Song: Slavery and Freedom in Maritime North Carolina* (University of North Carolina Press, 2001). He divides his time between two places he loves deeply, Durham, N.C., and his family's homeplace in Carteret County, N.C.

Dr. Elysa Engelman earned her Ph.D. in American and New England Studies from Boston University. She is the Director of Exhibits for the Mystic Seaport Museum, as well as a collaborating lecturer for the Williams-Mystic Maritime Studies Program and an adjunct professor at the University of Connecticut.

Kathryn Grover is an independent scholar whose books include *Make a Way Somehow: African-American Life in a Northern Community* (Syracuse University Press, 1994) and *The Fugitive's Gibraltar: Escaping Slaves and Abolitionism in New Bedford, Massachusetts* (University of Massachusetts Press, 2001).

Dr. Mirelle Luecke is Humanities Curator at the Mid-America Arts Alliance in Kansas City, Missouri. Her dissertation project (University of Pittsburgh, 2018) is entitled "Topsail Alley: Labor Networks and Social Conflict on the New York Waterfront in the Age of Revolution."

Megan Jeffreys is a doctoral candidate in the History Department at Cornell University and a project moderator for the Freedom on the Move (FOTM) runaway slave advertisement database. Her research focuses on self-liberation and fugitivity in Virginia, using runaway slave advertisements to understand the lives and experiences of enslaved individuals.

Dr. Cheryl Janifer LaRoche is a lecturer in Anthropology and American Studies at the University of Maryland. Her first book, *Free Black Communities and the Underground Railroad: The Geography of Resistance*, was published in 2014 by the University of Illinois Press.

Dr. Cassandra Newby-Alexander is Professor of History and Director of the Joseph Jenkins Roberts Center for the Study of the African Diaspora at Norfolk State University in Virginia. She is the author of *Virginia Waterways and the Underground Railroad* (Mt. Pleasant, SC: The History Press, 2017).

Dr. Michael D. Thompson, UC Foundation Associate Professor of History at the University of Tennessee, Chattanooga, is the author of *Working on the Dock of the Bay: Labor and Enterprise in an Antebellum Southern Port* (University of South Carolina Press, 2015).

Dr. Len Travers, Professor Emeritus of history at the University of Massachusetts, Dartmouth, was the project director of *Inhabitants and Estates of the Town of Boston, 1630–1800*, published by the New England Historical and Genealogical Society and the Massachusetts Historical Society (2001). Travers's current project focuses on New Bedford's antebellum population of color, using information gleaned from city directories.

Dr. Timothy D. Walker, Professor of History at the University of Massachusetts Dartmouth, is a scholar of maritime history, colonial overseas expansion, and trans-oceanic slave trading. Walker is a guest investigator of the Woods Hole Oceanographic Institution, a contributing faculty member of the Munson Institute of Maritime Studies, and Director of the NEH "Landmarks in American History" workshops series, titled "Sailing to Freedom: New Bedford and the Underground Railroad" (2011–2021).

INDEX

Page references in italics indicate figures.

abolitionism and abolitionists: assistance of, 11, 61, 65, 67, 84; destinations, 43; fugitive "rescues," 110–11, 115, 165, 169, 171–72; newspapers, 87, 142–43; northern Blacks and, 154–55; opposition, 43–44; slavery opponents, 150–51, 153–54; southern ports, 38, 64–65, 90; station houses, 147–48. *See also* Greenman family

Adams, William, 109

African Society Methodist Church, 86

Albemarle Sound, 57, 66

Alexandria, Virginia, 29, 113, 115–16, 183

alias, use of, 27–28, 30, 92–93, 133. *See also* Stowaway Joe

American Anti-Slavery Society, 45

American Beacon, 87–88, 90

American Colonization Society, 151

Amistad uprising, 16, 141, 148–49

Anacostia River, 113, 115

Anderson, Henry, 57

Annapolis, Maryland, 99, 112

antislavery: Liberty Party, 45; Quakerism and, 25–27

Armstead, Mary D. *See* Davis, Clarissa

Armstrong, John. *See* Hill, John

Ashe, Nelle, 209–10

Atkinson, C. F., 165

Atkinson, John and Mary, 92

Atlantic Ocean, 37, 81

Attucks, Crispus, 163

badges, slave or free, 36, 38, 41–42, 64, 72

Bagnall, William, 81, 93

Bailey, Frederick Augustus Washington. *See* Douglass, Frederick

Baltimore, Maryland: abolitionists in, 104; difficulty of escape, 111; enslaved African Americans in, 103–4; free Black community, 102–5, 118; pipeline to freedom, 102

Baltimore Harbor, 10–11; Black workers and mariners, 109; enslaved sailors in the, 102; Pratt Street slave traders, 102, 105

Baptist, Edward, 17, 200, 215n6

Bath, Maine, 171

Bath, North Carolina, 69

Bearse, Austin, 165–66

Beaufort, North Carolina, 20, 57, 68

Beecher, Henry Ward, 116, 122n53
Bell, Daniel, 115
Berkley, Margaret, 98n46
Berry, Lewis, 160–61, 172, 178n47
Berry, Wesley, 172–73
Bertie County (N.C.) Superior Court, 72
Black Jacks (Bolster), 15, 26
Blevins, John A., 91
Blight, David, 15, 148, 154
Blockson, Charles, 111–12
Bodams, Mathew, 57
Bolster, W. Jeffrey, 15, 26, 102–3, 133, 163, 183–84, 189
Bordewich, Fergus M., 4, 15–16
Boston, Eliza, 172
Boston, Massachusetts, 161; abolitionists in, 11, 161; captains and stowaways, 172; commerce with southern ports, 162–64; cradle of antislavery movement, 43, 161–62; directories, 184; free Black community, 154, 165; proslavery merchants, 44; return of slaves South, 31, 73, 145, 155; runaway destination, 26, 37, 41–42, 48, 59, 83, 161, 165, 169–70; Yankee network, 36, 69. *See also* vigilance committees
Bostwick, Andrew, 128
Bound for Canaan (Bordewich), 15
bounties and rewards, 42, 58–59, 70, 85, 87–88, 93, 104, 181; fugitive slave fund, 85–86
Bowley, John, 110–11
Bowley, Kessiah "Kizzy" Jolley, 110
Bragg, Thomas, 72
Brandegee, Augustus, 146
Brantford, Canada, 83
British Colonial Office, 16, 32n5
British Navy and maritime empire, 15–16
Brodess, John, 110
Broocher, Charles, 188
Brooks, S., 91
Brown, Elizabeth, 92
Brown, Henry "Box," 108
Brown, William Wells, 163, 216n13
Browne, John White, 168
Bryant, James L., 172
Burns, Anthony, 31
Bush, William, 183
Buzzard's Point, District of Columbia, 115

Cambridge, Maryland, 110
Camden County, North Carolina, 66
Cape Cod, Massachusetts, 11, 166, 170
Cape Fear and Cape Fear River, North Carolina, 54, 57, 64, 67–68, 71, 164
Cape May, New Jersey, *ii*
Cape Verde Islands, 29
Caribbean Sea, 139n57
Carney, William H., 27
Carter, Hill, 22
Carter, Joseph, 91
Carter, Josiah "Siah" Hulett, 20–21
Caulkins, Nehemiah, 60
Cecelski, David, 10, 15, 103, 144
census: African American population, 182; Canadian, 83; federal, 95n7; federal (1800), 128; federal (1840), 98n46, 195n5; federal (1850), 174nn17–18; federal (1860), 155
Chace, Elizabeth Buffum, 154
Charleston, South Carolina: fear of entrapment in, 37; fugitive episode, 205, 210–13, 218n30; jail requirement for Black sailors, 104; maritime escapes and, 144, 166; port activity, 38, 40, 46–47, 52nn43–44, 205; sea escapes of, 10, 36; vessel inspection, 45, 52n37; waterfront labor, 41–44. *See also* legislation, slavery
Charleston Courier, 40, 42, 44
Charleston Mercury, 209
Charous, H., 91
Chesapeake and Delaware Canal, 100, 105–6, 109, 115, 118, 119n18, 121n32
Chesapeake Bay, 6, 99–100, *101*, 116; aid to British, 102; Blacks' familiarity with, 118; escapes from, 6, 11, 106–7, 109, 112; perils of, 115; slaves seeking passage, 63; Tubman family, 110–11
Chester County, Pennsylvania, 112
Cheves, Langdon, 43
Choptank River, Maryland, 6, 100
Chowan County, North Carolina, 61
Civil War, 73; African American Fifty-Fourth Massachusetts Infantry

Regiment, 27; contraband slaves, 22; former slaves Union pilots, 69, 73; naval blockades, 20–21, 53n60
coastal water escape routes: advertisements in, 199–200, 208; Black watermen and, 54, 65; East Coast ports in, 55, 57; examination of, 10; geography of coast, 73, 100; havens for runaways, 59–60; interconnected maritime culture of, 149–50; Keene's route, 106–7; new research on, 4–5; New York Ship Inspection Law and, 49; Potomac route, 117–18; proximity to water, 6; southern ports and, 135; tidewater African communities and, 56
Cockburn, George, 102
Colley, John G., 44
Collins, Adam, 42
Collins, George, 98n37
Colored Sailors' Home, 45
Commissioners of Navigation and Pilotage on the Cape Fear River, 71
complicity: financial incentives for, 92–93; free Blacks and enslaved, 37, 40, 44, 60–61, 64–65, 71–72; seamen, 69; whites, 41–42, 48, 60–61, 93. *See also* abolitionism and abolitionists
Congdon, Charles T., 26
Congressional Medal of Honor, 27
Cooley, Mary Ann, 171
Cooper, Arthur and Mary, 172
Cooper River, South Carolina, 40, 49
Cornell Institute for Social and Economic Research (CISER), 200, 215
Cornfield Harbor, 116
Corps of Colonial Marines, 101
Cotton, Jack, 166
Craft, William and Ellen, 108, 216n13
Crapo, Henry Howland, 168, 184, 189, 195–96
Cuffe, Paul, 166–67
Cuffe, William, 29, 194
curfews on Black people, 90
Currituck Sound, 66, 73
Curry, James, 113

Daily Advertiser, 123, 134
dangers of seeking passage, 62–63, 72
Davis, Charles, 93
Davis, Clarissa, 93, 98n46
Davis, Mary Greenman, 147–48
Davis, Pardon, 151
Davis, William, Catharine, and Louisa, 81–82, 84, 93, 95
Davis Ridge, North Carolina, 69
Dawson, Kevin, 146
Deep South, 4, 25, 59, 102
Deep South ports, 102, 199
Deery, James, 209–13
Delaware River, 105–6
Delmarva Peninsula, 100
Dickenson, Ben, 63
disguises, 108, 132, 207; sailor garb, 133, 138n43
Douglass, Charles, 27
Douglass, Frederick: autobiographies of, 133, 180, 195n3, 199; Baltimore or plantation life, 103; with Edmonson children, 116; impression of New Bedford, 180, 192, 195; in New Bedford, 27, 154, 167, 181–85; New Bedford housing, 191, 194; Perryville escape, 18, 108–9; port town slave, 59; trade of caulking, 179, 182, 197n32; unskilled waterfront jobs, 186–87
Douglass, Frederick, Jr., 27
Douglass, Lewis, 27
Drayton, Daniel, 63, 113, 115–16, *117*
Ducker, Thomas, 115
Dudley, Edward, 59

Eastern Shore, Maryland, 6, 100, 110, 112
Eden, Richard, 63
Edenton, North Carolina, 57, 63–64
Edisto Island, South Carolina, 42, 210, 212
Edmonson, Mary and Emily, *114*, 115–16
Eglin, Harriet, 108
Elizabeth City, North Carolina, 57, 66
Elizabeth River, Virginia, 84, 90
Elk River, Maryland, 105, 115, 118
Elliott, Ben, 42
Elm Cemetery, Mystic, 156
Emancipator, The, 41–42, 49
Emerson, James, 104
Epic Journeys of Freedom (Pybus), 16

Ericsson Line, 109, 118, 121n32
escapes from slavery: as cargo, 109; masquerades, 108; *Pearl* schooner escape, 113–17, 122n50; Tubman family, 109–11
Ewing, A., 91

Fairhaven, Massachusetts, 29
Fayetteville, North Carolina, 70
Federal Writer's Project (FWP), 210
Fells Point, Maryland, 99–100, 102, 105, 110–11
Ferebee, London, 66
ferries and ferrymen, 18, 107, 118
Fields, Henry, 112
Finlay, Nancy, 148
flatboats, 57, 62, 65, 68, 86
Flowers, Charles, 29
Foner, Eric, 17, 136n8
Ford, Lewis, 151
Ford, Sheridan and Julia, 92–94
forests and forest industries, 62; survival in, 64
Forman, Isaac, Fanny, and William, 80–84, *89*, 92
Fort Albion, Tangier Island, Maryland, 101
Fortune, Thomas, 72
Fountain, Albert, 31, *56*, 57
Freedom on the Move (FOTM), 17, 208, 214; advertisement database, 17, 200; advertisements, study of, 202, 212, 215n11; crowdsourcing application, 201; geography of project, *201*, 203, 207; inland waterways, 216nn12–13; preliminary research, 216n15, 216n17; project origin, 12, 215nn6–8; project parameters, 203–5; search capabilities, 201, 216n16; trends in runaway escapes, 202, 205–6, 208, 213, 218n34; use of ships or vessels, 205–6; warnings to vessel masters, 217n23; work in progress, 200–201
Freeman, Ned, 209–13, 218n30
French, Rodney, 26
Frenchtown, Maryland, 115
Friends, Society of, 25–27, 54, 61, 65–67, 72, 164
From American Slaves to Nova Scotian Subjects (Whitfield), 15
fugitive assistants, 161
Fugitive's Gibraltar, The (Grover), 15
fugitive slave laws. *See* legislation, slavery
fugitive slave narratives: Atkinson, John and Mary, 92; Jackson, John Andrew, 36–38; Johnson, Charles, 133; Minkins, 95n7; slave assistance, 60; Smith, James Lindsey, 148; stationmaster accounts, 80–81; waterfront labor in, 41–42, 54–56, 66; waterway escapes, 1, 202–3. *See also* Siebert, Wilbur; Still, William
Fuller, Samuel, 67, 164
fumigation of vessels, 20, 59, 71, 91, 144

Galloway, Abraham, 63
Gara, Larry, 92, 154
Garrison, William Lloyd, 26, 43, 142, 150, 161, 172
Gateway to Freedom (Foner), 16
Gay, Sydney Howard, 167
Gellman, David, 124
Georgetown, D.C., 113
Georgetown, South Carolina, 147
German, Andrew, 146
Giles, Charlotte, 108
Goldsboro, North Carolina, 57
Gorham, Henry, 63
Grandy, Moses, 66
Great Alligator Swamp, 62
Great Dismal Swamp, 57, 60, 62, 84
Green, Lear, 109
Greenman family, 11, 141–42, 147–54, 156–57
Greenmanville Seventh Day Baptist Church, 150, 154
Gregory, Julia Ann, 92
Grimes, Harry, 63
Grimes, William, 19
Grinnell, Joseph, 189
Griswold, S. S., 150–51, 153–54
Gross, Gideon, 104
Groton, Massachusetts, 146
Grover, Kathryn, 11, 15, 26, 184
Gulf Stream, 8–9, 59

Haiti, 16
Haitian Revolution, 135
Hall, William, 88, 92
Hallsville, North Carolina, 68
Hamlin, Susan, 42
Hampton Roads, Virginia, 10, 16, 81–88, 90–91, 93–94, 96n14
Hand, Jonathan, 40
Hannum, James W., 168
Hanscom, S. P., 171
Harding, Vincent, 94
Harris, James W., 183
Harris, Leslie, 124, 130
Hattendorf, John B., 33n13, 33n15, 34n27
Havana, Cuba, 153
Havre de Grace, Maryland, 99, 107–8, 118
Heines, Peter, 57
Henrico County, Virginia, 85
Henry, William, 168–69
Higgins, James S., 167
Higginson, Thomas Wentworth, 165
Hill, Dempsey, 20–21
Hill, John, 83, 168–69
Hinton, Peter W., 88
hiring out, 61, 81, 85–87, 92
historiography, 1–4, 10, 14, 17, 32, 214
History of New Bedford (Ricketson), 27
Hodges, Graham Russell, 124
Hodges, James, 91
Holly, Sallie, 149
Holmes Hole, Massachusetts, 172
Hooper, G., 39
Howard Methodist Episcopal Church, 112
Huntington, A. J., 42
Hutchinson, Felix, 29
Hyde County, North Carolina, 57

Indian Ocean, 28
inland waterways, 18, 20, 57, 105
international waters, 206
Irving, Robert. *See* Ford, Sheridan and Julia

Jackson, Francis, 171
Jackson, John Andrew, 36–38, 41, 48
Jacksonville, Florida, 147, 171
Jacobs, Harriet Ann, 28, 57, 61, 63–64
Jacobs, John S., 28, 183, 194
James River, Virginia, 21, 84
Jennings, Paul, 115
Johnson, Charles, 133
Johnson, Ezra, 194
Johnson, Jane, 169
Johnson, "Lisbon," 29
Johnson, Nathan and Polly, 181, 187, 197n26
Johnson, William Henry, 183
Jones, Benjamin. *See* Stowaway Joe
Jones, Columbus, 145
Jones, Edgar (John Mason), 172
Jones, Thomas H., 20, 49n4, 61, 66, *126*
Jones, William Peel, 109
Jordan, William, 64

Keene, Joseph, and family, 106–7, 120n20
Key West, Florida, 145, 152
King's County, Virginia, 22
Knetsch, Joe, 16

Labaree, Benjamin Woods, 33n13, 33n15, 34n27, 158n30, 173n4, 173n8, 174n13
Lake Phelps, 62
Lancaster County, Pennsylvania, 112
Landers, Jane, 15
Landmarks in American History (NEH), 4, 200
Larson, Kate Clifford, 6
Latimer, Zebulon, 61
Lawrence, Joseph, 40
Lee, Edward, 91
legislation, slavery, 19; Act to Prevent the Abduction and Escape of Slaves, Florida, 19; capital offense in South Carolina, 40; Compromise of 1850, 116; Fugitive Slave Act of 1793, 22–23, 85; Fugitive Slave Act of 1850, 26–27, 31, 44, 73, 85, 141, 150–51, 155, 169, 217n24; Gradual Emancipation Act, New York (1799), 128–29; Gradual Emancipation Act, Pennsylvania, 136n7; gradual manumission law, New Jersey, 160; hiring out ban, Virginia, 86; Inspection of Vessels Act, Virginia (1856), 90–91, 97nn35–36; Negro Seamen Acts, 37–38, 45–46, 104, 111, 164;

legislation, slavery (*continued*)
New York fugitive slave law, 44, 46; slavery banned in Massachusetts, 166, 174n19; South Carolina fugitive slave laws, 45–46; South Carolina's New York Ship Inspection Law, 38, 45–49, 52n37, 52n40; transport forbidden to slaves, Maryland, 108–9; white sailor requirement, Maryland, 107
Levy, Moses, 43
Lewey, Henry and Rebecca, *89*, 169–70
Liberator, The, 142–43, 150–51
Liberty Line, The (Gara), 92
Library of Congress, 200
Light Street Wharf, 109
Little Choptank River, Maryland, 106
Liverpool, England, 43, 152
longshoremen, 4, 20, 187. *See* wharf workers
Lumpkin, Amie, 43
Lynah, James, 38

Madison, Dolly, 116
maritime commerce, 18, 47, 52n46, 131, 163–65
maritime labor: Black and white workers, 67–70, 86, 91, 163, 194–95; escaped slaves employment, 183–85; escape strategies, 123–24; ferrymen, 66; laws affecting Black pilots, 70; oystermen, 67; peddlers, 66; port and ship workers, 65–67, 84–85, 132; recruitment by "crimps," 189–90; skilled Black seamen, 107
Marshall, Wharfinger Thomas, 43
Martha's Vineyard, Massachusetts, 11, 166, 170–72
Mason, James, 85
Mason, John, 171–72
Mason-Dixon line, 8, 11, 44
Maxson, William Ellery, 150
McWhann, William, 38
Medley or New Bedford Marine Journal, 22, 24
Melville, Herman, 180, 191
Menemsha Bight, Martha's Vineyard, 171
Michel, Francis, 48
Millburn, Mary (Louisa F. Jones), 30
Miller, J. Root, 151
Minkins, John, 81, 83, 87, 92–93, 95n7
Mobile, Alabama, 48, 131, 152, 155, 163, 205
Moore, Furney, 72
Moore, Mariah, 83–84
Morris, James, 57
Morris, Robert, 170
Mr. Elliott, 67, 164
Mundy, Sarah and Elizabeth, 154–56
municipal ordinances, 71
Murdaugh, James, 91
Murray, Anna, 108
mutiny. *See Amistad* uprising; Haitian Revolution
mutiny, *Creole*, 16
Mystic, Connecticut, 11, 141–43, 147, 149–50, 152, 155
Mystic-Built (Peterson), 152
Mystic Pioneer, 150
Mystic River, Connecticut, 141, 146–47, 149, 152, 156
Mystic Seaport Museum, 141, 147–48

Nansemond River, Virginia, 84
Nantucket, Massachusetts, 11, 160–61; Black community of, 165–66, 172; whaling industry, 163–65
Narragansett, Rhode Island, 155
Narrative of the Life of Frederick Douglass (Douglass), 180, 182, 192
National Intelligencer, The, 100
National Park Service Network to Freedom, 99
Nell, William C., 169
Neuse River, North Carolina, 57, 65
Newark, New Jersey, 205
New Bedford, Massachusetts: abolitionism in, 25, 170–73; African American maritime labor, 11; African American neighborhoods, 191–92; Douglass escape to, 108, 179, 184; employment in, 181–83, 185–86, 194, 196n16; escaped slaves in, 182–83; Ford, Sheridan, escape to, 92–93; free Black community, 82, 154, 165, 180–82, 195, 195n3; Fugitive's Gibraltar, 26, 30, 181; fugitive slave incidents, 166–67; "golden age"

of whaling, 189; housing for mariners, 160, 191, 197nn25–26, 197n27; maritime commerce with southern ports, 162–65; poverty in, 192; racial prejudice in, 194; runaways on whaling vessels, 28–29; Seamen's Temperance Boarding House, 187; segregation in, 194; standard runaway slave advertisements, 22; textile mill employment, 27; Underground Railroad terminus, 26, 161, 180; whaling industry, 15, 165, 169, 190
New Bedford Anti-Slavery Society, 26
New Bedford Directory, The, 184–85; "Colored" employment in, 186–90, *186*, 195, 197n18; housing in, 191, *193*; population figures, 195n5
New Bedford Evening Standard, whaling industry, 164
New Bedford Whaling Museum, 29
New Bern, North Carolina, 57, 65, 69, 72, 167; wharf district, 69
Newby-Alexander, Cassandra, 17
New Haven, Connecticut, 148
New London, Connecticut, 11, 141–46, 156, 157n12
New Orleans, Louisiana, 102; advertisements in, 205, 207, 213, 218n34; cotton bales from, 47, 131; escapes from, 133, 168; jail for assisting escapes, 151; northern traders in, 152, 163; port of, 48; slaveholding region, 9–10; slave market of, 16, 105, 116
Newport, Rhode Island, 131, 152, 155, 166
newspaper articles and letters: editorials, 86, 91, 107; on housing, 192; letters to the editor, 88–90; notices and articles, 140–41, 143–45, 155–56, 170–71; speech by abolitionist, 149. *See also* runaway slave advertisements
New York, New York: abolitionism in, 45; advertisements in, 124–25, 138n38, 138n43; African American community network, 130–31; anonymity of, 132–34; Black history in, 127–28; Black occupations, 129, 137n27; city markets, 130; free Black community, 127, 129; goals of runaways, 131; Manumission Society, 128; maritime network, 11, 125–26, 133–34, 136n9; packet ships, 40; port activity, 130–33; preferred destination, 43, 204
New-York Gazette, 204
New-York Packet, 127
Niagara Falls, 83–84
Noank, Connecticut, 146, 154
Norfolk, Virginia: British Navy and, 100; enslaved port workers, 82, 87; escapes from, 20, 27, 30, 80, 83, 88; failed escapes, 72, 145; free Black seamen, 44; fugitive account, 95n7; maritime Underground Railroad, 10, 57, 84, 86, 169–70; northern traders in, 167; pilots in, 66; slave auctions, 150; slaves jailed, 81, 92
Norfolk and Portsmouth Herald, 85
Northampton County, Virginia, 28
North Carolina General Assembly, 62, 70; quarantine of ships, 71
Northup, Solomon, 199
Norwich, Connecticut, 146, 148, 157n12

occupations, water-connected, 4–5, 10. *See also* longshoremen; maritime labor; pilots; wharf workers
Ocracoke, North Carolina, 69, 73
Ontario, Canada, 82
Orlando, John, 145
Outer Banks, North Carolina, 21, 68, 73

Pamlico River, North Carolina, 29
Parker, Theodore, 171
Parsons, W. W., 88
Parson's Creek, Maryland, 106
Passages to Freedom (Blight), 15
Patapsco River, Maryland, 100
Pell, Aaron, 123
Pembroke, Massachusetts, 168
Pennock, Alex M., 88
Pennsylvania Anti-Slavery Society, 154
Pensacola, Florida, 145
Perryville, Maryland, 107–8, 112, 118
Peters, Samuel, 171
Petersburg, Virginia, 83, 86, 95n7, 104, 134, 169
Peterson, William, 147, 152

Philadelphia, Pennsylvania: advertisements in, 205; capture, escaped slaves, 27; free Black community, 81–82, 154; Keene's route, 106; League Island arrivals, *89*; maritime commerce with southern ports, 163–64; merchants, 163; overland route to, 18; runaway destination, 31, 57, 63–64, 108–9, 167, 169; stationmaster accounts, 1, 80, 94, 95n7; Tubman family escape, 111; Underground Railroad safe house, 30; Underground Railroad terminus, 83
Philadelphia, Wilmington, and Baltimore Railroad Steam Ferry, 107–8
Philbrick, Nathaniel, 33n12
Phillips, Stephen C., 168
Phillips, Wendell, 165
pilots, 38, 54, 66–67, 70–71, 100, 111, 164
Pinckney, Charles, 40
Piper, Philip, 29
Piper, William, 183
Pipkins, Jefferson, 91, 98n37
Plymouth, North Carolina, 57
Point Lookout, Virginia, 116
Port Deposit, Maryland, 112
Portsmouth, Virginia: assistance of skilled artisans, 91; departure point, 57, 86, 154; editorials, 89; escapes from, 20, 92–93; fugitive account, 95n7, 98n37; racial equality in, 69; restive slave population, 87; slave-owners in, 81
port towns. *See* Charleston, South Carolina; Edenton, North Carolina; Elizabeth City, North Carolina; New Bern, North Carolina; Norfolk, Virginia; Wilmington, North Carolina
Post, Amy Kirby, 169
Potomac River, 84, 100–101, 113, 115–17
Potter, Josephus, 143, 145–46
Potter, Sam, 70
Powell, William P., 160–61, 173, 187, 197n17
President Street Station, 108
Procknik, Mark, 29
proslavery newspapers, 90
protection papers, 133–34, *162*
Providence, Rhode Island, 132, 155, 166, 182, 184
Pybus, Cassandra, 16

Quakers. *See* Friends, Society of
Quarterly Anti-slavery Magazine, The, 191
Queen's County, Virginia, 22

Randall, Edinbur (John Mason), 171
Rappahannock River, Virginia, 84
Ray, Charles B., 166
Ray, Isaiah C., 175n29
Ray, James, 92
Redick, Willis and Lydia, 81–82, 84
Rediker, Marcus, 33n11, 138n49, 139n57, 217n20
Republican Standard, 170
Revolutionary War: Battle of Yorktown, 33n12; Dunmore's Proclamation, 128
rewards. *See* bounties and rewards
Reynolds, Joseph, 81, 95n3
Rice, Isaac, 155
Richmond, Virginia, 16, 31, 80, 85–86, 95n7
Ricketson, Daniel, 27
Ricketts, Cato, 91
Roanoke River, Virginia, 57, 72
Robinson, Peter, 66–67, 164
Robinson, William H., 54, 60, 66, 164
Rochester, New York, 169
Rodman, Samuel, 166
Rodman, William R., 183
Roselle, James, 29
Rotch, William, Sr., 166
Royal Gazette, 204
Ruggles, David, 139n59, 167
runaways, unsuccessful, 42–43, 85, 88, 116
runaway slave advertisements: in Annapolis, 112; in Charleston paper, 38–39, 42; coastal and seagoing vessel escapes, 204–5; descriptions in, 63; digital databases of, 200; groups of fugitives, 207–8, 217n25; historical source, 199; Keene family, 106–7, 120n20; for Lewis Berry, 178n47; locations of, 205, 212; military vessels, 205, 216n19; for Ned Freeman, 218n31; in New Bedford paper, 22–23, *24*; in New Bern paper, *58*; in New York newspapers, 133–34, 136n6; in New York paper, 123–24, 127, 130; reward announcements, 70, 87–88, 104;

rewards, 212–13; slave-owner documentation, 211; standard language of, 25; typical elements, 199, 208–10, 217n26; warnings to vessel masters, 59, 132, 207, 217n24; waterway escapes in, 203, 213–14, 216nn14–15, 216n17; work house return, 211. *See also* Freedom on the Move
Russell's Hotel, Toronto, Ontario, Canada, 82

Sabbath Recorder, The, 150, 155
"Sailing to Freedom: New Bedford and the Underground Railroad" (NEH workshops), 4
Salem, Massachusetts, 163, 166
"Saltwater Underground, The" (Bordewich), 15
Sams, William, 38
Sandwich Islands, 28, 69
Saunders, James, 83
Savannah, Georgia, 19, 40, 47–48, 131, 167
Savannah Georgian, 43
Savannah River, South Carolina, 47
Schirmer, Jacob, 43, 53n60
Schuylkill River, Pennsylvania, 30
Scott, Julius Sherrard, 130
Seekonk, Massachusetts, 166
self-emancipated slaves, 19, 23, 26
Seventh Day Baptists, 150, 154
Seward, William Henry, 44
Shepard, Joseph, 51n30
Siebert, Wilbur, 26, 84, 112, 165
Siebert, William H., 20
Sims, Thomas, 31
slave auctions, 60, 81, 110, 150
slave catchers, 156; dangers of, 59
slave mutiny, 16, 105
slave trade: northern reliance on, 151–53; waterway escapes, 216n14
Sloane, Samuel, 167
Slocum, John, 166
Slocumb Creek, North Carolina, 57
Smalls, Robert, 38, 39
Smith, Benjamin, 70
Smith, James Lindsey, 148
Smith, Joseph, 185, 194
Smith, Joseph H., 164
Smith, Joseph M., 182–83
Smith, Mary, 72–73
Smith, Oliver, 163
Smith, Peleg, Jr., 166
Smith, Philip, 172
Smith, Venture, 163
Snow Hill, Maryland, 167
Solomons, David, 133
Somewhat More Independent (S. White), 124
South Carolina, legislature: Committee on Federal Relations, 48–49, 53n56; Committee on the Colored Population, 49
South Carolina Association, 40
South Carolina General Assembly, 40
Southern Argus, 91, 107
"Southern Passage" (Landers), 15
Sparrow, Thomas, 72
Spy, Worcester, Massachusetts, 143
State Gazette of North Carolina, 58
St. Catharines, Canada, 92
Steam Ferry Landing site, 107
Steward, Henry, 169
Steward, Mary Ellen, 116
Still, William: Baltimore operations, 109, 111; correspondence of, 83, 91; Ericsson Line, 121n32; reasons for escapes, 94; stationmaster accounts, 1, 31, 63–64, 80–81, 92, 95n7, 98n37, 154; Vigilance Committee chairman, 30, 169
St. Marks, Florida, 152
Stoddard, Noah, 166
Stone, Lucy, 151
Stonington, Connecticut, 11, 163
Stowaway Joe, 141–47, 149, 153–57
Stowe, Harriet Beecher, 44, 118
stowing away, 20, 36–37, 41–42, 145; Charleston port, 48–49, 131
Summerville, Henry, 112
Susquehanna River, 84, 100, 107–8, 112

Taber, William C., 26, 166
Tangier Island, Virginia, 101
Tappan, Arthur and Lewis, 45
Tar River, North Carolina, 57
Temple, Lewis, 187
Temple, William, 185

There Is a River (Harding), 94
Thompson, John, 28
Thoreau, Henry David, 27
Toronto, Canada, 81; free Black community, 82
Torrance, John, 167
Torrey, Charles Turner, 167
Trent River, North Carolina, 57, 65
Tubman, Harriet, 6, 92, 107, 109–11, 118
Tubman, John, 110
Tubman, Tom, 110–11
Tyrrell County, North Carolina, 57

Uncle Tom's Cabin (Stowe), 44, 118
Underground Railroad: Black agency, 111; Black maritime laborers and, 54–55; Chesapeake Station, 100; conductors, 81, 92, 169; cotton bale hiding places, 165; definition of, 12n1; early fugitive cases, 164, 166–67; escape strategies, 107; maritime escapes and, 7–8, 10, 12n4; Maryland waterways, 99, 102; outside fugitive assistance, 161; quantitative data for, 12nn8–9; route maps, *2–3*; station and station keepers, 1, 84, 94, 112, 154–55; Washington, D.C., network, 117. *See also* Greenman family; New Bedford, Massachusetts
Underground Railroad in Massachusetts, The (Wilbur Siebert), 26

Valley Falls, Rhode Island, 20, 84, 154
Vanderhoop, Beulah, 171
Vanderhoop, Netta, 171–72
Vesey, Denmark, 40
vessels: *Acorn*, 168; *America*, 29; *Decatur*, 105; *Draper*, 28; *Ellen Barnes*, 93; *Mary of Duxbury*, 72–73; *Niagara*, 150, 152, 168; *Ocilla*, 152–53; *Pilgrim*, 152; *Rose Standish*, 152
vessels, bark: *Franklin*, 171–72; *Milwood*, 28
vessels, brig: *Bell*, 20, *126*; *Creole*, 16; *Florence*, 73; *John*, 132; *Ottoman*, 167–68; *Rolerson*, 145; *Rosetta*, 133–34; *William Purrington*, 172; *William Rathbone*, 152
vessels, British: *Coronet*, 43
vessels, Civil War: *Planter*, 38–39, *39*; USS *Monitor*, 21–22
vessels, Confederate: *Planter*, 39
vessels, design: Baltimore clipper, 103; Chesapeake Pilot Bay Schooner, 100; sail canoe, 106; steam-driven packet ships, 109
vessels, schooner: *Cato*, 134; *City of Richmond*, 31, 56, 80, 83, 87, 92–93; *Dolphin*, 72; *Eliza S. Potter*, 143, 145–47; *Fair Play*, 40; *Favourite Elsey*, 134; *Minerva Wright*, 72; *Pearl*, 113, 115–17; *Ranger*, 166–67; *Red Eagle*, 147; *Robert Center*, 44, 51n30; *Sally Ann*, 73; *Wellington*, 167
vessels, sloop: *Casket*, 19; *Union*, 24
vessels, steamboat: *Augusta*, 80; *Salem*, 116; *S. R. Spaulding*, 43
vessels, steam packet: *Marion*, 48
vessels, whaler: *Frances Henrietta*, 28, 29, 183; *Hope*, 168–69
vessels, whaling bark: *Edward*, 29; *Ocean*, 28
vessels, whaling brig: *Rising States*, 29, 194
vessels, yacht: *Wild Pigeon*, 165
vigilance committees, 161; Boston, 165, 167–72; New Bedford, 170; New York, 135–36, 139n59, 167; Norfolk, Virginia, 88; Pennsylvania, 30, 154; Philadelphia, 65, 92–93, 169; Portsmouth, Virginia, 88
Vineyard Gazette, 171
Vineyard Haven, Massachusetts, 171
Virginia State Penitentiary, 88, 97nn35–36
Virginia Waterways and the Underground Railroad (Newby-Alexander), 17
Voorhis, Robert, 166

Wainer, Michael, 167
Wainer, Thomas, 166–67
Wakefield, Rhode Island, 155
Walker, David, 43
Walker, Jonathan, 166
Wallace, James, 70

War of 1812, 100–102
Washington, D.C., 57, 105, 115, 117, 121n49
Washington, Madison, 16
Washington, North Carolina, 29, 57
waterfront labor, 10, 38, 41–42. *See* longshoremen; wharf workers
Waterman's Song, The (Cecelski), 15, 103
Webster, Daniel, 115
West Indies, 26, 46–47, 59, 69, 103, 135–36, 152
Weston, George, 28–29
Westport, Massachusetts, 29
whaling, 14; escaped slaves' employment, 6, 183, 185; freedmen employees, 26–28; fugitive slave identification, 29–30; "golden age" of whaling, 189
wharf workers, 36, 38, 41, 66; stevedores, 71, 86, 186. *See* longshoremen
Wheeler, Abigail, 86
Wheeler, John Hill, 169
White, Deborah Gray, 144
White, Miles, 57
White, Shane, 124, 131
Whitfield, Harvey Amani, 15
Wiggins, Dawson, 72
Williams, Avis, 187
Williams, John (John Mason), 172
Williams, Joseph, 156
Williamson, Passamore, 169
Wilmington, North Carolina: "asylum for Runaways," 57, 144; curfews on Black people, 64; escapes from, 30, 67; slaves outlawed from piloting, 71; slaves seeking passage, 63; waterfront, 20, 54, 64
Wilmington Aurora, 71
Wilmington Journal, 55, 71
Wilson, S. J., 81
Wilson, William H., 91
Wines, Moses, 86–87
Winsboro, Irvin D. S., 16
Withers, T. J., 48
women: advertisements for, 104, 131; disguises of, 108; "fancy girls," 108; occupations of, 129; sea escapes of, 82, 94, 131, 135; wharf workers, 30, 66
Wooby, Alfred, 72
Woolfolk, Austin, 105
Woolford, Levin, 106–7, 120n20
Worcester, Massachusetts, 141, 143, 146, 157n12
Worcester *Spy*, 143
Works Progress Administration (WPA), 42

York River, Virginia, 84

Zion African Methodist Church, 160